W9-BNN-303

HIDDEN MICKEYS

· ·

A Field Guide to

Walt Disney World®'s

Best Kept Secrets

· ·

6th edition

Steven M. Barrett

HIDDEN MICKEYS

A Field Guide to Walt Disney World®'s
Best Kept Secrets
6th edition

Published by
The Intrepid Traveler
P.O. Box 531
Branford, CT 06405
http://intrepidtraveler.com

Copyright ©2013 by Steven M. Barrett
Sixth Edition
Printed in Canada
Cover design by Foster & Foster
Interior Design by Starving Artist Design Studio
Maps designed by Evora Taylor
Library of Congress Control Number: 2012948587
ISBN-13: 978-1-937011-29-1

10 9 8 7 6 5 4 3 2

Trademarks, Etc. • • • • • • • • • • • •

Photo by Vickie Barrett

About the Author ● ● ● ● ● ● ● ● ● ● ● ● ●

Author Steven M. Barrett paid his first visit to Disney World in the late 1980s, after attending a conference in Orlando. He immediately fell under its spell, visiting it twice yearly with family and friends for the next several years, offering touring advice to the less initiated, and reading almost everything written about the WDW theme parks. When a job in his field opened up not far from WDW in 1998, Barrett, a Texas native, Air Force veteran, and former University of Oklahoma professor, relocated to the Orlando area from Houston, Texas. He began visiting the WDW parks every chance he got to enjoy the attractions, sample the restaurants, escort visiting friends and relatives, and find Hidden Mickeys! His interest in Hidden Mickeys led him to take pen in hand. The result is this book of Hidden Mickey scavenger hunts arranged to help you spend the least possible time waiting in line as you hunt for the elusive Mouse.

Dedication . . . .

I dedicate this book to my wife Vickie and our son Steven, who willingly accompanied me on countless research visits to Disney World and added invaluable insight to this book. Furthermore, updating this book would not be possible without the many wonderful Hidden Mickey fans I've met through my website and in the Disney parks. Thanks to you all.

True to their name, Hidden Mickeys are elusive. New ones appear from time to time and some old ones disappear (see page 17, paragraph 2). When that happens—and it will—I will let you know on my website:

HiddenMickeyGuy.com

So if you can't find a Mickey—or if you're looking for just a few more—be sure to check it out.

***

Thank You, My Fellow Hidden Mickey Hunters

No Hidden Mickey hunter works alone. Scores of dedicated Mickey sleuths have helped me find the elusive Mouse in WDW. Thanks to each and every one of you. You'll find your names in the Acknowledgements, beginning on page 281.

***

Finding Mickey Without Scavenger Hunting

Want to look for Hidden Mickeys in an attraction, restaurant, shop, or resort without scavenger hunting? Turn to the Index on page 290. If Mickey is hiding there, the Index will direct you to the page(s) with the appropriate Clues. If the venue isn't listed, Mickey isn't hiding there. Or if he is, I haven't yet found him.

– Steve Barrett

Table of Contents • • • • • • • • • • • • •

Read This First!   10

1. Hidden Mickey Mania   11

2. Magic Kingdom Scavenger Hunt   19
   Hints begin   43

3. Epcot Scavenger Hunt   69
   Hints begin   89

4. Disney's Hollywood Studios Scavenger Hunt   111
   Hints begin   131

5. Disney's Animal Kingdom Scavenger Hunt   151
   Hints begin   167

6. WDW Resort Hotel Scavenger Hunt   185
   Hints begin   213

7. Hither, Thither & Yon Scavenger Hunt   241
   (WDW Water Parks, Downtown Disney & Beyond)
   Hints begin   259

8. Other Mickey Appearances   275

9. My Favorite Hidden Mickeys   277
   My Top 10   277
   10 Honorable Mentions   278

10. Don't Stop Now!   280

Acknowledgements   281

Index to Mickey's Hiding Places   290

Maps

   Magic Kingdom   20
   Epcot   70
   Disney's Hollywood Studios   112
   Disney's Animal Kingdom   152
   Walt Disney World® Resort   186, 242

Tip: To find a specific attraction, restaurant, shop, or resort, turn to the Index, page 290.

Read This First! . . . .

My guess is that you have visited Disney World before, perhaps many times. But if I've guessed wrong, and this is your first visit, then this note is for you.

Searching for Hidden Mickeys is lots of fun. But it's not a substitute for letting the magic of Disney sweep over you as you experience Walt Disney World (WDW) for the first time. For one thing, the scavenger hunts I present in this book do not include all the attractions in WDW. That's because some of them don't have Hidden Mickeys! For another, this book doesn't cover many things the first-time visitor should know and do to make that first trip to Disney World as magical as possible.

That doesn't mean you can't search for Hidden Mickeys, too. Just follow the suggestions in Chapter One of this book for "Finding Hidden Mickeys Without Scavenger Hunting."

CHAPTER 1

Hidden Mickey Mania

Have you ever marveled at a "Hidden Mickey"? People in the know often shout with glee when they recognize one. Some folks are so involved with discovering them that Hidden Mickeys can be visualized where none actually exist. These outbreaks of Hidden Mickey mania are confusing to the unenlightened. So let's get enlightened!

Here's the definition of an official Hidden Mickey: a partial or complete image of Mickey Mouse that has been hidden by Disney's Imagineers and artists in the designs of Disney attractions, hotels, restaurants, and other areas. These images are designed to blend into their surroundings. Sharp-eyed visitors have the fun of finding them.

The practice probably started as an inside joke among the Imagineers (the designers and builders of Disney attractions). According to Disney guru Jim Hill (JimHillMedia.com), Hidden Mickeys originated in the late 1970s or early 1980s, when Disney management wanted to restrict Disney characters like Mickey and Minnie to the Magic Kingdom. The Imagineers designing Epcot couldn't resist slipping Mickey into the new park, and thus "Hidden Mickeys" were born. Guests and "Cast Members" (Disney employees) started spotting them and the concept took on a life of its own. Today, Hidden Mickeys are anticipated in any new construction at Walt Disney World, and Hidden Mickey fans can't wait to find them.

Hidden Mickeys come in all sizes and many forms. The most common is an outline of Mickey's head formed by three intersecting circles, one for Mickey's round head and two for his round ears. Among Hidden Mickey fans, this image is known as the "classic" Hidden Mickey, a term I will adopt in this book. Other Hidden Mickeys include a side or oblique (usually three-quarter) profile of Mickey's face and head, a side profile of his entire body, a full-length silhouette of his body seen from the front, a detailed picture of his face or body, or a three-dimensional Mickey Mouse. Sometimes just his gloves, handprints, shoes or ears appear. Even his name or initials in unusual places may qualify as a Hidden Mickey.

And it's not just Mickeys that are hidden. The term "Hidden Mickey" also applies to hidden images of other popular characters. There are Hidden Minnies, Hidden Donald Ducks, Hidden Goofys, and other Hidden Characters in Disney World, and I include many of them in this book.

The sport of finding Hidden Mickeys has caught on and adds even more interest to an already fun-filled Walt Disney World vacation. This book is your "field guide" to more than 1,200 Hidden Mickeys in WDW. To add to the fun, instead of just describing them, I've organized them into six scavenger hunts, one for each of the major theme parks, one for the Walt Disney World Resort hotels, and one for all the rest of WDW: the water parks, Downtown Disney, WDW Speedway, and beyond. The hunts are designed for maximum efficiency so that you can spend your time looking for Mickeys rather than cooling your heels in lines. Follow the Clues and you will find the best Hidden Mickeys WDW has to offer. If you have trouble spotting a particular Hidden Mickey (some are extraordinarily well camouflaged!) you can turn to the Hints at the end of each scavenger hunt for a fuller description.

Scavenger Hunting for Hidden Mickeys

To have the most fun and find the most Mickeys, follow these tips:

★ **Arrive early** for the theme park hunts, say 30 minutes before the official opening time. Pick up a Guidemap and a Times Guide and plot your course. Then look for Hidden Mickeys in the waiting area while you wait for the rope to drop. You'll find the Clues for those areas by checking the *Index to Mickey's Hiding Places* in the back of this book. Look under "Entrance areas." If you arrive later in the day, you may want to pick up a FASTPASS for the first major attraction and then skip down a few Clues to stay ahead of the crowds.

★ "Clues" and "Hints"

Clues under each attraction will guide you to the Hidden Mickey(s). If you have trouble spotting them, you can turn to the Hints at the end of the hunt for a fuller description. The Clues and Hints are numbered consecutively, that is, Hint 1 goes with Clue 1, so it's easy to find the right Hint if you need it. In some cases (*The Great Movie Ride* in Disney's Hollywood Studios is a good example), you may have to ride the attraction more than once to find all the Hidden Mickeys.

★ Scoring

All Hidden Mickeys are fun to find, but all Hidden Mickeys aren't the same. Some are easier to spot than others. I assign point values to Hidden Mickeys, identifying them as easy to find (a value of 1 point) to difficult to find the first time (5 points). I also consider the complexity and uniqueness of the image: the more complex or unique the Hidden Mickey, the higher the point value. For example, the brilliantly camouflaged Mickey hiding in The Garden Grill Restaurant mural in Epcot is a five-pointer.

★ Playing the game

You can hunt solo or with others; competitively or just for fun. There's room to tally your score in the guide. Families with young children may want to focus on one- and two-point Mickeys that the little ones will have no trouble spotting. (Of course, little ones tend to be sharp-eyed; so they may spot familiar shapes before you do in some of the more complex patterns.) Or you may want to split your party into teams and see who can rack up the most points (in which case, you'll probably want to have a guide for each team).

Of course, you don't have to play the game at all. You can simply look for Hidden Mickeys in attractions as you come to them (see "Finding Hidden Mickeys Without Scavenger Hunting," below).

★ Following the Clues

The hunts often call for crisscrossing the parks. This may seem illogical at first, but trust me, it will keep you ahead of the crowds. Besides, it adds to the fun of the hunt and, if you're playing competitively, keeps everyone on their toes.

★ *Waiting in line*
Don't waste time in lines. If the wait is longer than 15 minutes, get a FASTPASS (if available and you're eligible), move on to the next attraction, and come back at your FASTPASS time. Exception: In some attractions, the Hidden Mickey(s) can only be seen from the Standby (regular) queue line, and not from the FAST-PASS line. (I've not suggested FASTPASS in the Clues section when that is the case.) The lines at these attractions should not be too long if you start your scavenger hunt when the park opens and follow the hunt Clues as given. If you do encounter long lines, come back later during a parade or in the hour before the park closes. Alternatively, if you need to board an attraction with a long wait without a FASTPASS, use the Single Rider queue if available (check your Guidemap for a big "S" symbol next to the attraction).

★ *Playing fair*
Be considerate of other guests. Many Hidden Mickeys are in restaurants and shops. Ask a Cast Member's permission before searching inside sit-down restaurants, and avoid the busy mealtime hours unless you are one of the diners. Tell the Cast Members and other guests who see you looking around what you're up to, so they can share in the fun.

Finding Hidden Mickeys Without Scavenger Hunting

If scavenger hunts don't appeal to you, you don't have to use them. You can find Hidden Mickeys in the specific rides and other attractions you visit by using the *Index to Mickey's Hiding Places* in the back of this book. For easy lookup, in addition to being listed alphabetically, attractions in Magic Kingdom, Epcot, and Disney's Animal Kingdom are listed under their appropriate "lands" or "areas" (for example, Fantasyland in Magic Kingdom, Future World East in Epcot, and Asia in Animal Kingdom). In Epcot, attractions are also listed by pavilion. To find Hidden Mickeys in the attraction, restaurant, hotel or shop you are visiting, simply turn to the *Index*, locate the appropriate page, and follow the Clue(s) to find the Hidden Mickey(s).

Caution: You won't find every WDW attraction, restaurant, hotel or shop in the Index. Only those with confirmed Hidden Mickeys are included in this guide.

Hidden Mickeys, "Gray Zone" Mickeys, Wishful Thinking

The classic (three-circle) Mickeys are the most controversial, for good reason. Much debate surrounds the gathering of circular forms throughout Walt Disney World. The sideways classic Mickey made of blue bubbles on the *Living with the Land* entrance-queue wall mural (Clue 93 in the Epcot Scavenger Hunt) is surely the work of a clever artist. However, three-circle configurations occur spontaneously in art and nature, as in collections of grapes, tomatoes, pumpkins, bubbles, oranges, cannonballs, and the like. Unlike the bubbles Hidden Mickey in Epcot, it may be difficult to attribute a random "classic Mickey" configuration of circles to a deliberate Imagineer design.

So which groupings of three circles qualify as Hidden Mickeys as opposed to wishful thinking? Unfortunately, no master list of actual or "Imagineer-approved" Hidden Mickeys exists. Purists demand that a true classic Hidden Mickey should have proper proportions and positioning. The round head must be larger than the ear circles (so that three equal circles in the proper alignment would not qualify as a Hidden Mickey). The head and ears must be touching and in perfect position for Mickey's head and ears.

On the other hand, Disney's recent mantra is: "If the guest thinks it's a Hidden Mickey, then by golly it is one!" Of course, I appreciate Disney's respect for their guests' opinions. However, when the subject is Hidden Mickeys, let's apply some guidelines. My own criteria are looser than the purists' but stricter than the "anything goes" Disney approach. I prefer to use a few sensible guidelines.

To be classified as a real classic Hidden Mickey, the three circles should satisfy the following criteria:

1. Purposeful (sometimes you can sense that the circles were placed on purpose).

2. Proportionate sizes (head larger than the ears and somewhat proportionate to the ears).

3. Round or at least "roundish."

4. The ears don't touch each other, and the ears are above the head (not beside the head).

5. The head and ears touch or are close to touching.

6. The grouping of circles is exceptional or unique in appearance.

7. The circles are hidden or somewhat hidden and not obviously intended to be part of the décor.

Having spelled out some ground rules, allow me to now bend the rules in one instance. Some Hidden Mickeys are sentimental favorites with Disney fans, even though they may actually represent "wishful thinking." (My neighbor, Lew Brooks, calls them "two-beer Mickeys.") Who am I to defy tradition? For example, the nuts in the jar along the queue at *Jungle Cruise* in the Magic Kingdom are all about the same size. Nevertheless, although the image doesn't meet our classic Mickey criteria, many guests and even Cast Members call the jar nuts a Hidden Mickey. So I include the jar-nuts Mickey in the Magic Kingdom Scavenger Hunt in Chapter 2 (Clue 140).

Hidden Mickeys vs. Decorative Mickeys

Some Mickeys are truly hidden, not visible to the tourist. They may be located behind the scenes, accessible only to Cast Members. You won't find them in this field guide, as I only include Hidden Mickeys that are accessible to the guest. Other Mickeys are decorative; they were placed in plain sight to enhance the décor. For example, in a restaurant, I consider a pat of butter shaped like Mickey Mouse to be a decorative (aka décor) Mickey. Disney World is loaded with decorative Mickeys. You'll find images of Mickey Mouse on items ranging from manhole covers, to laundry room soap dispensers, to toilet paper wrappers and shower curtains in the hotels. I do not include these ubiquitous and sometimes changing images in this book unless they are unique or hard to spot.

Hidden Mickeys can change or be accidentally removed over time, by the process of nature or by the continual cleaning and refurbishing that goes on at Disney World. For example, the "Steamboat Willie" Hidden Mickey in the star map in Mickey's Star Traders shop in Tomorrowland disappeared when the shop was remodeled. Moreover, Cast Members themselves sometimes create or remove Hidden Mickeys.

My Selection Process

I trust you've concluded by now that Hidden Mickey Science is an evolving specialty. Which raises the question, how did I choose the Hidden Mickeys in the scavenger hunts in this guide?

I compiled my list of Hidden Mickeys from all resources to which I had access: my own sightings, friends, family, Cast Members, websites, and books. (Cast Members in each specific area usually — but not always! — know where some Hidden Mickeys are located.) Then I embarked on my own hunts, and I took along friends or family to verify my sightings. I have included only those Hidden Mickeys I could verify.

Furthermore, some Hidden Mickeys are visible only intermittently or only from certain vantage points in ride vehicles. I don't generally include these Mickeys, unless I feel that adequate descriptions will allow anyone to find them. So the scavenger hunts include only those images I believe to be recognizable as Hidden Mickeys and visible to the general touring guest. It is likely, though, that one or more of the Hidden Mickeys described in this book will disappear over time.

I'll try to let you know when I discover that a Hidden Mickey has disappeared for good by posting the information on my website:

HiddenMickeyGuy.com

17

If you find one missing before I do, please

email me care of my website to let me know.

I have enjoyed finding each and every Hidden Mickey in this book. I'm certain I'll find more as time goes by, and I hope you can spot new Hidden Mickeys during your visit.

So put on some comfortable walking shoes and experience Walt Disney World like you never have before!

Happy Hunting!

— Steve Barrett

CHAPTER 2

Magic Kingdom Scavenger Hunt

Clue 1: As you approach the security area, look down for Mickey under your feet.
3 points

(Check your Times Guide for any morning, afternoon, and evening parades. There are generally both decorative and Hidden Mickeys on the floats and banners.)

Clue 2: Once you are in the park, examine the scrollwork of the roof of the Main Street Train Station.
2 points

★ While you are waiting for the park to open you may want to hunt for Hidden Mickeys on **Main Street, U.S.A.** (See Clues 160 to 176.)

★ Head for Fantasyland and walk fast to **Enchanted Tales with Belle**.

Clue 3: Look near the fireplace in the first room for two Hidden Mickeys. (You can exit back through the entrance queue to look for more Hidden Mickeys in Fantasyland or stay and enjoy the performance if you wish.)
5 points for both

★ Go to **Peter Pan's Flight**.

Clue 4: Study the overhead attraction sign at the entrance for two decent Mickey images.
5 points for spotting both

Clue 5: Just before you get to the entrance queue turnstile, look closely at the bark of the trees facing the loading area to find a classic Hidden Mickey.
3 points

Clue 6: Keep looking down for a brown classic Mickey on the ground.
5 points

19

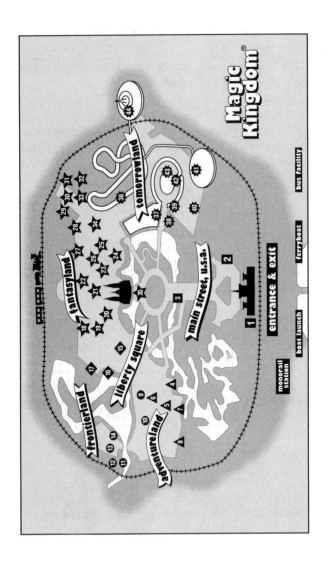

main street, u.s.a

1 WDW Railroad
2 Mickey's Meet 'N Greet in Town Square Theater
3 Guest Information Board

adventureland

4 Swiss Family Treehouse
5 Walt Disney's Enchanted Tiki Room
6 The Magic Carpets of Aladdin
7 Jungle Cruise
8 Pirates of the Caribbean

frontierland

9 Frontierland Shootin' Arcade
10 Country Bear Jamboree
11 Splash Mountain
12 WDW Railroad
13 Big Thunder Mountain Railroad
14 Raft to Tom Sawyer Island

liberty square

15 The Hall of Presidents
16 Liberty Square Riverboat
17 Haunted Mansion

fantasyland

18 "it's a small world"
19 Peter Pan's Flight
20 Mickey's PhilharMagic
21 Prince Charming Regal Carrousel
22 Enchanted Tales with Belle
23 Princess Fairytale Hall (Opening 2013)
24 Fairytale Garden
25 The Many Adventures of Winnie the Pooh
26 Seven Dwarfs Mine Train (Opening 2014)
27 Under the Sea ~ Journey of The Little Mermaid
28 Ariel's Grotto
29 Pete's Silly Sideshow
30 Casey Jr. Splash 'N' Soak

31 WDW Railroad
32 The Barnstormer
33 Dumbo the Flying Elephant
34 Mad Tea Party
35 Castle Forecourt Stage

tomorrowland

36 Tomorrowland Speedway
37 Stitch's Great Escape!
38 Monsters, Inc. Laugh Floor
39 Buzz Lightyear's Space Ranger Spin
40 Galaxy Palace Theater
41 Walt Disney's Carousel of Progress
42 Tomorrowland Transit Authority PeopleMover
43 Astro Orbiter
44 Space Mountain

★ If you're lucky, you may spot Mickey on the rotating moon and earn yourself some bonus points.

5 bonus points

Clue 7: Search for a classic Mickey near mermaids.
3 points

★ Line up for **The Many Adventures of Winnie the Pooh**. Study Mr. Sanders' big tree.

Clue 8: Search for a Mickey made of rocks embedded in the tree.
3 points

Clue 9: Look for a submarine image in the wood of the tree. (Tip: This is a Hidden Tribute rather than a Hidden Mickey.)
4 points

Clue 10: Find a side profile of Mickey in the bark.
4 points

Clue 11: Locate Mickey on a wooden post by a window outside.
5 points

Clue 12: Next check out two Hidden Mickeys inside the entryway play area.
4 points for both

★ Now hop in your honey pot and find five Hidden Characters.

Clue 13: Examine the flower-pot marker in Rabbit's Garden.
3 points

Clue 14: In Owl's house, find the picture of Mr. Toad and Owl.
3 points

Clue 15: Near the end of Owl's house, locate a picture of Mole with Winnie the Pooh.
3 points

★ Walk to **Under the Sea ~ Journey of The Little Mermaid**.

Note: Many collections of circular rock impressions in both the entrance and exit areas and inside this attraction suggest classic Hidden Mickeys. I include my favorite images, which seem intentional, below.

Clue 16: Spot a Hidden Mickey on a rock just outside the Standby entrance queue.
4 points

Clue 17: In the outside Standby queue, be alert for another Hidden Mickey on a rock near a waterfall.
5 points

Clue 18: Also in the outside Standby queue, study the rock walls for a submarine image. (Not a Hidden Mickey, but an awesome Hidden Image!)
5 points

Clue 19: In the inside Standby entrance queue, at a large opening in the rock ceiling on your right and just past a carved wooden figure, stay alert for a classic Mickey in light on the lower wall to your left. This Hidden Mickey is designed to appear only on November 18 (Mickey's birthday) around noon, but it just might appear other times of the year!
10 bonus points

Clue 20: Along the inside Standby entrance queue, find a Hidden Mickey in the rock wall above some bottles on your left.
5 points

Clue 21: On the ride, look for a purple-coral classic Mickey on your right.
5 points

Clue 22: Don't miss the frogs with Hidden Mickeys!
4 points for one or more

Clue 23: Along the inside exit, study the walls to your left for Mickey.
4 points for one or more

Clue 24: Outside the cave exit, look around for Steamboat Willie!
5 points

★ Stroll over to **Ariel's Grotto**.

Clue 25: Be on the lookout for Mickey on the wall along the entrance queue of *Ariel's Grotto*.
5 points

★ Cross over to Frontierland and get a FASTPASS to ride *Splash Mountain* later. Then ride **Big Thunder Mountain Railroad**.

Clue 26: During the first climb, search the cavern floor to the right of the coaster.
4 points

Clue 27: Look for a classic Hidden Mickey and a Hidden Winnie the Pooh on the ground to your right near the end of the ride.
4 points for both

Clue 28: Study the reddish rock along the exit walkway for a Hidden Tinker Bell.
4 points

★ Return to **Splash Mountain** at your allotted FASTPASS time. Hop aboard and keep your eyes peeled for one Hidden Mickey in the queue, six on the ride, and at least two more after you exit.

Clue 29: Along the queue, look to your left for a red Mickey hanging on the wall.
3 points

Clue 30: Soon after you start, search for barrels that form a classic Mickey.
3 points

Clue 31: Just as your boat goes outside, spot a tiny classic Mickey on a "moonshine" barrel!
5 points

Clue 32: Just past Brer Frog, find the fishing bobbers that form a Hidden Mickey.
4 points

Clue 33: In the room with jumping water, spot the hanging rope classic Mickey.
4 points

Clue 34: As your boat ascends toward the big drop, look toward the opening for a side profile of Mickey's face.
3 points

Clue 35: In the riverboat scene after the big drop, find the Hidden Mickey in the clouds.
4 points

Clue 36: Along the exit walkway, look for the birdhouse with at least two acorn classic Mickeys.
3 points for two or more

Clue 37: After the ride, take another look at the mountain from the outside viewing area to spot that Clue 34 side profile (again).
3 points

★ Head for **Haunted Mansion** in Liberty Square. Find six classic Mickeys, two Donald Ducks, and a Mr. Toad!

Clue 38: Along the interactive "Scenic" left-side entrance queue, search for a Mickey made of barnacles.
4 points

Clue 39: In the first room inside the entrance, look for some classic Mickeys in the border design around a portrait.
3 points

Clue 40: During the ride, be alert for Donald Duck on two different chairs.
4 points each

Clue 41: Find the Mickey on the ghostly banquet table.
2 points

Clue 42: Spot plates on the floor in the attic.
4 points

Clue 43: Look closely at the "Grim Reaper" by the opera-singing lady.
5 points

Clue 44: Outside, as you exit, look for a classic Mickey next to a gate.
3 points

Clue 45: Find Mr. Toad along the exit walkway.
3 points

★ Enter **Columbia Harbour House** restaurant and look for a classic Hidden Mickey. (Be considerate of the diners.)

Clue 46: Check the art on the downstairs walls.
2 points

★ Enjoy lunch. Some suggestions: The Plaza Restaurant off Main Street for sit-down, Columbia Harbour House for sandwiches or salads, or Cosmic Ray's Starlight Café in Tomorrowland for chicken or burgers.

★ Walk into Adventureland. Choose the left entrance queue for **Pirates of the Caribbean** and find four Hidden Mickeys. Then find nine classic Hidden Mickeys on the ride and four more after the ride.

Clue 47: Spot some cannonballs along the left queue.
3 points

Clue 48: Look near a faux fireplace along the queue for a Hidden Mickey.
5 points

Clue 49: Now search for two classic Mickey locks in the left queue.
4 points for spotting both

Clue 50: When Davy Jones appears on the ride, look up for a classic Mickey.
5 bonus points

Clue 51: Try to spot the classic Mickey shadow above the drunken pirate's cat.
4 points

Clue 52: Near the end of the ride, look left at the recessed doors in the wall.
4 points

Clue 53: Don't miss the treasure room's open door.
4 points

Clue 54: Now glance at the wall behind Jack Sparrow.
4 points

Clue 55: As you exit the ride, search for some coins and jewels.
5 points for both

Clue 56: In the gift shop, spot a classic Mickey in a painting.
3 points

Clue 57: In a small camera shop near the *Pirates* ride, look around for a classic Mickey.
3 points

★ Stop by the **Frontierland Shootin' Arcade**.

Clue 58: Find a classic Mickey in front of the target area.
1 point

★ Then turn right to **Liberty Square** and cross the street.

Clue 59: Find the classic Mickey at the *Liberty Square Riverboat* entrance.
1 point

★ Now cross the bridge to Tomorrowland and go to the **Tomorrowland Speedway**.

Clue 60: Look for a shadow on the pavement near the *Tomorrowland Speedway* that's shaped like a classic Mickey.
3 points

★ Walk over and get yourself a FASTPASS for **Buzz Lightyear's Space Ranger Spin**.

Clue 61: Spot the classic Mickey on the FASTPASS machine.
2 points

★ Go to the outside of the **Monsters, Inc. Laugh Floor**.

Clue 62: Find the moon with classic Mickey craters.
1 point

Clue 63: Spot the asteroid shaped like a classic Mickey.
1 point

★ Get in line for *Monsters, Inc. Laugh Floor*.

Clue 64: As you enter the waiting area, search for a classic Mickey in a window display.
4 points

★ Go to **Walt Disney's Carousel of Progress** (open seasonally and on busy holidays). Check the first scene for Clue 65, the third scene for Clue 66, the last scene for Clues 67 to 72, and the exit for Clue 73.

Clue 65: Admire a classic Mickey on a mirror.
3 points

Clue 66: Search for Mickey's blue hat.
4 points

Clue 67: Observe a painting on the rear wall.
4 points

Clue 68: Find a Mickey nutcracker.
2 points

Clue 69: Spot a Mickey Mouse doll.
2 points

Clue 70: Search around for green Mickey ears.
4 points

Clue 71: Look fast for a classic Mickey on a spaceship.
5 points

Clue 72: View an object with Mickey ears in the kitchen.
3 points

Clue 73: Don't miss Hidden Mickeys along the exit walkway.
2 points

★ Go to **Buzz Lightyear's Space Ranger Spin** at your allotted FASTPASS time and be on the lookout for ten Hidden Mickeys along with another Hidden character.
Note: Some of the planets with Hidden Mickeys appear in several places along the entrance queue and on the ride.

Clue 74: Inside the building on the right wall, find the planet with a continent shaped like the side profile of Mickey Mouse.
3 points

Clue 75: On this same poster, spot classic Mickey craters.
3 points

Clue 76: Look for the side-profile Mickey continent further along the entrance queue to the left.
2 points

Clue 77: Search for a Hidden Mickey in Sector 2 nearby.
3 points

Clue 78: Pay attention to the right wall in the very first interactive room on the ride for a tiny classic Mickey in the stars. (This one is tough to spot.)
5 points

Clue 79: During the first part of the ride, spot another side profile of Mickey. Look to the left of your vehicle in the room with batteries.
3 points

Clue 80: Also in the battery room, to the right of your vehicle, stare at the star field to the right of the cone over Zurg to find a blue classic Mickey star.
5 points

Clue 81: Catch another view of the planet with a side-profile Mickey in the space video room.
3 points

Clue 82: Just past the space video room, look straight ahead to spot that side-profile Mickey planet one more time.
2 points

Clue 83: Along the exit, look for an alien pointing to a classic Mickey.
2 points

Clue 84: Spot Stitch's spaceship nearby.
3 points

★ Walk to the far side of **Astro Orbiter** and search carefully for a small classic Mickey traced in the cement nearby.

Clue 85: Check the side facing *Space Mountain*.
5 points

★ Walk over to **The Hall of Presidents** in Liberty Square.

Clue 86: In the waiting room for the show, study the paintings for a tiny classic Mickey.
4 points

★ Now go to the **Liberty Square Riverboat** (it sometimes closes at 5:00 p.m. or at dusk). If the wait is 10 minutes or more, grab a snack from a vendor in Liberty Square or Frontierland and refresh yourself while you wait to ride the boat.

Clue 87: From the boat, look for a classic Mickey rock formation at the right end of the bridge in Frontierland. (Note: This Hidden Mickey is also visible from *Tom Sawyer Island*.)
4 points

★ From near *Big Thunder Mountain Railroad*, float on the **raft** over **to Tom Sawyer Island**.

Clue 88: Search one of the caves for Goofy.
3 points

Clue 89: In the same cave, spot Mickey not far from Goofy.
3 points

Clue 90: In Fort Langhorn, look around in the rear right Rifle Roost for a Mickey in wood.
4 points

★ Float back to Frontierland and then walk to Fantasyland to see **Mickey's PhilharMagic**. Or get a FASTPASS to enjoy it later if the wait is too long.

Clue 91: In the first waiting area inside, squint at the wall mural.
4 points for two or more

Clue 92: Inside the main theater, examine the border of the video screen.
2 points

Clue 93: Look for a shadow Mickey on a table.
4 points

Clue 94: Stare at Ariel's jewels for a classic Mickey in a ring.
5 points

Clue 95: During the show, keep alert for a classic Mickey during the magic carpet ride.
5 points

Clue 96: Stop in the gift shop at the exit and find a classic Mickey.
3 points

★ Enter **Pinocchio Village Haus** restaurant.

Clue 97: Look for a tiny, dark classic Mickey on the wall near the exit to the restrooms.
4 points

Clue 98: Keep searching on this wall for a tiny, white classic Mickey.
5 points

★ Stroll over to **Fairytale Garden**.

Clue 99: Find a classic Mickey on a light pole.
3 points

Clue 100: Search for a Hidden Character on a wall.
4 points

★ Go to **"it's a small world"** and try to spot two classic Hidden Mickeys.

Clue 101: In the Africa room, look up at the vine with purple leaves.
3 points

Clue 102: In the South Pacific Room, search for an animal classic Mickey.
3 points

★ As you exit, head **toward Peter Pan's Flight**.

Clue 103: Find grapes arranged like a classic Mickey.
2 points

★ Walk over to **Sir Mickey's Store**.

Clue 104: Observe a classic Mickey outside the store.
1 point

Clue 105: Gaze inside a display window of the store to find more classic Mickeys.
4 points for two or more

★ Enter the **Castle Couture shop**.

Clue 106: Search high on a wall for a bronze frieze with a tiny classic Mickey on a bush.
5 points

★ Now walk to the **exit area** of the **Fantasyland Train Station** in Storybook Circus.

Clue 107: Check the pavement near the exit from the Station for at least two Hidden Mickeys.
5 points for two or more

★ Stand outside **Casey Jr. Splash 'N' Soak Station**.

Clue 108: Look over the boxcars in Casey Jr. Splash 'N' Soak for a classic Mickey.
5 points

★ Cruise over to **The Barnstormer**.

Clue 109: Find a classic Mickey near a picture of Goofy outside The Barnstormer.
3 points

Clue 110: Study a large billboard outside The Barnstormer for a Hidden Mickey.
5 points

★ Walk back to **Pete's Silly Sideshow**.

Clue 111: Search for a classic Mickey on a poster outside Pete's Silly Sideshow.
5 points

★ Check out the **FASTPASS area** for **The Barnstormer** and **Dumbo the Flying Elephant**.

Clue 112: Locate tiny Mickey balloons.
5 points for finding eight balloons

★ Return to the **area near Dumbo the Flying Elephant**.

Clue 113: Look for a classic Mickey near the entrance to the Dumbo FASTPASS queue.
3 points

★ Amble over to the entrance area for **Be Our Guest Restaurant**.

Clue 114: Examine a short rock wall for a classic Mickey near the check-in station at the entrance walkway to Be Our Guest Restaurant.
5 points

Clue 115: As you enter Be Our Guest Restaurant, search the room to the right for a Hidden Mickey.
5 points

Clue 116: Look for Mickey bubbles on a wall in the Rose Gallery seating area to the right of the restaurant's Ballroom.
5 points

Clue 117: Find Mickey in a fabric hanging in the West Wing seating area, also to the right of Be Our Guest Restaurant's Ballroom.
5 points

★ Outside again in Fantasyland, find **Gaston's Statue**.

Clue 118: Study the statue for a Hidden Mickey.
5 points

★ Gaze around inside the **Bonjour Village Gifts** shop.

Clue 119: Find a Hidden Mickey on a wall.
2 points

★ Stroll over to Town Square Theater on Main Street, U.S.A. and visit **Mickey's Meet 'N' Greet**. (Get a FASTPASS if the line is too long.)

Clue 120: Inside Mickey's Greeting Room, take a flash photo of the "Electricity" display and see what happens to Mickey!
4 points

Clue 121: Find a Mickey made of rings.
2 points

Clue 122: Spot another classic Mickey in Mickey's magic chest (it's sometimes covered by a scarf).
2 points

Clue 123: Don't miss Oswald the Lucky Rabbit!
5 points

Clue 124: Look around for sorcerer Mickey.
4 points

Clue 125: In the gift shop at the exit, find Mickey on a table.
2 points

Clue 126: In the gift shop, search for Mickey on a house.
3 points

★ Stop near **The Yankee Trader** shop in Liberty Square.

Clue 127: Look down at the hoofprints.
4 points

Clue 128: Look around the Square for a tiny Hidden Mickey on a shopping stand.
4 points

★ Walk over and look inside **Ye Olde Christmas Shoppe**.

Clue 129: Spot a stack of logs with a Hidden Mickey.
2 points

★ Walk into the **Liberty Tree Tavern**.

Clue 130: Search for a classic Mickey in the waiting area.
3 points

Clue 131: Now look for a classic Mickey in a painting in one of the seating areas to the left of the waiting area. (Psst! You'll have to climb some stairs to find this Hidden Mickey.)
4 points

★ Enter the **Frontier Trading Post** in Frontierland.

Clue 132: Look for two rope classic Mickeys.
3 points for spotting both

Clue 133: Spot a cowboy with a Hidden Mickey.
3 points

★ Check out the inside of **Pecos Bill Tall Tale Inn and Cafe**.

Clue 134: Squint for a classic Mickey on a plate that's sitting on a ledge.
4 points

★ Head for Adventureland and stop inside **Tortuga Tavern**.

Clue 135: Search for a candle image.
3 points

★ Pick up a FASTPASS for *Jungle Cruise*, if available. Then head on over to enjoy **Walt Disney's Enchanted Tiki Room**.

Clue 136: Find classic Mickeys at the bottom of two bird perches. One is in the left corner as you enter, and you'll find the other in the right corner as you exit.
3 points each

Clue 137: Near the entrance to *Walt Disney's Enchanted Tiki Room*, look around for a Hidden Mickey on a statue.
3 points

Clue 138: Study the cement for a tiny classic Mickey between the Agrabah Bazaar shop and *The Magic Carpets of Aladdin* ride.
4 points

★ Eat an early dinner either before or after riding *Jungle Cruise*. One choice: The Crystal Palace buffet. Disney characters visit your table there, but reservations are usually needed unless you're both early and lucky.

★ Ride *Jungle Cruise* during your FASTPASS window and search for six Hidden Mickeys and two Hidden Donalds.

Clue 139: Study the sign outside for a Hidden Mickey.
2 points

Clue 140: Along the entrance queue, spot some nuts that resemble Mickey.
2 points

Clue 141: Study a tree across the river from the loading dock for a small white classic Mickey.
4 points

Clue 142: Watch for Donald Duck's face on a canoe.
4 points

Clue 143: Look to the right of a rhinoceros for a Hidden Mickey.
5 points

Clue 144: Stay alert for a Hidden Mickey on an airplane.
4 points

Clue 145: Search the riverbanks for Donald Duck's face on a native.
4 points

Clue 146: Coming out of the temple, look hard at the first undecorated column on the left for a chipped area of brick that forms part of a profile of Mickey's head and face. (This is a tough one!)
5 points

★ Walk through the *Swiss Family Treehouse*.

Clue 147: Keep alert for Mickey on the tree trunk.
5 points

Clue 148: Look around outside the attraction for Mickey on a rock.
4 points

★ Check out the shields on the **Adventureland bridge to the hub** in front of Cinderella Castle.

Clue 149: Find two Hidden Mickeys.
3 points for both

★ Now cross the park to Tomorrowland and go to **Tomorrowland Transit Authority People-Mover**. Find a Hidden Mickey as you ride.

Clue 150: In the last part of the ride, observe the accessories of the woman getting her hair done.
3 points

★ Walk to the **Merchant of Venus** shop.

Clue 151: Find a classic Mickey on a wall mural.
2 points

Clue 152: Can you spot a Mickey hat?
2 points

★ Now scan the wall mural inside **Mickey's Star Traders** shop.

Clue 153: Look for the train on the mural.
2 points

Clue 154: Find the Hidden Stitch.
3 points

Clue 155: Spot Mickey hats on a building.
2 points

Clue 156: Look up higher at the satellite dishes.
2 points

Clue 157: Scan the road layout.
3 points

Clue 158: Find three clear domes.
2 points

Clue 159: Follow the mural around to another classic Mickey on a building.
1 point

★ Cross the nearest bridge to **Main Street, U.S.A.** and search for 18 or more classic Mickeys as you stroll toward the park entrance.

Clue 160: Look around the outside of The Crystal Palace restaurant.
3 points

Clue 161: Check out a classic Mickey image in the Main Street Bakery.
3 points

Clue 162: As you enter the short side street off of Main Street, study the area near the bricks outside the entrance to the Crystal Arts store for a tiny classic Mickey.
5 points

Clue 163: Near the Emporium store outside, search for Hidden Mickeys on a sign.
3 points for all

Clue 164: Find Mickey in stained-glass windows high on the Emporium exterior.
3 points

Clue 165: Study the outside display windows of the Emporium store for a Hidden Mickey in a logo.
4 points

Clue 166: Inside the Emporium store, study the merchandise stands.
2 points

Clue 167: Look for a tiny Mickey on a building in an outside display window of the Emporium store.
5 points

Clue 168: Observe the overhead moving candy bins in the Main Street Confectionery near Town Square.
3 points

★ Closely examine the **Caffe Italiano coffee cart** (present seasonally) near Tony's Town Square Restaurant to earn some bonus points.

2 bonus points

Clue 169: Inside Tony's Town Square Restaurant, spot Mickey on a bookshelf.
3 points

Clue 170: Study the floor inside Tony's for a classic Mickey.
5 points

Clue 171: Now look around inside the restaurant for a classic Mickey under a painting.
3 points

Clue 172: Look up for a classic Mickey as you exit the restaurant.
3 points

Clue 173: Find Hidden Mickeys on Main Street's horse-drawn trolley.
2 points

Clue 174: Stand in Town Square plaza and look for a classic Mickey on a ceiling.
2 points

Clue 175: Look around the Main Street Train Station for a Hidden Mickey on a ticket.
4 points

Clue 176: Find a Hidden Mickey on the wall inside the Main Street Train Station.
3 points

★ Ride the **WDW Railroad** around the park to search out another Hidden Mickey.

Clue 177: Try to spot the reclining Mickey in the clouds as your train chugs through *Splash Mountain*.
4 points

★ Enjoy the **evening parade**. You'll likely find a few Hidden Mickeys (and several decorative Mickey images) on the floats.

Clue 178: If it's the *Main Street Electrical Parade*, search for a classic Mickey on the front of a vehicle. 2 points

★ You can often spot a classic Mickey in the sky during the evening **Wishes fireworks** show. If you see one, give yourself bonus points!

5 bonus points for spotting one or more

★ Keep your eyes peeled for another Hidden Mickey or two as you end your day in the park.

Clue 179: As you leave Main Street under the train station, search for Mickey on a gate. 2 points

★ Ride the **ferryboat** from the Magic Kingdom to the Transportation and Ticket Center.

Clue 180: As you walk onto the ferry and as you exit the ferry at the TTC, look around for a classic Mickey. 4 points

★ If you go through the **Transportation and Ticket Center** (TTC), check out a cool Hidden Mickey and earn some bonus points.

Clue 181: Study the TTC ceiling skylights. 5 bonus points

Now turn the page and tally your score.

Total Points for Magic Kingdom =

How'd you do?

Up to 247 points – Bronze
248 to 493 points – Silver
494 points and over – Gold
618 points – Perfect Score

If you earned bonus points in *Peter Pan's Flight, Under the Sea ~ Journey of the Little Mermaid, Pirates of the Caribbean,* on Main Street, U.S.A., at the fireworks, or in the TTC, you may have done even better!

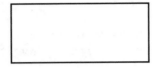

**Caution:
Don't peek at this
section unless you
really want help!**

Magic Kingdom Entrance

Hint 1: Classic Mickeys are formed in the bell clapper designs of some of the commemorative bricks in the walkways in front of the Magic Kingdom.

Main Street, U.S.A. – Train Station

Hint 2: The periphery of the Main Street Train Station roof, second level, has scrollwork that repeats a classic Mickey motif.

Fantasyland

– *Enchanted Tales with Belle*

Hint 3: Inside the first room of Maurice's cottage, a stack of firewood stands to the left of the fireplace. An upright classic Mickey made of three logs is at the lower middle of the stack, and a sideways classic Mickey is at the upper middle left of the stack. Other combinations of logs also resemble classic Mickeys.

– Peter Pan's Flight

Hint 4: At the lower right of the entrance-sign cloud formation is an incomplete classic cloud Mickey. All you can see is the top of the head and the ears. It's just to the right of the "t" in "Peter," and Peter Pan is standing between Mickey's ears.

Hint 5: Close to the entrance turnstile, a group of trees faces the loading area. The fourth tree from the far end has a dark classic Mickey in the bark about half-way up the trunk.

Hint 6: Three brown rocks in the yard in front of the doghouse form a classic Mickey. The rocks are in the brown dirt section of the yard. Mickey's smiling face may be on the "head" rock, but it's hard to spot!

Bonus Points Hint: When the rotating moon is in just the right position, you can see a dark classic Mickey on the moon, above the silhouettes of the flying Peter Pan and his entourage. Unfortunately, since the moon rotates, you can't spot this Hidden Mickey on every ride through the attraction.

Hint 7: On the rocky edge of the mermaid lagoon, three flowers on the grass form a classic Mickey; the "head" is yellow and the "ears" are light orange.

– The Many Adventures of Winnie the Pooh

Hint 8: Inside the big tree, a classic Mickey is formed by embedded rocks above the frame of the smaller children's entrance.

Hint 9: Above the frame of the larger entrance inside the big tree is a depression in the wood shaped like a submarine: a tribute to the previous *20,000 Leagues Under the Sea* attraction at this location; thus, a Hidden Tribute rather than a Hidden Mickey.

 Hint 10: On the outside of the big tree, in back, a side profile of Mickey is carved

into the bark. It's at the upper left corner above the lower window.

Hint 11: Outside on the far side of the big tree, behind the fence, a classic Mickey is etched into the wood in the middle of a vertical brown post on the left side of a window.

Hint 12: Two Hidden Mickeys are in Rabbit's Garden along the entry area (accessed through the Standby queue):
- A head of lettuce and two tomatoes form a classic Mickey, and
- Three watermelon drums are positioned to create a classic Mickey

Hint 13: At the beginning of the ride, in Rabbit's Garden, the small marker with radishes (in the middle pot to the left of the "Letus" sign) has one radish shaped like a classic Hidden Mickey.

Hint 14: At the beginning of the left wall of Owl's house (the second room on the ride) is a picture of Mr. Toad handing the deed to the house over to Owl (a tribute to the previous attraction in this building, *Mr. Toad's Wild Ride*).

Hint 15: Near the end of this room, on the right side of the floor, is a picture of Mole standing with Winnie the Pooh.

– Under the Sea ~ Journey of The Little Mermaid

Hint 16: A classic Hidden Mickey made of three circular impressions in the rock is to the upper right of the sign at the Standby entrance to the attraction.

Hint 17: On the right side along the outside Standby entrance queue, a classic Mickey made of impressions is at the top right side of a rock that sits in the middle of the small lagoon in front of the waterfall.

Hint 18: At the left side of the outside Standby entrance queue, a Nautilus submarine impression is in a rock wall behind a small pond. When you reach a fence on your left strewn with ropes and nets, look back to your left and study the rear rock wall near the waterline. First spot the round porthole that resembles an eye; the nose of the submarine points to the left.

Note: "Nautilus" is the submarine, commanded by Captain Nemo, in Jules Verne's novel *Twenty Thousand Leagues Under the Sea*. It was the ride vehicle in the WDW ride of the same name, which closed in 1994.

Hint 19: Each year on Mickey Mouse's birthday (November 18) the noontime sun shines through holes carved in the rockwork above you at just the right angle to form a classic Mickey on the wall of the inside entrance queue. The Mickey light lasts for several minutes. The top of Mickey's head is formed by the carving in the highest rock and the lower part of his head, by the carving in the rock closer to you. Stay alert, because the sunlight just might shine through both rock openings at other times of the year to form Mickey!

Hint 20: Along the left side of the inside Standby entrance queue, a classic Mickey tilted to the left is formed by holes in the rock above some bottles on a table.

Hint 21: In the first part of the room where the song "Under the Sea" is playing, three oval purple corals clinging to a rock to the right of your ride vehicle form a classic Mickey. They're just past and behind the singing chorus line of fish that are standing on their tails.

Hint 22: Toward the end of the ride, check the pond (to your right) for frogs with dark green spots on their backs that form sideways classic Mickeys. The frogs are perched on lily pads to the left of Ariel and Eric in a boat.

Hint 23: Along the inside exit queue from the ride, a classic Mickey is formed of three impressions in the rock wall to your far left. To spot it, look to the far wall through an opening in the near left wall. The image is tilted to the left. It's about halfway up the wall and below a ceiling light. (Note: You'll probably find other rock impressions along the exit that resemble classic Mickeys.)

Hint 24: At the end of the exit walkway from *Under the Sea,* turn to your right to spot an amazing Hidden "Steamboat Willie" Mickey Mouse. The Imagineers sculpted this image on a series of rocks. His left leg and shoe are closest to you, then his right leg and shoe are on the next rock. Two holes in the rocks represent the buttons on his shorts. His whitish face is on a flat rock, and he's looking left. His tall hat is the last rock above his head. There's even a ship's wheel in the rock to the left of his face!

– Ariel's Grotto

Hint 25: Soon after you make the last right turn inside the entrance queue for *Ariel's Grotto,* on the lower part of the rear wall near the floor on your left, a side profile of Mickey Mouse looking to the left is sculpted in relief on the wall.

Frontierland

– Big Thunder Mountain Railroad

Hint 26: Three stalagmites in the cavern to your right at the beginning of the ride form a classic Mickey. Look down at the left side of the floor of the cavern to spot it.

Hint 27: At the end of the ride, just past the dinosaur bones on the right side of the track, you'll see sets of gear wheels lying on the ground. The first set of gears resembles a classic Hidden Mickey and the second set looks more like Winnie the Pooh. (You can also spot these gears from the FASTPASS queue.)

Hint 28: On the left side as you exit the ride (in the exit closest to the Standby line entrance), a cutout in the reddish rock resembles a side profile of Tinker Bell. She's behind the fence, behind a cactus, and between two metal carts.

– Splash Mountain

Hint 29: A red classic Hidden Mickey is painted on a yoke that hangs on a left wall of the entrance queue. It's in the first tunnel. Start looking for it when you reach the part of the tunnel with lights on the wall. You can spot it from both the Standby and FASTPASS queues.

Hint 30: Halfway up the second crankhill, on the right side, three barrels in the lower right corner of a stack of barrels form a classic Mickey.

Hint 31: During the first part of the ride, when your boat is outside, look to your right for a barrel with "Muskrat Moonshine" painted on the side. A classic Mickey is formed by holes in the paint, above the "s" in "Muskrat."

Hint 32: Look for a picnic basket up on a small ledge. You'll spot it just past Brer Frog, who is sitting on an alligator and fishing with his toe. Near the basket are three red-and-white-striped fishing bobbers in the shape of a classic Hidden Mickey.

Hint 33: On the right side of your boat, in the room with jumping water, a classic rope Mickey is hanging halfway down from the ceiling. It's in the shadows behind a lantern and just past a turtle lying on a geyser.

Hint 34: The hole in the mountain at the top of the big drop is sculpted to form a side profile of Mickey's face. As you approach the big drop in your boat, Mickey's nose juts out from the left side of the hole. (You can also see this one from the outside viewing area; see Hint 37.)

Hint 35: Near the end of the ride, the upper outline of one of the white clouds on the right side of the riverboat scene is shaped like Mickey Mouse lying on his back, with his head to the right. (This Hidden Mickey is also visible from the *Walt Disney World Railroad* train as it passes through *Splash Mountain*; see Clue and Hint 177.)

Hint 36: As you pass the photo viewing area on your way out, look over to the entrance queue to spot two classic Mickeys formed by acorns on a birdhouse with a rope ladder. One classic Mickey formation is above a door and below blue roof slats. The other is near the peanut-shell chimney, above the curve of the red rail.

Hint 37: Walk in front of *Splash Mountain* after your ride. The hole in the mountain for the big drop forms a side profile of Mickey's face. From the outside, Mickey's nose juts out from the right side of the hole.

Liberty Square

– Haunted Mansion

Hint 38: Along the interactive "Scenic Route," a classic Mickey made of barnacles is on a huge bathtub with the words "Here Floats Captain Cul-pepper Clyne." The classic Mickey is tilted right and is below and between the letters "r" and "C" in the name.

Hint 39: Just inside the entrance to the first room, you'll find some small classic Mickeys in the oval border design around the portrait of the dressed-up aging man above the fireplace.

Hint 40: As you pass by the library room (at the beginning of the ride) and then the "endless hall-way" on your right, check out the backs of two purple chairs for an abstract Donald Duck. Near the top of the chairs, you can see his cap, which sits above his distorted eyes, face, and bill. (Note that the chairs may change locations at times.)

Hint 41: A plate and two saucers on the ghostly banquet table are arranged to form a classic Mickey. They're usually at the bottom left corner of the table.

Hint 42: In the first part of the attic area, on the floor to your left under a small table with shelves, plates form a classic Mickey.

Hint 43: To the right of the opera-singing lady (her left) is a ghost resembling the Grim Reaper. He is holding up his left arm. Hanging from his left hand is a cloth with markings at the top that form a classic Hidden Mickey.

Hint 44: Outside, at the left end of the covered walkway, a classic Mickey metal latch holds a wrought iron gate open.

Hint 45: In the pet cemetery on the left side of the outside exit walkway, a Mr. Toad tombstone stands at the rear left corner.

– Columbia Harbour House restaurant

Hint 46: In the downstairs table area, a wall across from the food-order counters is decorated with three small circular maps covered by a single piece of glass. (The central map is labeled "Charles V.") The three circles form a classic Mickey.

Adventureland

– Pirates of the Caribbean

Hint 47: About halfway along the left queue, a pile of cannonballs appears on the floor to your left. A classic Mickey made of cannonballs is on the lower left area of the pile.

Hint 48: Along the left entrance queue is a room with a faux fireplace on the right side. A classic Mickey is in the plaster on the sloping area to the right and above the fireplace mantle. It's about seven feet up from the floor.

Hint 49: Tall gun cabinets stand on both sides of the left entrance queue. On two of the cabinets are classic Mickey-shaped locks (one on each side).

Hint 50: At the beginning of the ride, Davy Jones's image is sometimes projected on a wall of mist in front of the boat. Look up at the left side of his hat (his right side, viewers' left). Below and to the left of the bottom of the "V" at the

50

front of his hat, three tiny gold balls form a classic Mickey.

Hint 51: About halfway through the ride and past the red-haired lady, a cat behind an intoxicated pirate casts a classic Hidden Mickey moving shadow on the corner of the wall above and behind it.

Hint 52: As your boat approaches the last scene (the treasure room), a classic Mickey lock hangs on large wooden recessed doors to the left.

Hint 53: As the treasure room comes into view, a classic Mickey lock hangs at the middle of the wooden door that's swung open on the left. A long key with a cord hanging from it juts out of the keyhole of the lock.

Hint 54: Classic Mickey locks hang on the cabinets behind Captain Jack Sparrow in the treasure room.

Hint 55: Just as you enter the gift shop after exiting your boat, several classic Mickeys are formed by either coins or jewels in hanging plates near the right wall. Look along the edges of the plates for some of the best images.

Hint 56: After you exit the ride, turn left and find a painting at the lower right of a wall map on the rear wall of the gift shop. In the painting, a lady in a multicolored gown has a classic Mickey on her left shoulder.

Hint 57: Rocks forming a classic Mickey are in The Crow's Nest shop, inside and on the right of the front display case. This shop is at the edge of Adventureland, near Frontierland.

Frontierland

– Frontierland Shootin' Arcade

Hint 58: In the front center of the target area is a group of cactus plants. One near the middle, just below the gray tombstone, has three lobes forming a classic Hidden Mickey.

Liberty Square

– Stocks near the Liberty Square Riverboat entrance

Hint 59: Padlocks on the stocks near the entrance are shaped to resemble classic Hidden Mickeys (even though the "ears" are a bit small).

Tomorrowland

– Near Tomorrowland Speedway

Hint 60: A tall lamp post casts a classic Mickey shadow on the pavement. It's best seen on a sunny day in the late morning or early afternoon.

– Buzz Lightyear FASTPASS machines

Hint 61: On the right side of the display at the top of the FASTPASS machines for *Buzz Lightyear's Space Ranger Spin* is a classic Mickey with red ears.

– Monsters, Inc. Laugh Floor

Hint 62: On the outside wall, a picture advertising a Recreational Rocket has a moon with craters shaped like an upside-down classic Mickey.

Hint 63: Also on the outside wall, a sign advertising a Space Collectibles Convention includes an asteroid shaped like a classic Mickey.

Hint 64: As you enter the attraction, look for a window display of a city on the rear of the right-hand wall just past the entrance doors to the second room. A classic Mickey is under the apex of the triangular roof segment on the building in the front center of the window display.

– Walt Disney's Carousel of Progress

Hint 65: In the first scene, on the right side of the stage, where the daughter is getting ready for the evening (on Valentine's Day), a classic Mickey made of cloth decorates the top of her mirror.

Hint 66: In the third scene, Mickey's Sorcerer's Hat sits at the right side of the room, next to the girl in the shaker machine.

Hint 67: In the last scene, an abstract Mickey Mouse as the Sorcerer's apprentice from the film *Fantasia* is in a painting on the dining room wall. To spot it, look immediately to the left rear of the scene as it rotates into view. The painting is on the dining room's right rear wall.

Hint 68: On the left side of the room, a nutcracker shaped like Mickey Mouse stands on the left side of the mantelpiece.

Hint 69: Under the Christmas tree, a plush Mickey Mouse is behind the wrapped boxes.

Hint 70: On the last stage, one of the Christmas presents under the tree (near the grandfather's chair) is decorated with a large classic Mickey head cut out of green paper and glued to the side of the gift. The gift is partially hidden by another present, so you see the ears and part of the top of Mickey's head. The green Mickey ears are to the right of Grandpa's lower leg.

Hint 71: A classic Mickey appears (just for a few seconds) on the top of a spaceship in the middle of the television screen. Look for it just as the game starts on the TV, before Grandma starts playing.

Hint 72: A pepper grinder on the kitchen counter has Mickey ears. Look for it as you exit the room.

Hint 73: Along the exit ramps, classic Mickeys are on the backs of the round signs for the attraction.

HINTS HINTS HINTS HINTS HINTS HINTS HINTS HINTS HINTS HINTS HINTS HINTS HINTS

– Buzz Lightyear's Space Ranger Spin

Hint 74: Just inside the building, in the entrance queue, the second poster on the right wall is called "Planets of the Galactic Alliance." In Sector 1, the central continent on the planet "Pollost Prime" is shaped like a side profile of Mickey Mouse's head.

Hint 75: At the right lower corner of this poster, a purple planet ("Planet Z") has three craters that form a sideways classic Mickey with "ears" to the left.

Hint 76: The side-profile Mickey continent appears in the top left of a recessed wall further along the entrance queue, to the left of the large View Master.

Hint 77: Sector 2 in this same mural contains a planet made of many spheres, some of which form classic Mickeys. One of them is at the outer edge of the planet at about the "10 o'clock" location.

Hint 78: On the ride, in the very first interactive room with targets, a tiny classic Mickey with a green head and blue ears is on the first part of the lower right wall. You have to rotate back and to the right in your vehicle to see it. The Hidden Mickey is below and between two five-point green stars.

Hint 79: You go through three different rooms during the first part of this ride. When you enter the room with lots of batteries, look to the left of the ride vehicle. You'll see a side profile of Mickey's head in the rear left under the words, "Initiate Battery Unload."

Hint 80: Also in the battery room, look to the right of your vehicle and high over Zurg's left (your right) shoulder to spot a tiny blue classic Mickey star, tilted to the left. It's in the star field to the right of the large blue and yellow cone suspended over Zurg.

Hint 81: As the ride vehicle moves through the space video room, planet "Pollost Prime," with continent Mickey, flies by on the right wall.

Hint 82: Just past the space video room, in the final battle scene on the ride,

"Pollost Prime" shows up yet again on a wall straight ahead and to the upper left.

Hint 83: A yellow classic Mickey is on the wall across from the video monitors that show ride photos. An alien is pointing up to it.

Hint 84: Stitch's spaceship is flying through space in a corner of the first mural on the right wall as you exit the ride.

– Astro Orbiter

Hint 85: A small classic Mickey is traced in the cement close to a support beam near *Astro Orbiter* on the side toward *Space Mountain*, between Cool Ship and The Lunching Pad.

Liberty Square

– The Hall of Presidents

Hint 86: On a wall painting in the waiting room for the show, a tiny classic Mickey is at the end of the object George Washington holds in his left hand.

– Liberty Square Riverboat

Hint 87: At the right end of the bridge from Frontierland (as you face it from the boat), three rocks form a classic Mickey. They're located between the last two vertical posts that support the handrail, about one foot down from the top of the rocks. (Note: This Hidden Mickey is also visible from *Tom Sawyer Island*.)

Frontierland

– Tom Sawyer Island

Hint 88: Halfway through Old Scratch's Mystery Mine, bright shining gems embedded in the wall form a side profile of Goofy. He's looking to your right.

Hint 89: To the left of the Goofy gems, black stones on the ground against the far left of the rear wall form an upside-down classic Mickey.

Hint 90: In Fort Langhorn, enter the Rifle Roost at the far right corner (as you stand at the entrance to the fort). On top of the right handrail, about halfway up the steps to the top of the Rifle Roost, there is a Hidden Mickey created by: a wood knot, an additional mark, and an indentation in the wood.

Fantasyland

– Mickey's PhilharMagic

Hint 91: In the first waiting area inside, the wall mural with musical instruments has several small white classic Mickeys.

Hint 92: On the right vertical border of the video screen in the main theater, a classic Mickey hides inside a French horn.

Hint 93: In the "Be Our Guest" portion of the movie, there is a point where you are watching Lumiere dancing on the table with other characters. The view goes to an overhead shot and there are shadows cast on the table from the candle hands of Lumiere. These shadows come together at times to form what appears to be a Hidden Mickey.

Hint 94: In "The Little Mermaid" segment, Ariel throws out jewels in the water in front of her. Stay focused on the right side of the screen (your right), to spot a ring as it rotates slowly from a rim position to an open circle. A dark classic Mickey image is visible just as you first spot the open center of the ring. The image disappears as the ring finishes its rotation.

Hint 95: Watch closely as Aladdin and Jasmine ride their magic carpet in the sky. Stare at the bottom left of the screen for a quick glimpse of three round buildings on the ground. They're clustered to form a classic Mickey.

Hint 96: Music stands shaped like classic Mickeys are on shelves high up above the merchandise in Fantasy Faire at the exit of *Mickey's PhilharMagic*.

– Pinocchio Village Haus restaurant

Hint 97: As you head from the dining area to the restrooms, a tiny dark classic Mickey appears above the word "dreams" on the "When You Wish Upon A Star" mural. You'll find it on the left wall near the exit to the restrooms.

Hint 98: On the left side of the same mural, a tiny white classic Mickey hides near a sparkling star. It's to the left of the Fairy, at the level of her mid right thigh, and her right thumb points to it.

– Fairytale Garden

Hint 99: At the base of the first light pole on the right as you enter, a classic Mickey that looks like a piece of different colored stucco is in the cement on the side next to the fence.

Hint 100: A side profile of Pluto's head is on the wall, upper left of the stage. It's left of the brick circle and above the stairs.

– "it's a small world"

Hint 101: Toward the end of the Africa room, vines on the right above the giraffes and to the left of your boat have purple leaves shaped like classic Mickey heads.

Hint 102: Near the end of the South Pacific room, several koala bears hang on a tree. As you approach the bears on your left, the back of the blue bear's head forms a classic Mickey.

– Near Peter Pan's Flight

Hint 103: Between *Peter Pan's Flight* and the restrooms nearby (next to Liberty Square), you'll find paintings of grape clusters on the walls. The lower three grapes in the second cluster from the right at the bottom form a classic Mickey.

– Sir Mickey's Store

Hint 104: You'll find a classic Mickey toward the top of the store's sign-shield. The shield is hanging under a vine, across from Tinker Bell's Treasures shop.

Hint 105: In a display window to the right of the main entrance to the store, classic Mickeys are on the border of the archer's collar in a painting on the rear wall of the display. You can also usually find classic Mickeys made by arrangements of buttons on the floor of the display.

– Castle Couture shop

Hint 106: To find a tiny classic Mickey on the wall, walk through the entrance doors to the right of the Cinderella fountain. Then turn right and look up at the bronze horizontal frieze near the ceiling. You'll spot a series of arches over bushes with flowers. Walk forward to the far end of the frieze and count back six arches to a bush with three flowers at its upper left that form a classic Mickey. If you have trouble spotting it, ask a Cast Member to point it out for you.

– Storybook Circus area

Hint 107: Between the exit of the Fantasyland Train Station and the nearby restrooms is a trail of large and small (mother and baby) elephant tracks. These prints in the pavement come together at times to form classic Mickeys.

Hint 108: On the "Giraffes" boxcar in *Casey Jr. Splash 'N' Soak Station*, a classic Mickey is hidden in the clouds behind a giraffe in a painting on the side of the boxcar facing the restrooms. The cloud Hidden Mickey is behind the lower neck of the tall giraffe and it's tilted to the right.

Hint 109: Under the entrance sign to *The Barnstormer*, two classic Mickeys are in the scrollwork below Goofy's picture. The

images are at the top corners on each side of the faux ticket booth window.

Hint 110: On the huge billboard on the right side of *The Barnstormer* (the billboard the ride train hurtles through), a tiny gray classic Mickey hides in the middle of the propeller of the lower plane on the far right side of the billboard.

Hint 111: A poster of Daisy Duck ("Madame Daisy Fortuna") is outside to the left of the entrance to *Pete's Silly Sideshow*. A faint classic Mickey is traced on the upper part of her light green blouse, just to the right of her right index finger.

Hint 112: Eight Mickey balloons are scattered around the large "Storybook Circus" painting at the rear of the tent over the FASTPASS machines for *The Barnstormer* and *Dumbo the Flying Elephant*. This tent is next to *Pete's Silly Sideshow*.

Hint 113: A classic Mickey is formed by a manhole cover (the "head") and two elephant tracks (the "ears") near the entrance to the FASTPASS queue for *Dumbo the Flying Elephant*.

– Enchanted Forest area:
Be Our Guest Restaurant

Hint 114: A faint classic Mickey in swirls is on top of a short rock wall to the left of the check-in station at the beginning of the entrance walkway to Be Our Guest Restaurant. It's on top of the last flat rectangular stone before the wall ends at the left side of the station.

Hint 115: Just inside the entrance to Be Our Guest Restaurant, as you enter into the room with suits of armor, the ax blade at the far right has a classic Hidden Mickey hole cut out of it.

Hint 116: On the left side of the rear wall of the Rose Gallery seating area (to the right of the restaurant's Ballroom dining room), look for a small painting of Mrs. Potts and Chip. Chip plays in a dish filled with bubbles. Three of those bubbles form a classic Mickey.

Hint 117: Inside the Be Our Guest Restaurant, walk to the West Wing room and stand in front of the rose at the rear of the room. Now turn and look up to your right to spot an amazing Hidden Mickey hole in tattered fabric hanging from the ceiling.

– Gaston's Tavern area

Hint 118: A tiny classic Mickey made of dark impressions in the rock is on the back side of Gaston's Statue in front of Gaston's Tavern. It's near the water line below Gaston's left leg.

Hint 119: Groups of circles in several antique maps on the wall inside the Bonjour Village Gifts shop resemble classic Mickeys. The most convincing image is on the "Terrestrial Globe" map on the left wall, on which a globe forms the head of an upside-down classic Mickey.

Main Street, U.S.A.

– Town Square Theater

Hint 120: When you take a flash photo of Mickey in the Electricity display in the Greeting Room, he turns into a skeleton Mickey in your photo.

Hint 121: A classic Mickey made of metal rings lies in the right upper compartment of Mickey's open magic chest in the Greeting Room.

Hint 122: Inside Mickey's magic chest, on the right, there's a classic Mickey lock on a chain (it's sometimes covered by a scarf). Additional Mickey-shaped locks can often be spotted in various locations in the Greeting Room.

Hint 123: Oswald the Lucky Rabbit is drawn on a piece of paper at the upper right of a bulletin board at the back of the room. He's to the right of a drawing of Mickey Mouse.

Hint 124: To the right of the exit door from the Greeting Room, three large Mickey Mouse playing cards are held upright by

a long clip on the floor. In the middle of the clip, a classic Mickey wearing a triangular "hat" resembles a sorcerer Mickey.

Hint 125: Classic Mickey locks hang from the side of a metal display table in the gift shop.

Hint 126: A birdhouse from the now-closed Mickey's Toontown Fair sits on a tall merchandise cabinet at the left side of the shop (as you enter from Mickey's greeting area). The front door of the birdhouse is shaped like a classic Mickey.

Liberty Square

– Outside The Yankee Trader shop

Hint 127: A classic Mickey with hoofprints for ears and a water utility cover for a head can be found in the cement equidistant between The Yankee Trader shop and the Columbia Harbour House restaurant, near the red cement.

Hint 128: A tiny red classic Mickey is painted on a finger of one of the hands on the side of Madame Leota's shopping stand.

– Ye Olde Christmas Shoppe

Hint 129: In the framed log collage under a register in the middle of the store, a classic Hidden Mickey formed by three logs hides in the upper left corner of a stack of logs.

– Liberty Tree Tavern

Hint 130: Look for a spice rack to the right of the fireplace on the rear wall of the waiting area. Three grapes in a small still-life painting on the spice rack form a classic Mickey.

Hint 131: Turn left from the waiting area and go up the stairs. Then turn right and enter a brown room with a fireplace on the inside. Go up to the fireplace (you'll have to climb a few more steps) and look for a classic Mickey in the clouds. You'll find it on the left side of the upper part of the painting that's hanging to the left of George Washington's portrait.

Frontierland

– Frontier Trading Post store

Hint 132: A "How to Pin Trade" sign, behind a register inside the store to the right, sports a rope classic Mickey. Another rope classic Mickey is attached to a pole. It stands above the merchandise, facing the middle entrance to the store.

Hint 133: In the "How to Pin Trade" posters, a cowboy's lanyard has a black classic Mickey.

– Pecos Bill Tall Tale Inn and Cafe

Hint 134: Inside the cafe, find the plates sitting upright along a ledge near the ceiling behind the middle of the serving counter. On the third plate from the left, at the upper left of the inside circle of the plate, three red spots behind the white bird form a classic Mickey.

Adventureland

– Tortuga Tavern

Hint 135: In a window display about pirates inside the Tortuga Tavern restaurant, three candles stuck in a bowl form a classic Hidden Mickey.

– Walt Disney's Enchanted Tiki Room

Hint 136: Upside-down classic Mickeys are camouflaged in the designs at the bottom of two bird perches. One perch is in the left corner as you enter the theater. The other is to the right of the exit door.

Hint 137: To the right of the entrance to *Walt Disney's Enchanted Tiki Room*, a statue with several faces has classic Mickeys formed by beads in the middle of the forehead, above the nose.

– Near The Magic Carpets of Aladdin

Hint 138: A charm embedded in the cement between *The Magic Carpets of Aladdin* exit and the Agrabah Bazaar shop contains a tiny classic Mickey. It's near a shop pole that has a strip of blue paint at the top of its base.

– Jungle Cruise

Hint 139: Check the big sign outside. On the side of the sign that faces the attraction, three barnacles under the "J" in "Jungle Cruise" form a classic Mickey.

Hint 140: Along the entrance queue, on a shelf facing the cruise boats, three walnuts in a jar resemble a classic Mickey.

Hint 141: Across the river from the loading dock, look for a hut with a tall tree behind it that leans to the right. There's a white classic Mickey marking on the tree bark above the hut. To spot it, follow the right-leaning tree trunk high up to the Mickey marking. It's about two-thirds of the distance up the trunk, where the trunk angles slightly more to the right.

Hint 142: Along the right side of the boat, watch for the Pygmy War Canoes sitting on a beach. The bow of the middle canoe resembles Donald Duck.

Hint 143: At the front middle of the scene with the safari group climbing a pole above a rhinoceros, three gray rocks on the ground form a classic Mickey.

Hint 144: After the waterfall, a wrecked silver plane sits to the right of the boat. Look back to spot three circles etched in the metal at the lower right of the visible section of fuselage. The circles are all the same size, but many folks and Cast Members consider them a Hidden Mickey.

Hint 145: Along the left side of the boat, be alert for menacing natives with spears. The last isolated native of the group wears a Donald mask.

Hint 146: The first undecorated column on the left wall (the third column from the end as you come out of the temple) has a chipped area of brick on the third block from the top. The chipped area forms part of a profile view of Mickey's head and face. Don't get discouraged if you have trouble spotting it; this one is tough to find — especially the first time.

– Swiss Family Treehouse

Hint 147: A side profile of Mickey, facing to the right, is on a section of the tree trunk that touches a wall of the treehouse. Mickey is in a clearing inside a large patch of green algae. You'll find it on the right as you descend the steps from the boys' bedroom and on the left as you walk down from the very top of the trail.

Hint 148: On the outdoor stone seating area near the Swiss Family Treehouse, a classic Mickey is etched in a rock. The rock rests on the seating area against a wooden pole. Mickey's head is made of circles and his ears are depressions in the rock.

– Adventureland bridge to the 'hub'

Hint 149: Shields are propped at the sides of the bridge connecting Adventureland with the hub in front of Cinderella Castle. Two classic Mickeys with smiley faces for "ears" appear on separate shields. One with white ears is at the bottom of one shield, while the other, an upside-down classic Mickey with blue ears, is at the top of a second shield.

Tomorrowland

– Tomorrowland Transit Authority PeopleMover

Hint 150: The woman getting her hair done sports a belt buckle with a classic Hidden Mickey.

– Merchant of Venus shop

Hint 151: Face the cash registers and look at the mural on the wall behind the left side register. In the foreground is one of Stitch's cousins holding a Mickey balloon. (Mickey's face is on the balloon).

Hint 152: In the same mural, another cousin of Stitch is wearing Mickey ears.

– Mickey's Star Traders shop

Hint 153: On the mural, the headlights of a train form a classic Mickey.

Hint 154: Stitch races beside a train in the mural.

Hint 155: Mickey hats sit atop windows halfway up the sides of a building.

Hint 156: Satellite dishes form a classic Mickey on top of this building.

Hint 157: Across the room on another mural, the middle circle of freeway loops forms a classic Mickey.

Hint 158: Over one of the entrance doors, clear domes form a classic Mickey.

Hint 159: The blue glass dome covering one building is a classic Mickey with ears.

Main Street, U.S.A.

Hint 160: On the roof of The Crystal Palace restaurant, the circles in the middle row of the tower above the main entrance resemble Mickey ears.

Hint 161: Along the left side of the Main Street Bakery entrance queue, a Mickey-shaped serving platter is partially hidden in the upper left of a display case. Other plate arrangements in the display cabinet aren't proportioned properly to be Hidden Mickeys.

Hint 162: A tiny classic Mickey is impressed in the cement outside the Crystal Arts store entrance. It's on a gray flagstone between the red cement and the bricks of the side street off of Main Street. Find a long crack (between red cement sections) that's parallel to Main Street and starts in front of the entrance pillars at the store entrance. The gray flagstone is at the end of this crack, and the Hidden Mickey is at the lower right corner of the flagstone as you face the store.

Hint 163: Outside along Main Street, just to the right of the Emporium shop and near the Athletic Club, a sign on a door has two classic Mickeys, at the top and bottom along the border.

Hint 164: The cupola above the Emporium, in the middle recessed area of the store, has stained-glass windows just below the highest eaves. The central flower circle in each window is joined with two frosted "ear" panels to form classic Mickeys.

Hint 165: In an outside display window in the middle recessed area of the Emporium store, a classic Mickey image hides on a piano above the words "Steinmouse & Sons." The display window is under a sign that says "Collectibles."

Hint 166: In the Emporium store, metal poles that hold up merchandise shelves sport classic Mickey holes.

Hint 167: In the outside Aladdin display window of the Emporium store, you'll find a small classic Mickey window in a building wall.

Hint 168: Candy bins in the Main Street Confectionery move along a track suspended from the ceiling. On the lower front and back sides of the bins, holes form classic Mickeys.

Bonus Points Hint: The sign on the Caffe Italiano cart, which appears seasonally in front of Tony's Town Square Restaurant, includes a classic Mickey in its design.

Hint 169: Inside Tony's Town Square Restaurant, as you enter the main dining area from the entrance waiting area, three white flowers form a classic Mickey on a bookshelf to the upper left.

Hint 170: When you enter Tony's inside dining area, look left to the corner and find the second floor tile to the right of the corner. There's a classic Mickey impression at the center right side of this black tile. If you view the Hidden Mickey from the seating area, it will appear upside-down.

Hint 171: A classic Mickey made of bread rolls is to the right as you enter the dining area inside Tony's Town Square Restaurant. It's sitting on an armoire under a painting from *Lady and the Tramp*.

Hint 172: A small classic Hidden Mickey is on the middle back of the overhanging entrance sign to Tony's Town Square Restaurant. Look up as you exit the restaurant.

Hint 173: Several classic Mickeys adorn the gear on the horse pulling the Main Street Trolley.

Hint 174: In Town Square plaza, walk about seven or eight steps away from the island curb towards the train station. As you approach the station, a classic Mickey is formed by circles on the train station ceiling. You might call this a "positional" classic Mickey because you have to be in just the right position to see it.

Hint 175: At the Main Street Train Station's faux ticket office upstairs, an image that looks like Mickey is on a baggage ticket next to the letter "K" inside the front window to the right. (Walk up the outside stairs to the office window, which faces Main Street.)

Hint 176: A classic Mickey-shaped lock can also be found inside the faux ticket office. Look for the lock hanging on the right wall behind the windows.

– From the WDW Railroad

Hint 177: In the riverboat scene near the end of the *Splash Mountain* ride, the upper outline of one of the white clouds on the right is shaped like Mickey Mouse lying on his back, his head to the right.

Note: This Hidden Mickey is also visible from the *Splash Mountain* ride; see Clue and Hint 35.

– Evening Parade

Hint 178: In the *Main Street Electrical Parade*, a classic Mickey is formed by circles on the front of the train Goofy is driving.

– Train Station Exit from Main Street

Hint 179: Classic Mickeys are repeated atop a tall gate, which is usually folded inside a recess beside the entrance and exit tunnel walkway under the Main Street Train Station.

Ferryboat Landing at Magic Kingdom

Hint 180: Ropes coiled into classic Mickeys can often be spotted at the ferry loading docks at the Magic Kingdom and at the Transportation and Ticket Center. Look next to a large post on either side as you walk onto or leave the boat at either loading dock. Cast Members usually maintain these rope images.

Transportation and Ticket Center

Hint 181: An imprint of Mickey's face, full frontal image, has remained over the years. It looks as though it was made by a balloon that melted against the glass. This Hidden Mickey is in the second overhead glass bubble from the tram, in the first row of bubble skylights to the right as you walk from the trams toward the monorail entrance ramps.

CHAPTER 3

Epcot Scavenger Hunt

••••••••••••••••••••••••••••

Note: Many of the Hidden Mickeys in this park are in restaurants and shops. Be considerate of fellow guests and Cast Members as you search. Tell them what you're looking for, so they can share in the fun. Avoid searching restaurants at busy meal times unless you are one of the diners.

★ Walk briskly to **Test Track**.

Clue 1: In the Standby entrance queue, look for a classic Mickey traced on the wall.
5 points

Clue 2: Now spot a white classic Mickey on the wall.
4 points

Clue 3: Watch for an interactive touch screen on the right wall of the Standby entrance queue. Make your own classic Mickey on top of the car!
5 points

Clue 4: On the ride, watch for a road sign on your right to spot a Hidden Mickey.
5 points

★ Cross Future World to The Land pavilion and get in line for **Soarin'**. (Ask a Cast Member at the entrance if the interactive games are playing along the Standby entrance queue. If they aren't, the Cast Member can call to activate the games.)

Clue 5: Along the entrance queue, five screens show changing artistic landscapes. (Note: These landscapes are not the interactive games; the games appear every few minutes on these same screens). Search for Mickey in the landscape with the purple mountain ridge in the lower background.
4 points

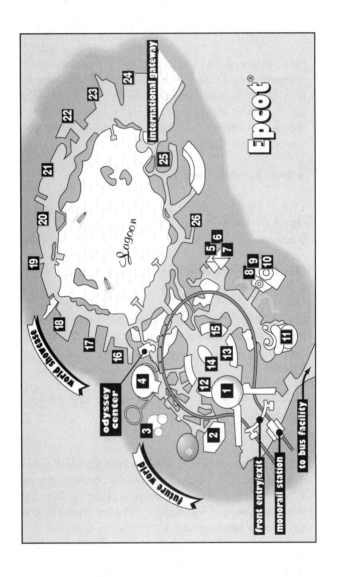

FUTURE WORLD

1 Spaceship Earth Pavilion
2 Universe of Energy Pavilion
3 Mission: SPACE Pavilion
4 Test Track Pavilion

Imagination! Pavilion
5 Captain EO
6 Journey Into Imagination with Figment
7 ImageWorks

The Land Pavilion
8 Living with the Land
9 The Circle of Life
10 Soarin'

11 The Seas with Nemo & Friends Pavilion
Turtle Talk with Crush
12 Innoventions East
13 Innoventions West
14 Innoventions Plaza
15 Epcot Character Spot

WORLD SHOWCASE

16 Mexico: Gran Fiesta Tour
17 Norway: Maelstrom
18 China: Reflections of China
19 Germany
20 Italy
21 The American Adventure: The American Adventure show
22 Japan
23 Morocco
24 France: Impressions de France
25 United Kingdom
26 Canada: O Canada!

Clue 6: Interactive games appear at times on these screens on the right wall of the entrance queue. Watch for the snowman!
4 points

Clue 7: In the "Bird Race" interactive game, stay alert for a Mickey image in a rock archway over a river.
5 points

Clue 8: In the pre-show video, spot the Mickey ears.
2 points

Clue 9: In the pre-show video, stay alert for Hidden Character clothing logos.
4 points for spotting two

Clue 10: While soaring, look left for a Mickey balloon.
4 points

Clue 11: Then look right for a Mickey shadow.
4 points

Clue 12: Don't blink at the golf ball!
5 points

Clue 13: A huge classic Mickey in the sky greets you at the end of your *Soarin'* ride.
3 points

★ Walk over to the **Mission: SPACE** Standby queue. Three Hidden Mickeys wait to be found.

Clue 14: Along the entrance queue, search for a Hidden Mickey on a planet.
4 points

Clue 15: Spot a Hidden Mickey in "status lights" on a monitor.
4 points

Clue 16: Look for waveform images on a monitor that form a Hidden Mickey.
4 points

Clue 17: Just before launch, keep your eyes

open for two identical Hidden Mickeys.
4 points

Clue 18: As you land on Mars, glance around for a
Hidden Mickey on a building.
4 points

Clue 19: After the ride, look for a Hidden Mickey on a
video console in the exhibit area.
2 points

Clue 20: Spot a Hidden Mickey on the ceiling of the
gift shop at the attraction exit.
4 points

Clue 21: Search for Donald and Pluto on the ceiling.
4 points for spotting both

Clue 22: Study the spaceship in a mural in the gift
shop.
3 points

Clue 23: Now squint for a small Hidden Mickey in the
same mural.
3 points

Clue 24: While you're at it, examine the mural for an
upside-down classic Mickey.
3 points

Clue 25: Now glance low for classic Mickeys near the
floor.
2 points

Clue 26: Find two classic Mickeys and a side-profile
Mickey on the wall of the gift shop.
2 points for spotting all three

Clue 27: Outside in the front plaza, search for a classic Mickey on the moon.
3 points

Clue 28: Look down for a classic Mickey in the blue
tile area out front.
5 points

Clue 29: In a blue tile stripe out front, spot a white classic Mickey near a gray disk.
4 points

Clue 30: Find two more classic tile Mickeys near a drain cover.
4 points for spotting both

★ Walk across Future World to The Seas with Nemo & Friends pavilion. Check out **Turtle Talk With Crush**.

Clue 31: Study the undersea images on the show screen for a classic Mickey.
3 points

★ Stroll to the Imagination! pavilion. Enjoy the **Captain EO** show.

Clue 32: Check out Captain EO's ship for a Hidden Mickey.
3 points

★ When World Showcase opens, take the path to the right of *Test Track*, heading toward World Showcase. Stop by the **Odyssey Center building**.

Clue 33: Glance inside for Mickey.
3 points

★ Go to **Maelstrom** in the Norway pavilion. Study the loading area mural to find two Hidden Mickeys. Then enjoy the ride and movie and find three more.

Clue 34: Find the Viking wearing Mickey ears.
3 points

Clue 35: Look for the cruise director with Mickey's face outlined in the creases of her shirt. (This is a hard one to spot.)
4 points

Clue 36: During the first part of the ride, find Mickey on the ground in front of a Viking.
5 points

Clue 37: While on the ride, check out a leaf-shadow Mickey on a rock archway above you.
5 points

Clue 38: During the movie after the *Maelstrom* ride, stay alert for Mickey above the trees.
4 points

★ Eat an early lunch to avoid the crowds. The San Angel Inn Restaurante in the Mexico pavilion is an ideal choice if you have 11:30 a.m. or so reservations. If not, try fast food at Mexico's Cantina de San Angel or the Kringla Bakeri Og Kafe in Norway.

★ If you eat in the San Angel Inn, look for classic Mickeys in the smoke rising from the volcano (see Clue 44).

★ Go to **Gran Fiesta Tour Starring the Three Caballeros** in Mexico and keep your eyes peeled for classic Mickeys.

Clue 39: At the beginning of the ride, take a close look at the smoke rising from the volcano.
4 points

Clue 40: In the first tunnel, search for Mickey on a necklace.
5 points

Clue 41: Find Mickey on a video screen on the wall.
5 points

Clue 42: Spot classic Mickeys in a small blue pond to the left of the boat.
4 points

Clue 43: Don't miss Mickey in a barge!
3 points

★ After exiting the ride, walk to the San Angel Inn Restaurante (if you haven't already been there) and look for classic Mickeys that appear and disappear.

Clue 44: Observe the smoke rising from the volcano. Ask the attendants to let you walk

to the fence by the river if you need a closer look.
4 points

★ Stroll over to **China**.

Clue 45: Search for Hidden Mickeys on posts in the courtyard.
4 points

★ Now study the water for possible bonus points.

2 bonus points for one or more Hidden Mickeys

★ Cross over the bridge to the **Outpost**.

Clue 46: Check out the wooden poles.
3 points

★ Walk left to **Germany** to find five classic Hidden Mickeys.

Clue 47: As you walk into the plaza, look for the classic Mickey on a suit of armor on the building to your right.
3 points

Clue 48: Spot Mickey behind a large bell.
3 points

Clue 49: Search for Mickey near a lion.
3 points

Clue 50: Study the woodwork inside Karamell-Küche for a Hidden Mickey.
5 points

Clue 51: Look for a Hidden Mickey in the exhibit's landscaping.
3 points

★ Continue to check out the landscaping around the train attraction to earn yourself some possible bonus points. (Note: These Hidden Mickeys come and go.)

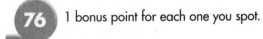

1 bonus point for each one you spot.

★ Stop at **Italy** to inspect the shops, statues, and restaurants.

Clue 52: Classic Mickeys are near the wine!
2 points

Clue 53: Look for Mickey behind a statue.
3 points

Clue 54: Find Mickey in the waiting area of Tutto Italia Ristorante.
3 points

★ Go to **The American Adventure** pavilion and step inside.

Clue 55: Search the walls for a classic Mickey in roses.
4 points

★ Now inspect the rear wall of the rotunda, upstairs and down, for classic Hidden Mickeys.

Clue 56: Study a picture in the rotunda for Hidden Mickeys on two metal beams.
3 points for spotting both

Clue 57: Take a good look at the bronze eagle reliefs in the rotunda.
2 points for each floor; 4 points total

★ Now watch **The American Adventure show** and keep an eye out for three hard-to-spot classic Hidden Mickeys. (Tip: Try to sit on the right side of the theater for the best view of the Hidden Mickeys.)

Clue 58: At the beginning of the film, look at the rocks behind a kneeling female pilgrim.
4 points

Clue 59: Stay alert for a Mickey image on a stockade.
3 points

Clue 60: At the end, watch the fireworks' explosions behind the Statue of Liberty Torch.
4 points

Clue 61: Outside, enjoy the Fife and Drum Corps and find four Hidden Mickeys. Check your Times Guide for performance times.
5 points for all spotting four

★ Stroll over to **Japan**.

Clue 62: Search for a classic Mickey in the koi fish pond.
2 points

Clue 63: Check out the grates at the bases of the trees in the courtyard.
2 points

Clue 64: Look around for Mickey in the bushes by the lagoon.
3 points

Clue 65: On your way to Morocco, don't miss the rock Mickey near the Mitsukoshi store!
5 points

★ Meander to **Morocco**.

Clue 66: Gaze at the front of the shop on the promenade for Hidden Mickeys.
2 points for one or more

Clue 67: Now look at the roof of this shop.
4 points

Clue 68: Search for Mickey on a hat in an inside display.
4 points

Clue 69: Find a Mickey made of basket lids on the wall of a shop.
4 points

Clue 70: Study a mural at the rear of the pavilion for three Hidden Mickeys.
5 points for spotting all three

Clue 71: Look for Aladdin's lamp near an outside shop.
3 points

★ Go to **France**.

Clue 72: Examine the grates at the bases of the trees in the courtyard.
2 points

Clue 73: Find the classic Mickey bush on the right side of the ornamental garden.
3 points

Clue 74: Look high for classic Mickeys on the outside of a shop.
2 points

Clue 75: Search for Remy the rat inside a shop in the pavilion.
4 points

Clue 76: Examine the inside of a shop for a red, white, and blue classic Mickey.
3 points

Clue 77: In the movie *Impressions de France*, spot Mickey's head and ears in the background of the wedding scene.
4 points

★ Enter the **United Kingdom**.

Clue 78: Check out a classic sports Mickey from the street.
2 points

Clue 79: Look around for Mickey stickers hidden inside merchandise cabinets in a UK store.
5 points for three or more

★ Now walk over to **Canada** to find more classic Mickeys.

Clue 80: Examine the totem pole on the left near the steps into the pavilion.
3 points

Clue 81: Inside a store, search for a classic Mickey on an animal.
4 points

Clue 82: Study the front of the stone steps near the theater for a classic Mickey.
4 points

Clue 83: Step inside Le Cellier Steakhouse for a Mickey made of wine.
3 points

★ Stroll over to the **Disney Traders** store in Showcase Plaza.

Clue 84: Enter the store and discover a running Mickey.
2 points

★ Return to Future World and walk to Club Cool at the end of Innoventions West. Enjoy free exotic and refreshing soft drinks from foreign countries.

★ Get a FASTPASS for the *Living with the Land* ride in The Land pavilion.

★ Head over to **The Seas with Nemo & Friends** to find ten or more Hidden Mickeys.

Clue 85: Look up along the entrance queue for the ride for a Hidden Mickey.
3 bonus points (This image is not always present.)

Clue 86: Keep alert on the ride for a Mickey in the rock. Look below the fifth video screen to spot it.
5 points

Clue 87: Walk upstairs and search for one or more Hidden Mickeys on the aquarium floor.
5 points for one or more

Clue 88: Downstairs, find two Hidden Mickeys in bubbles on the wall near the manatees.
5 points for spotting both

Clue 89: In Bruce's room downstairs, look around for classic Mickeys in two different windows.
4 points for spotting both

80

★ In the waiting area for **Turtle Talk**

With Crush, search for two Hidden Mickeys.

Clue 90: Spot a tiny Mickey in the coral on the wall.
5 points

Clue 91: Admire a Hidden Mickey on a starfish.
4 points

Clue 92: Now search for Mickey near the exit gift shop.
3 points

★ Head right to the **Living with the Land** ride at your FASTPASS time. Study the wall murals to find three classic Hidden Mickeys.

Clue 93: Take a good look at the bubbles in the mural at the rear of the entrance queue.
3 points

Clue 94: Examine the mural behind the loading area near the farmer's hat.
3 points

Clue 95: Now check the lower part of the mural behind the loading area.
3 points

Clue 96: On the ride, keep alert for a Cast Member with a Hidden Mickey on a video screen.
4 points

Clue 97: Search for a garden hose classic Mickey. (This Hidden Mickey is also visible on the "Behind the Seeds" tour.)
4 points

Clue 98: Spot Mickey in a horizontal water tube.
4 points

Clue 99: Along the ride, stay alert for one or more plastic gourds shaped like Mickey.
3 points

Clue 100: Look for plants arranged to form a Hidden Mickey.
4 points

Clue 101: Toward the end of the ride, find the green Hidden Mickey in the round test tube holder in a lab room.
3 points

Clue 102: Spot Mickey's name in this same lab room.
2 points

★ Go inside **The Garden Grill** restaurant upstairs and take a good look at the back wall.

Clue 103: Find and then marvel at the green face of Mickey Mouse on the left side of the large mural of vegetation. He's in three-quarter profile on the right side of a single fern and he's well camouflaged by the fern's leaves.
5 points

Clue 104: Observe Hidden Mickeys on the characters' clothing.
3 points

★ Go to the **interior railing** to the left of the pavilion's main entrance.

Clue 105: Focus on the side of one of the globes hanging over the lobby to spot another Mickey.
3 points

★ Now walk **outside** under the overhang and **face the entrance doors**.

Clue 106: Study the mosaic mural on the right wall for a classic Mickey in jewels.
4 points

Clue 107: Search the same mosaic mural for a classic Mickey in grapes.
4 points

★ Walk down the sloping walkway (from the pavilion) until you come to "The Land" sign out front.

Clue 108: Search for a classic Mickey in the stones embedded in a support for "The

Land" sign. (Tip: The support is covered with tiles and stone designs.)
4 points

Clue 109: If you take the "Behind the Seeds" tour, stay alert for a photo of the lettuce classic Mickey that you may have spotted earlier during the ride. While on the tour, you can also check on the garden hose Mickey (Clue 97).
3 points

★ Keep your reservations for dinner. If you don't have reservations, eat at the Food Court in The Land.

★ Go to the Imagination! pavilion and ride **Journey Into Imagination with Figment**.

Clue 110: Find a Hidden Mickey on a greaseboard. (Note: It's not always there.)
5 bonus points

Clue 111: Squint for a black pair of Mickey ears in the Sight Room.
4 points

Clue 112: Look up at Figment's bathtub for a classic Mickey.
3 points

Clue 113: Now look up again in Figment's bathroom for another classic Mickey near the bathtub.
3 points

Clue 114: Find a classic Mickey on a cloud in the rainbow room.
3 points

Clue 115: Search for a Mickey in snow.
5 points

Clue 116: Look for a classic Mickey on the wall along the exit hallway.
3 points

★ When you reach **ImageWorks** . . .

Clue 117: Look down inside for a classic Mickey.
4 points

★ Now cross through Innoventions West and head for **Spaceship Earth**. Line up for the ride.

Clue 118: During the ride, keep alert for classic Mickey light patterns on the floor to your right.
5 points

Clue 119: Now look quickly to your left for a Hidden Mickey in scrolls.
5 points

Clue 120: During the ride, notice the Hidden Mickey on the document in front of the sleeping monk.
4 points

Clue 121: In the Renaissance section, look quickly to your left to spot the classic Mickey formed by paint circles on a tabletop near a painter.
4 points

Clue 122: Look for a chalkboard with the name of a famous Mickey Mouse cartoon.
4 points

Clue 123: As you enter the large computer room, find a Mickey image on a desk to your right. (You can spot this image again in the large mirror on the rear wall as you pass by!)
5 points for spotting both the image and its reflection

Clue 124: After you exit the ride vehicle, look up for Mickey in the "Project Tomorrow" area.
3 points

★ Cross back through the Innoventions buildings to the **Universe of Energy**. Find a Hidden Mickey as you take in the show and ride.

Clue 125: After the dinosaur section of the ride, watch the movie and look for the shadow of Disney's Hollywood Studios'

"Earful" Tower (the tower with Mickey ears) in the door of a church in the background.
5 points

★ Walk to **Innoventions East** and look around for a nearby **restaurant**.

Clue 126: Spot Mickey on a menu.
3 points

★ Stroll inside Innoventions West to the **"Where's the Fire?"** attraction.

Clue 127: Look for Mickey in the logo.
3 points

Clue 128: Stare at a computer monitor screen.
3 points

Clue 129: Search for a classic Mickey near books.
2 points

Clue 130: Don't forget Goofy! (Tip: He's upside down.)
4 points

Clue 131: Walk by **"The Great Piggy Bank Adventure"** attraction and spot a Hidden Mickey on the wall.
3 points

★ Now go to **Club Cool**.

Clue 132: At the front entrance, look near the outside sign for Mickey.
3 points

Clue 133: Search inside Club Cool for a classic Mickey in the interior design.
3 points

Clue 134: Spot Mickey outside at the rear entrance.
3 points

★ Go to the **MouseGear shop**, where you'll find a number of Hidden Mickeys and décor Mickeys.

Clue 135: Before you enter MouseGear, find the classic Mickey in the sign above the shop entrance.
1 point

★ Now step inside, and keep your eyes peeled.

Clue 136: Examine the nuts on the display racks' bolts.
1 point

Clue 137: Then look for classic Mickeys at the ends of the display racks.
1 point

Clue 138: Now check out the bolt ends themselves.
2 points

Clue 139: Observe the gauges on the wall.
1 point

Clue 140: Search for Donald's shadow.
3 points

Clue 141: Spot a set of Hidden Mickey gears.
2 points

Clue 142: Can you find an image of Donald Duck with a classic Mickey on him?
2 points

Clue 143: Finally, look at the tops of the garment display mannequins.
1 point

★ Walk outside the shop toward *Test Track* and take the first right onto a **walkway leading to World Showcase**.

Clue 144: Stare at the cement as you walk until you discover a Hidden Mickey.
5 points

★ Walk to **Epcot Character Spot** and then walk on through the front entrance.

Clue 145: Look above the entrance doors to *Epcot Character Spot* for a Hidden Mickey.
3 points

Clue 146: Search for Mickey's hat in four different places in and around *Epcot Character Spot*.
5 points for spotting all four

Clue 147: Find Goofy and his Hidden Mickey.
3 points

Clue 148: Look around for a yellow classic Mickey made of buttons.
3 points

Clue 149: Don't miss a classic Mickey on a gray metal device.
3 points

Clue 150: Now find Mickey wearing earphones.
2 points

Clue 151: Spot Mickey's gloves.
2 points

Clue 152: Don't miss Mickey in the stars!
3 points

Clue 153: Find Mickey's ears.
1 point

Clue 154: Search for Mickey in the clouds.
3 points

Clue 155: Study your **Epcot Guidemap** for a tiny Hidden Mickey.
4 points

Now turn the page and tally your score.

Total Points for Epcot =

How'd you do?
Up to 211 points – Bronze
212 to 421 points – Silver
422 points and over – Gold
528 points – Perfect Score

If you earned bonus points along the entrance queue for *The Seas with Nemo & Friends*, in *Journey Into Imagination with Figment*, in China, and/or around Germany's miniature train exhibit, you may have done even better!

**Caution:
Don't peek at this
section unless you
really want help!**

Test Track

Hint 1: On the wall, along the right side of the Standby entrance queue is a photo collage of artists and designers. A classic Mickey is traced on a transparent drawing board, just above the right hand of a man wearing glasses and drawing with a Magic Marker.

Hint 2: In the middle of the photo collage of artists and designers, a tiny white classic Mickey lies above a white vertical dashed line. This Hidden Mickey is above the left forearm of a girl who is drawing on white paper.

Hint 3: A bit further along on the right wall of the Standby queue, look for an interactive screen with design criteria (efficiency, etc.) listed above a car. Touch the area along the top of the car and circles will appear. You can arrange these circles with your finger to form a classic Mickey.

Hint 4: On the ride, about halfway along the inside track, a classic Mickey hides on the first road sign on your right.

The Land

– *Soarin'*

Hint 5: Along the right side of the entrance queue, five screens show changing artistic landscapes. In the landscape with the purple mountain ridge in the lower background, a large green tree halfway up the right side of the screen hosts a classic Mickey group of flowers.

Hint 6: Watch for the interactive games on the screens along the right wall of the Standby entrance queue. In the game with the snowy scene, a snowman appears at the left side of the screen. His head is a side profile of Mickey Mouse.

Hint 7: In the "Bird Race" interactive game, watch as the bird follows a river. More than halfway through the game, a side-profile Mickey looking to the left appears as a cutout in the rock archway over the river.

Hint 8: In the pre-show video, a man who is wearing Mickey Mouse ears is asked to take them off.

Hint 9: In the pre-show video, a boy sitting in his ride seat is wearing a red shirt with a Grumpy logo and shorts sporting Mickey Mouse.

Hint 10: On the ride, when you soar over the hills and spot a golf course, look immediately to your lower left and find a golf cart. The man standing on the other side of the cart is holding a blue Mickey balloon.

Hint 11: Now look to the right side of the golf course. About halfway along the fairway a slightly distorted classic Mickey shadow is cast on the green grass by a cluster of three trees. The "ears" of the shadow Mickey touch the right side of the white cart path.

Hint 12: Look straight ahead and then down to the golf course. Spot the man who is about to swing a golf club. When he strikes the golf ball, it will head directly toward you. Watch the ball's rotation to see the dark classic Mickey on the surface of the ball.

Hint 13: As you complete your *Soarin'* ride over Disneyland, the second burst of fireworks forms a huge classic Mickey in the sky.

Mission: SPACE

Hint 14: On the far right and left (outer) video monitors in the Mission Control room, classic Mickey circles appear on the lower part of the surface of Mars.

Hint 15: Continue to watch the video loops as three "status lights" form a classic Mickey at the lower right side of the rightmost monitor screen.

Hint 16: During the video loop on either of the middle monitors, three small waveform images merge into a classic Mickey on the lower left of the screen.

Hint 17: You'll see identical faint classic Hidden Mickeys above a horizontal bar on both sides of the launch door before it opens and before you see the sky.

Hint 18: As your spacecraft is landing on Mars, look sharp for a classic Mickey made of satellite dishes on top of the second building from the end, on the right side of the landing strip.

Hint 19: In the Expedition Mars section of the exit exhibit area, you'll find small classic Mickeys in the design of the video-game joystick consoles at the upper left and upper right corners.

Hint 20: In the center of the gift shop near the exit doors, a large side profile of Mickey Mouse is painted on the ceiling in the middle square.

Hint 21: On either side of Mickey's side profile on the ceiling are side profiles of Donald Duck and Pluto (or is it Goofy?).

Hint 22: On the right side of the mural behind the gift shop's cash register, the three round thrusters behind the blue X-2 spaceship form an upside-down classic Mickey.

Hint 23: Look for Minnie Mouse in the same mural. There's a small classic Mickey in the dirt under her left foot.

Hint 24: On the left side of the mural behind the gift shop's cash register, you'll find an upside-down classic Mickey on the lower part of the moon.

Hint 25: The bases of some of the merchandise stands near the gift shop exit contain "support arches" in the shape of Mickey.

Hint 26: You can spot Hidden Mickeys in the electrical tubing on the wall on both sides of the exit door from the gift shop. There's a classic Mickey on one side and both a classic Mickey and a side-profile Mickey on the other.

– In the entrance plaza

Hint 27: Spot three craters that approximate a classic Mickey at the upper left of the Luna 8 landing site on the back side of the moon.

Hint 28: In the middle of a blue tile area, very near and to the left of a gold strip (as you face the attraction), you'll find a tiny tile classic Mickey (black head and blue ears).

Hint 29: A small classic Mickey formed of white tiles is toward the bottom of a blue tile stripe. Look for a gray disc in the cement, near the lowest part of the stripe. Mickey is hiding about four feet from the disc as you go toward the Mars planet.

92

Hint 30: Two more tile or stone classic Mickeys (black head and white ears) lie next to a drain cover. Look for the cover in a circle of tiles to the left of the *Mission: SPACE* sign.

The Seas with Nemo & Friends

– Turtle Talk With Crush

Hint 31: Look closely at the middle left side of the rear screen, near the edge, to spot a classic Mickey made of coral circles on the rock. Mickey's ears are angled to the left.

Imagination!

– Captain EO

Hint 32: In the movie, the three lower thrusters on the back of Captain EO's spaceship form a classic Hidden Mickey.

Odyssey Center

Hint 33: In the Odyssey Center building, classic Mickeys are in the carpet inside the doors that are nearest the bridge to the Test Track area. The largest circles are the "heads," and the smaller circles next to them form the "ears" of classic Mickeys.

Norway

– Maelstrom

Hint 34: On the left side of the large loading area mural, a Viking in a ship wears Mickey ears. He's sitting below the middle red stripe of the sail.

Hint 35: Toward the right side of the same mural, a woman cruise director holds a clipboard. To the left of the top of her clipboard, the creases in her white shirt form a side profile of Mickey's face. His face is slightly distorted and he's looking to your left.

Hint 36: At the beginning of the ride, to the right of your boat, look for the Viking blowing a horn. On the ground in front of him is a rope twisted into a classic Mickey.

Hint 37: On the ride as your boat is going backwards, just after you pass a huge polar bear on your left, you will pass through a rock archway. As your boat comes out from under it, stare at the archway. Leaves near the end of a vine on the left middle of the arch cast a classic Mickey shadow on the rock below the vine.

Hint 38: Toward the end of the movie after the *Maelstrom* ride, a red Mickey balloon floats on the right side of the screen. The single balloon is visible above the trees for a few seconds as the movie camera pans down a street filled with parade celebrants.

Mexico

– Gran Fiesta Tour
Starring the Three Caballeros

Hint 39: At the beginning of the boat ride, smoke rises from the volcano. Every half minute or so, holes in the smoke form classic Mickeys that quickly disappear.

Hint 40: Along the left wall inside the first tunnel, look at the fifth man from the end. He is wearing green shorts and has a partially covered blue classic Mickey on the front of his necklace.

Hint 41: Watch for a video screen to the right of your boat that shows a broad expanse of water in the foreground and, in the background, a shoreline edged with modern buildings set against the backdrop of a mountain. Donald Duck is parasailing over the water, but you want to focus on the buildings on the shoreline. One building on the right side of the scene has a dark classic Mickey tree in front of it.

Hint 42: About halfway through the ride, in the small blue pond to the left of the boat, classic Mickeys appear in the bubbles after Donald is taken away. Look above and also to the lower left of the octopus.

Hint 43: Toward the end of the ride, as you enter the fireworks room, three drums form a classic Hidden Mickey at the lower right of the "Viva Donald" barge to the left of your boat.

– San Angel Inn Restaurante

Hint 44: Smoke rising from the volcano by the river forms classic Mickeys that quickly disappear.

China

Hint 45: Classic Mickey-shaped flowers are sculpted on the bases of several decorative light posts on the outside front of the pavilion.

Bonus Points Hint: In the ponds, the floating lily pads sometimes come together to form recognizable classic Mickeys.

Outpost
between China and Germany

Hint 46: At the Outpost, three of the short wooden posts at the corner closest to the bridge form a classic Mickey.

Germany

Hint 47: On the second floor of the building to your right, to the right of the glockenspiel clock, are three suits of armor. The one closest to the glockenspiel has a classic Mickey on its crown.

Hint 48: In the rear of the courtyard, a three-circle classic Mickey formation is in the ironwork support behind the bell on the front of the clock tower. It's formed by the circular metal support (not by holes in the metal) and is tilted to the left.

Hint 49: At the left of the entrance to the Biergarten Restaurant, you can see a wrought iron lion behind a lamp on the outside wall. The lion's front and rear paws are resting on an upside-down classic Mickey.

Hint 50: Inside the Karamell-Küche shop, a small orange classic Hidden Mickey is painted on the side of the framework holding the merchandise shelves closest to a back door. The image is about halfway up on a vine on the right side of the framework.

– Landscaping around the miniature train exhibit

Hint 51: Near the small town at the front of the exhibit, look for a shrub shaped like a classic Mickey. It's planted close to the center walkway that separates the small town from the background of streams and hills. Disney landscapers try to maintain the Mickey shape of this bush as it grows.

Bonus Points Hint: Check the dirt, grass, and decorations for other Hidden Mickey images that come and go during the year.

Italy

Hint 52: In the wine shop, Enoteca Castello, classic Mickeys appear in the woodwork along the relief design of the upper front counter.

Hint 53: Behind the statue on the right side of the walkway in front of the restaurants, a classic Mickey impression hides on the left side of the rock wall.

Hint 54: In the waiting room of Tutto Italia Ristorante, the scrollwork at the middle bottom of the mirror frame forms a classic Mickey.

The American Adventure

Hint 55: A classic Mickey made of roses decorates a lady's hat in a painting on the first floor on the far left wall (as you enter). Look for the painting in which a man is speaking to a crowd in front of a hardware store. The lady with the rose-trimmed hat is at the lower middle of the painting and the Hidden Mickey is on the right side of her hat.

Hint 56: A picture on a first-floor wall at the right rear of the rotunda (indoors) shows

workers building a skyscraper. The tops of two vertical beams behind the workers sport classic Mickeys.

Hint 57: On the rear wall of the rotunda, first and second floors, large bronze eagle reliefs have classic Mickeys in the corners.

– The American Adventure show

Hint 58: At the beginning of the film, a classic Mickey appears on the rock behind (and to your right of) a kneeling female pilgrim.

Hint 59: Early in the show, a classic Mickey lock hangs on the right side of a stockade in a scene of the American Revolution time period.

Hint 60: At the end of the show, fireworks light up the sky behind the Statue of Liberty Torch as it rises from the floor. One of the last fireworks at the upper right fizzles into a classic Mickey head (best seen from the right side of the theater).

– Fife and Drum Corps

Hint 61: Four classic Mickeys appear on the Fife and Drum Corps drums. A black one is on the lower front of the big bass drum. Three more decorate the smaller snare drum: two black (one on each side of the lower part of the drum) and a small blue one (traced on a blue banner on the right rear middle).

Japan

Hint 62: In the koi fish pond across from the Mitsukoshi store, a drain cover in the water near the bamboo fence sports a classic Mickey.

Hint 63: The trees in the courtyard are encircled by metal grates with classic Mickey designs.

Hint 64: Out on the promenade, next to the lagoon, three round bushes to the left of the Torii Gate form a classic Mickey.

Hint 65: A classic Mickey formed by three rocks is deep inside a hole in a large bush. It's on the right side of the pavilion, next to the far right sidewalk to the Mitsukoshi store, and near a juniper tree.

Morocco

Hint 66: Three brass plates are arranged to form a classic Mickey on the left green door at the entrance to the Souk-al-Magreb "Gifts of Morocco" shop on the promenade. (Sometimes, the plates are on the nearby red door, and you might find more than one plate classic Mickey on the doors!)

Hint 67: You'll find a black classic Mickey on both sides of the red-and-green design on the lower part of the fabric cover atop the Souk-al-Magreb "Gifts of Morocco" shop. (Note: The fabric cover is sometimes removed temporarily.)

Hint 68: A classic Hidden Mickey design is repeated along the top of a hat in the exhibit "Moroccan Style – The Art of Personal Adornment" in the pavilion's Gallery of Arts and History. The gallery is at the front left of the pavilion, and the hat with classic Mickeys is displayed at the far left of the gallery.

Hint 69: Basket lids usually form a sideways classic Mickey on the wall inside the Brass Bazaar shop (located at the right side of the Morocco pavilion behind the Tangierine Café). As you face the rear of the pavilion from inside the shop, look above the right side of the archway.

Hint 70: Across from Restaurant Marrakesh, three small classic Mickeys are on a mural on the rear wall of a small room. One is at the top of a tower on the right side of the mural's street. Another is on the left side of the street, next to a double archway. The third is a tiny black Mickey in an upper doorway on the left middle part of the mural.

Hint 71: Outside on the promenade, look for a wooden cart at the side of a tarp-covered display booth. Aladdin's lamp is on the back of the cart.

France

Hint 72: The trees in the courtyard are encircled by metal grates with classic Mickey patterns.

Hint 73: In the patterned hedge (parterre) garden, a bush in the middle right area (on the side nearest the canal) is trimmed to the shape of a classic Mickey.

Hint 74: Classic Mickey images are high on the outside molding of Les Vins de France shop, near the entrance to *Impressions de France*.

Hint 75: Inside Les Vins de France, a small plush figure of Remy (the rat from the movie *Ratatouille*) sits in a basket on a shelf near the ceiling, behind the service counter.

Hint 76: A classic three-circle Hidden Mickey hangs in the shop that adjoins Les Vins de France wine shop. It's at the upper left of a bulletin board on a wall opposite the entrance to the shop, and it's red, white, and blue!

– Impressions de France

Hint 77: In the movie's outdoor wedding scene, you can see a Mickey head and ears in a second floor window of the house in the background. It's in the center screen.

United Kingdom

Hint 78: Outside the Sportsman's Shoppe, a sign has a classic Mickey with a tennis racket head, a soccer ball for one ear, and a rugby ball for the other.

Hint 79: In The Crown & Crest shop, you'll find three Mickey stickers inside merchandise cabinets. In each case, you will have to put your head inside the cabinet to spot the Mickey sticker. So please be careful that you don't knock over any merchandise while you're searching. We want these images to hang around.

• The first Hidden Mickey is stuck to the wood of the cabinet that's just inside The Crown & Crest shop's entrance door and immediately to your right as you enter from outside. This black classic Mickey is taped to the back center of the cabinet's upper horizontal header (the fascia board). Stick your head inside the cabinet (careful of the merchandise!) and look up and back to find Mickey.

• A second Hidden Mickey sticker (this one a full-body Mickey) is in the cabinet immediately to the left of the entrance door. Again, you must put your head inside and look up and back behind the center of the fascia board.

• You'll find a third Hidden Mickey on a cabinet to the left of the cash register. He's on the back of the cabinet's support post. Stick your head inside the cabinet and look around the post. Mickey is facing the wall.

Canada

Hint 80: Past the steps into the pavilion, the left totem pole has black classic Mickeys on both sides near the top by the raven's beak.

Hint 81: A small black classic Mickey is on the side of a fish, which is hanging on the outside of a box at the left rear of the first room as you enter the Northwest Mercantile shop.

Hint 82: A classic Hidden Mickey is etched on the front facing of a stone step inside Canada, close to the theater. Start at the theater and walk up the steps. You will come to a landing with a light and a trail that branches off to the left. Continue walking up the steps. The Mickey image appears before you reach the next landing.

Hint 83: Behind the check-in desk at Le Cellier Steakhouse, three horizontal bottles at the center top of a wine display form a classic Mickey.

Showcase Plaza

– Disney Traders store

Hint 84: Mickey can be seen running around the equator of the globe that's hanging from the ceiling of Disney Traders (one of the two stores at the front of Showcase Plaza).

The Seas with Nemo & Friends

Hint 85: As you reach the wooden rails of the walkway along the inside entrance queue for the ride, a classic Mickey made of blue moving water circles lies above you on the right side. (Note: This image isn't always present.)

Hint 86: On the ride, a classic Mickey impression in rock lies below the fifth video screen from the start. It's slightly above and between two pink clusters of standing corals, to the right of center in the rock ledge.

Hint 87: Spot one or more classic Mickeys formed of rocks at the bottom of the aquarium. They're best seen from the viewing corridor and the circular viewing area upstairs. Recently, one of the images had starfish-shaped rocks for its "ears." Note: These rock Mickeys may change locations on the aquarium floor, and some may disappear at times. You may need to look through several windows in the observation area to find them.

Hint 88: In the manatee viewing room, lower level, bubbles in wall paintings form two classic Mickeys. One is on the left wall (as you exit), in the left middle square containing the words "Manatee Zone … Slow Speed." Another is on the right wall as you exit, in the lower left square with the polar bear.

Hint 89: As you enter Bruce's room on the lower level, check out the second windows on both the right (labeled "Did You Know?")

and left (labeled "Bruce's Scrapbook"). In both windows, an oyster contains three pearls arranged as a classic Mickey.

Hint 90: In the waiting room for *Turtle Talk With Crush*, a tiny classic Mickey is in the pink and brown coral in the first window painting to the right as you enter the room. At the lower part of the painting, the Mickey is left of the third tallest (leftmost) blue tube, about one quarter of the distance up the side of the tube.

Hint 91: Also in the *Turtle Talk With Crush* waiting room, look at the upper left of the second window to the right (as you enter the room) to spot "Peach" the starfish. An upside-down classic Mickey lies above the left side of Peach's "eyebrow."

Hint 92: Bubbles come together to form several classic Mickeys on the garbage cans you see in the pavilion.

The Land

– Living with the Land

Hint 93: In the middle section of the giant wall mural at the rear of the queue, bubbles align to form a classic Mickey, ears angled to the left.

Hint 94: A classic Mickey is formed by shrubs (the "head" has yellow dots on it) to the right of the brim of the farmer's hat near the top of the loading dock mural.

Hint 95: In the lower right area of the mural behind the boat loading area, three circles form a small classic Mickey (a purple circle forms the head and blue circles form the ears). The head is tilted slightly to the right.

Hint 96: In the first part of the ride, a female Cast Member on the last video screen on your left has a Mickey Mouse face hiding on the upper part of her name tag.

Hint 97: A garden hose is coiled into a classic Mickey to the right of the boat about

halfway through the fish farming section. (Cast Members usually arrange this Mickey image every morning.)

Hint 98: A classic Mickey made of wire mesh can be found in the aquaculture section. Cast Members generally place it in one of the horizontal display tubes that are part of the landscape on either side of your boat.

Hint 99: Along the ride, you can often spot hanging plastic gourds shaped like classic Mickeys. They're used to grow fruit or vegetables into Mickey shapes.

Hint 100: Plants of different colors are usually arranged in groups to form a classic Mickey in the greenhouses. Often the plants are lettuces.

Hint 101: Toward the end of the ride, a large circular test-tube holder on the right side of a "Biotechnology Lab" room has a green classic Mickey in the center. Mickey is formed by the test tubes' green stoppers.

Hint 102: On one of the tables in this biotech lab, a sign advertises the plant product, "Mickey's Mini Gardens."

– The Garden Grill

Hint 103: On the left side of the large wall-mural of vegetation inside the restaurant, a Mickey is hiding behind the most prominent fern that extends all the way to the top of the mural. Counting up horizontally from the bottom of the fern, his face is mostly behind the fifth through eighth leaves on the fern's right side. He's looking slightly downward and to the right in a three-quarter profile. Two black circles that form his eyes are visible above the sixth fern leaf on the right, more than halfway to the end of the leaf. Mickey's ears jut above the seventh leaf, and his mouth and nose are below the sixth leaf. His face and ears are green, and his mouth is slightly open. This Hidden Mickey is a real classic!

103

Hint 104: In the restaurant, Chip 'n' Dale wear red bandannas with small, dark classic Mickeys in the design.

– Around The Land's main entrance

Hint 105: From the upper level railing, just to the left as you walk in the main entrance, a classic Mickey is on the Earth above the lobby. It's in water swirls, to the left of the tip of South America.

Hint 106: A classic Mickey is in the mosaic mural on the pavilion's right outside wall (as you enter). Find the word "LAND" on the mural and look slightly above and to the right about six feet or so to a reddish plateau. Just above the left side of the flat upper part of the plateau are three jewels, a green "head" and two reddish "ears."

Hint 107: In the same mosaic mural, look for a cluster of grapes to the upper left of the word "LAND." A classic Mickey, tilted to the right and almost upside down, is formed by three grapes. The grape Mickey is partially beneath the translucent signboard.

Hint 108: The Land sign outside the pavilion's entrance rests on two large stone- and tile-covered supports. On the end of the right-hand support, embedded stones decorate the upper portion of the green-tiled area. A small classic Mickey, formed of three stones, lies near the center of the stone decoration.

Hint 109: About halfway along the "Behind the Seeds" tour in the greenhouses, an electrical box on the right side of the tour path sports a photo of a lettuce classic Mickey. You may have spotted one similar to it during the *Living with the Land* ride; see Clue and Hint 100.

(Note: While on the tour, you can also admire the garden-hose classic Hidden Mickey in the aquaculture section; see Clue and Hint 97.)

Imagination! Pavilion

– Journey Into Imagination with Figment

Hint 110: As you enter the Sight Room, a tiny dark classic Mickey is hidden at the lower right of a greaseboard on a wall to your right. The greaseboard is below the words "Focus Group." (Note: This Hidden Mickey may change locations on the board or even disappear at times.)

Hint 111: In the center of the Sight Room, headphones on the left of two tables have Mickey ears on an earpiece!

Hint 112: Three bubbles make a classic Mickey near Figment's hand on the edge of his bathtub.

Hint 113: In Figment's Upside-Down House, his toilet forms a classic Mickey with two red circles on the floor.

Hint 114: When you feel a blast of air and the walls open, you'll see a rainbow and balloons. Look down and to the right to see classic Mickey circles appear on a cloud at the bottom right of the stage.

Hint 115: In this same scene at the end of the ride, find the letters that spell "Action" that stand in the middle of the scene. Snow covers the top of the letter "A," and a classic Mickey sits in the snow at the bottom left of the snow cap. The Hidden Mickey image tilts to the left.

Hint 116: On the left wall of the exit hallway, a sideways classic Mickey is behind and between the "I" and "m" of the ImageWorks sign.

– ImageWorks

Hint 117: Behind a pillar in the middle of *Image-Works*, a classic Hidden Mickey is on the floor made of tan-colored tile.

Spaceship Earth

Hint 118: After the fall of Rome, you see three Islamic scholars seated around a table on the floor. They are illuminated by lights that form patterns on the floor. The outer circle of light patterns form classic Mickeys.

Hint 119: Across from the Islamic scholars, on a wall to your left, are shelves with cubbyholes full of scrolls. In one of the last cubbyholes you pass before you leave the scene, the round ends of three stacked scrolls lying horizontally form a classic Mickey. It's on the second shelf, in the right lower corner of the second cubbyhole from the wall.

Hint 120: During the ride, in a scene to the left, monks are writing at desks. In front of the sleeping monk is a document with a small ink blot at the upper right corner. The blot is shaped like a classic Mickey and becomes visible as your vehicle passes by.

Hint 121: Just after the Gutenberg printing press scene, in the first part of the Renaissance section, look for the first painter to the left of your ride vehicle. Three white paint circles form a classic Mickey on the top left of the table near the painter. You have to look fast for this one.

Hint 122: On the right side, as you're passing the section showing black and white movies, a chalkboard marquee on the ground lists upcoming features. One is "The Band Concert," a famous Mickey Mouse cartoon.

Hint 123: As soon as you enter the large computer room, look to the right of your vehicle to spot a coffee mug on a desk. The desk has a label on the side that says "Think." You'll see the edge of a Mickey sticker on the coffee mug. As you pass by the desk, look back to your right into the large mirror at the rear of the room. You can see the whole Mickey sticker on the mug!

Hint 124: At the exit of *Spaceship Earth*, several classic Mickeys float along on overhead blue screens in the Project Tomorrow interactive area.

Universe of Energy

Hint 125: After the dinosaur section of the ride, the movie shows a man driving a car out of a barn and towards a church building in the background (the fourth building from the left). A shadow of the Disney's Hollywood Studios' "Earful" Tower appears in the door of the church.

Innoventions East

– *Electric Umbrella*

Hint 126: Look for a menu outside or inside the restaurant. An apple between "Kids'" and "Picks" has a classic Mickey image formed by bites out of the apple. This "Kids' Picks" apple image is found in many restaurants around Walt Disney World.

Innoventions West

– *"Where's the Fire?"*

Hint 127: A partial classic Mickey is at the lower left of the *"Where's the Fire?"* logo, which appears between shows on all the monitors in this attraction.

Hint 128: In one of the rooms, look for a computer monitor screen on a desk. You can make out classic Mickeys in the changing graphics on the screen.

Hint 129: A classic Mickey bookend is visible on the desk in the Kids' Bedroom.

Hint 130: Goofy is on an upside-down magazine draped over a lamp in the Kids' Bedroom.

– *"The Great Piggy Bank Adventure"*

Hint 131: On the yellow wall inside the attraction, circles below the sign "Start saving early" form a classic Mickey tilted to the left. You can see the image from the outside walkway.

– Club Cool near Innoventions West

Hint 132: Holes in the metal bracket supports behind the outdoor sign form classic Mickeys.

Hint 133: Above you, on a colorful decorative border in the middle of the club, green circles form an upside-down classic Mickey.

Hint 134: A classic Mickey is near the bottom of the blue banners that are located outside and above the rear entrance to Club Cool.

Innoventions Plaza

– MouseGear shop

Hint 135: The signs above the shop entrances have classic Mickeys with two round ears above the letter "G" as the head.

Hint 136: The large wing nuts on the bolts of the display racks form Mickey ears.

Hint 137: At the ends of some of the display racks, bolts next to larger holes form classic Mickeys.

Hint 138: The ends of some of the large bolts that jut out from the stippled panels on the merchandise cases are stamped with classic Mickeys.

Hint 139: Some of the gauges on the wall are arranged as classic Mickeys.

Hint 140: The shadows of Donald Duck and his relatives are on the upper part of a wall in the center of the store.

Hint 141: Classic Mickey gears hang above a display on a wall opposite the cash registers.

Hint 142: Look for a large Donald Duck on a wall in the part of the store near the main walkway to the east side of Future World to find a classic Mickey made of gears.

Hint 143: Some of the garment display manne-quins have classic Mickeys at the top.

Hint 144: Outside and behind MouseGear is a classic Mickey in the walkway cement. Exit the shop at the rear heading toward Test Track, then take the first right onto a walkway (heading toward World Showcase). Just before the path changes to an octagonal shape, look down near the left railing to find a small classic Mickey in-dented in the concrete.

Epcot Character Spot

Hint 145: A small white classic Mickey is on the inside wall among the stars above the entrance doors to *Character Spot*. It's to the upper right of the exit sign.

Hint 146: A Mickey hat appears in several places: near the right end of the inside wall mural in the waiting queue, outside on window murals near the entrance doors and over the exit doors, and on the outdoor sign, where it is behind and below the "CH" on the side of the sign that faces The Land pavilion.

Hint 147: Goofy is on an upper inside window, across from the second greeting bay. There's a small, white classic Mickey on his spacesuit.

Hint 148: The yellow buttons on a giant cell phone on the right side of the middle greeting bay form a classic Mickey.

Hint 149: Behind the giant cell phone, at the right rear of the middle greeting bay, you'll find a clas-sic Mickey on a gray metal device.

Hint 150: At the left rear of the middle greeting bay, a metal 3-D Mickey head wears earphones.

Hint 151: Mickey's gloves are on a robot light switch in the next to last greeting bay.

Hint 152: A constellation classic Mickey is on the right rear wall of the last greeting bay.

Hint 153: In the last bay on the right, a green alien wears Mickey Mouse ears.

Hint 154: A side-profile cloud Mickey floats in the sky mural on an upper inside window across from the last greeting bay.

Epcot Guidemap

Hint 155: Look by the water under the number 5 on the park map (the 5 on the Innoventions West building). In the notch on the right side of the lake, there is a tiny bush or flowerbed shaped like Mickey's head (red and green "head" and green "ears").

Disney's Hollywood Studios Scavenger Hunt

• •

Note: Many of the Hidden Mickeys in this park are in restaurants and shops. Be considerate of fellow guests and Cast Members as you search. Tell them what you are looking for, so they can share in the fun. Avoid searching restaurants at busy meal times unless you are one of the diners.

★ Your scavenger hunt in Disney's Hollywood Studios (aka "the Studios") starts even **before you enter the park**.

Clue 1: Look closely at the brackets on the signs above the ticket windows.
2 points

Clue 2: Examine the fence at the entrance turnstiles.
1 point

★ Walk first to **Toy Story Midway Mania!**

Clue 3: Search carefully for a blue classic Mickey along the Standby (i.e., regular) entrance queue.
5 points

Clue 4: As your ride starts, glance back at a big book for Donald and Mickey. (Sometimes, the book is positioned so that these images cannot be seen from the vehicle).
5 bonus points for both

Clue 5: On the interactive screens, look behind the target balloons in front of the volcano for a classic Mickey.
5 points

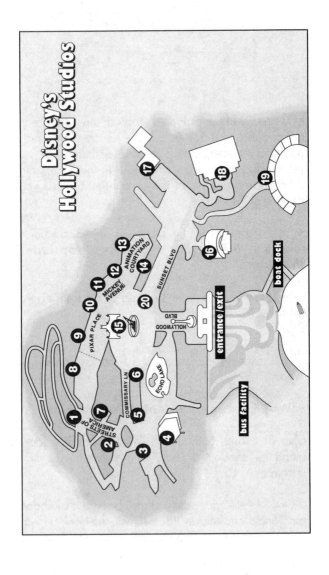

1. Lights, Motors, Action!® Extreme Stunt Show
2. MuppetVision 3D
3. Star Tours
4. Indiana Jones™ Epic Stunt Spectacular!
5. ABC Sound Studio
6. The American Idol Experience
7. "Honey, I Shrunk the Kids" Movie Set Adventure
8. Studio Backlot Tour
9. Toy Story Midway Mania!™
10. The Legend of Captain Jack Sparrow
11. Walt Disney: One Man's Dream
12. Voyage of The Little Mermaid
13. The Magic of Disney Animation
14. Disney Junior — Live on Stage!
15. The Great Movie Ride
16. Beauty and the Beast — Live on Stage!
17. Rock 'n' Roller Coaster® Starring Aerosmith
18. The Twilight Zone Tower of Terror™
19. Fantasmic!
20. Guest Information Board

Clue 6: On another screen, watch the white plates for a classic Mickey image.
3 points

Clue 7: Stay alert for a classic Mickey below an exclamation point on the wall.
5 points

Clue 8: Along the exit walkway, spot another classic Mickey on a wall.
2 points

Clue 9: Study a book along the exit for a tiny classic Mickey.
5 points

Clue 10: Outside of the attraction, look around for popcorn Mickey.
3 points

Clue 11: Then search outside for Mickey on a plate.
2 points

★ Now go to **Rock 'n' Roller Coaster Starring Aerosmith**. (You can find the Hidden Mickeys here without riding the coaster, the first nine by exiting before the ride, two in the gift shop by walking in through the exit from outside, and three outside in the courtyard.)

Clue 12: Look down at the carpet along the entrance queue for Hidden Mickeys.
4 points

Clue 13: Don't miss the tiny Mickey on a wall poster just before the pre-show room.
4 points

Clue 14: Search around the pre-show room for a classic Mickey.
4 points

Clue 15: After the pre-show, look for three Mickeys on a poster.
4 points for spotting all three

114

Clue 16: Before boarding, spot Mickey hiding near the ceiling.
4 points

Clue 17: Look across the track for Mickey on the wall.
5 points

Clue 18: At the loading gate, look at the rear license plates of the limo ride vehicles. (Then exit if you wish.)
4 points

Clue 19: At the exit, find a box with a classic Mickey. (If you haven't taken the ride, walk in through the gift shop to the video monitor area to find this Mickey.)
4 points

Clue 20: In the gift shop, a mannequin wears this Mickey!
4 points

Clue 21: Outside in the courtyard, search for three Hidden Mickeys on the wall.
5 points for spotting all three

★ Walk to **The Twilight Zone Tower of Terror** and explore the entry queue area and pre-show for three Hidden Mickeys.

Clue 22: During the pre-show film in the library, find the plush Mickey Mouse doll held by a little girl.
3 points

Clue 23: Linger in the left library to spot the words "Mickey Mouse" on sheet music on a desktop.
4 points

Clue 24: Notice a classic Mickey stain on the wall in the boiler room.
4 points

(Tip: For the best vantage point for the ride Hidden Mickeys (Clues 25 to 27), take the right queue when the line for the ride splits. Then tell the Cast Member you're hunting for Hidden Mickeys and ask to be seated in the rightmost ride vehicle.)

Clue 25: At the first stop on the ride, search for a Hidden Mickey above you.
4 points

Clue 26: Also look for a Mickey Mouse doll here.
4 points

Clue 27: Stare at the star field (the doors to the elevator shaft just before they open!) to spot a classic Hidden Mickey in the stars.
5 points

Clue 28: After you leave your elevator, keep alert for a classic Mickey near the photo selection area.
3 points

Clue 29: As you exit, spot Mickey on the floor!
4 points

Clue 30: Outside the gift shop at the exit, check out the rock wall at the smoking area for a classic Mickey.
4 points

★ Walk down Sunset Boulevard and turn right to *Voyage of The Little Mermaid*.

Clue 31: Look for a classic Mickey in the inside waiting room. (You can stay for the show in the theater or exit out the doors you just entered to continue your Hidden Mickey search.)
3 points

★ Stroll over to *The Great Movie Ride*. First find two classic Mickeys among the celebrity impressions in the cement in front of the Chinese Theater and then take the ride.

(If the wait is more than 15 minutes, go on to *Star Tours — The Adventures Continue* and try *The Great Movie Ride* later. Best times: during a parade or two hours before park closing.)

Clue 32: Check Harry Anderson's square.
3 points

Clue 33: Now see if you can spot a Mickey in Carol Burnett's square.
3 points

Clue 34: In the middle of the loading dock mural, search for the Hidden Minnie above a tree stump. (Psst! It's visible at loading and unloading.)
5 points

Clue 35: On the right side of this mural, squint for a tiny black Hidden Mickey.
5 points

Clue 36: As you start down Gangster Alley, look for Mickey's brown shoes under a James Cagney poster.
4 points

Clue 37: At the end of Gangster Alley, find Mickey's shadow in a window near the top of the "Chemical Company" building.
5 points

Clue 38: In the "Western" section, spot two references to Pocahontas.
5 points for both

Tip: To spot all of the Hidden Images in the "Raiders of the Lost Ark" room (Clues 39 to 42, below) look quickly first to your left, then to your right, then left, and finally right again as your vehicle moves through the room.

Clue 39: Look left for R2-D2 and C-3PO on the wall!
5 points

Clue 40: Stare to the right of your vehicle for a small white classic Mickey on a tablet below the ark container.
5 points

Clue 41: Find Mickey and Donald on the left wall, at the end of the "Raiders of the Lost Ark" room. (Psst! Mickey is facing Donald.)
5 points

Clue 42: Now glance quickly to your right for a hiero-glyphic Mickey.
5 points

Clue 43: In the "Tarzan" room, stare at the trees high above and to your right for a classic Mickey.
3 points

Clue 44: In the "Wizard of Oz" room, search for Mickey in the flowers.
3 points

Clue 45: Look up to spot Mickey in the trees in the "Wizard of Oz" room.
5 points

Clue 46: After you exit, study the design above the outside entrance door for a classic Mickey image.
3 points

★ Outside the exit, walk past the Sorcerer's Hat and turn right (with Echo Lake on your left) to **Star Tours — The Adventures Continue**.

Clue 47: Don't miss a classic Mickey on a tree along the outside queue.
5 points

Clue 48: Along the inside entrance queue, look for a Hidden Mickey near C-3PO.
3 points

Clue 49: Now wait for a shadow Hidden Mickey in a video on a wall display along the entrance queue. (Note: You may have to cool your heels awhile to spot this one!)
4 points

Clue 50: Next, study the entrance queue luggage scanner for Mickey and other Disney characters and images.
5 points total for finding Mickey and two or more other Disney images

Clue 51: At the end of the ride, if you land on the Coruscant planet (as opposed to

other random end destinations for the ride), look for classic Mickeys on a rear wall.
5 bonus points

Clue 52: Spot a blue-light classic Mickey on a counter in the gift shop at the exit.
4 points

Clue 53: Find classic Mickey on the front of another counter in the gift shop.
3 points

★ Catch the next performance of **Lights, Motors, Action! Extreme Stunt Show**.

Clue 54: Don't miss classic Mickeys along the entrance walkway.
4 points for one or more

Clue 55: Search for a small full-body Mickey Mouse at the rear of the set.
5 points

Clue 56: Find a classic Mickey in a set window.
5 points

Clue 57: Stay alert for fiery Mickey ears.
5 points

Clue 58: Exit to the left for Mickey beyond the fence.
4 points

★ Take a lunch break. Keep your reservations if you have them. If not, try the Backlot Express for burgers and sandwiches, the Pizza Planet Arcade for pizza, or the ABC Commissary for salads and stir-fry.

★ Check your Times Guide for convenient show times for The American Idol Experience and Beauty and the Beast — Live on Stage. While you're seated, **scan your Studios Guidemap** for a Hidden Mickey.

Clue 59: Turn the Disney's Hollywood Studios map upside down and search for Mickey.
4 points

Clue 60: Now study the map right side up for tiny side profiles of Mickey and Minnie.
3 points

★ After lunch, go to **MuppetVision 3D** and find five Hidden Mickeys and a Hidden Surprise.

Clue 61: Look for a Mickey Mouse in the fountain outside MuppetVision.
2 points

Clue 62: On the wall near the far turn of the long outside waiting queue, check out the poster about 3D glasses to find a classic Mickey.
3 points

Clue 63: During the first part of the pre-show on the video monitors, observe the test pattern.
4 points

Clue 64: Try to spot the Mickey balloons while Kermit rides in on a fire truck.
3 points

Clue 65: Study the license plate on the fire truck for a Hidden Surprise.
4 points

Clue 66: Find a Mickey image just outside the theater exit doors.
3 points

★ Walk up the Streets of America. Turn right and pass by the *Honey, I Shrunk the Kids Movie Set Adventure* to the **Studio Backlot Tour**.

Clue 67: Don't miss a drawing of Walt Disney and two images of Mickey Mouse on the wall.
3 points for spotting all three images

(Caution: If the waiting queue is short, you may be directed past the winding aisles of the prop storage area. To check out the Hidden Mickeys in Clues 68 to 72, step past the ropes to explore the aisles away from the crowds.)

Clue 68: Search for Mickey's gloves and shoes in the prop storage area.
3 points for spotting both

Clue 69: Look closely at the refrigerator on the right side of the first aisle in the prop storage area.
3 points

Clue 70: In the second aisle, locate a green classic Mickey.
3 points

Clue 71: In the second aisle, don't miss Sleeping Beauty!
3 points

Clue 72: Find Mickey and Minnie together in the second aisle.
3 points

Clue 73: While on the tram, stay alert for Mickey on the wall of the sewing room to your left.
3 points

Clue 74: While on the tram, spot a classic Mickey on an airplane.
3 points

Clue 75: Study a mural in the exit displays (after the tram ride) for three Mickey images.
5 points for spotting all three

★ Walk to **Studio Catering Co.**

Clue 76: Search for a Hidden Mickey on a wall.
3 points

★ Walk down Mickey Avenue to **Walt Disney: One Man's Dream**.

Clue 77: During your walk through the attraction, look around for a Hidden Donald near Walt, who is holding a pointer.
3 points

Clue 78: Now find Mickey on the wall near Walt.
3 points

★ Check out the show **Disney Junior – Live on Stage!** in Animation Courtyard.

Clue 79: Watch for Mickey in the lighting and stage effects.
3 points for two or more

★ Continue down Mickey Avenue, then up the steps or through the arch. Veer left to **The Hollywood Brown Derby** restaurant. Admire the mural on the wall outside, above the restaurant.

Clue 80: Look for two classic Mickeys in the mural.
4 points for spotting both

★ Now look at the pictures in the waiting area inside the restaurant.

Clue 81: Spot the man with Mickey Mouse ears.
3 points

★ Catch a performance of **The American Idol Experience**.

Clue 82: Find two Mickeys on the stage backdrop.
5 points each

Clue 83: Watch for a Hidden Mickey in a video of Jordin Sparks.
4 points

★ Turn left as you leave and **head down Sunset Boulevard**.

Clue 84: Search for a classic Mickey in scrollwork on a blue building.
4 points

★ Walk to **Rosie's All-American Café**.

Clue 85: Look around the food order area for Mickey.
4 points

Clue 86: Look around for Mickey behind Rosie's service counter.
3 points

★ Now catch a performance of **Beauty and the Beast – Live on Stage**.

Clue 87: Watch for Mickey on the back of one of the characters.
3 points

★ Turn left onto Hollywood Boulevard, then right to **Hollywood & Vine restaurant**.

Clue 88: Seek a Hidden Character above the entrance.
3 points

★ Enter the restaurant and examine the left wall.

Clue 89: Find a stick-figure Mickey.
2 points

Clue 90: Search the wall for some classic Mickeys.
3 points

★ Step inside the waiting area for the **50's Prime Time Café** and look closely at the tables.

Clue 91: Check out what's holding them together.
1 point

★ Check your Times Guide for a convenient performance of **Mulch, Sweat & Shears**.

Clue 92: Look for a Hidden Mickey in the props.
4 points

★ Enter the **Backlot Express** restaurant.

Clue 93: Look for standing Mickeys.
4 points for finding four or more

★ Ask a restaurant Cast Member to let you check out the **Sci-Fi Dine-In Theater Restaurant** inside.

Clue 94: Look for a classic Mickey in the waiting area of the Sci-Fi Dine-In Theater Restaurant.
3 points

Clue 95: Find a full-body Mickey in the waiting area.
3 points

Clue 96: Search for Mickey in the left hallway to the dining area.
4 points

Clue 97: Study the right rear mural. Look for two Hidden Mickeys along the treetops.
5 points for both

Clue 98: Stare at a small mosaic mural at the rear of the restaurant for a side profile of Mickey Mouse.
5 points

Clue 99: Watch the movie reel for three Hidden Characters.
8 points for spotting all three

Clue 100: Stay alert for a classic Hidden Mickey on a spacesuit.
4 points

Clue 101: Find a Hidden Mickey on a dining car.
3 points

★ Get yourself some coffee or other refreshment at **The Writer's Stop**. Look up while you enjoy it.

Clue 102: See anything on the overhead theater lights?
2 points

★ Mosey over to the **Pizza Planet Arcade** and find three Hidden Mickeys.

Clue 103: Search for a small classic Mickey in the stars above the counter registers. Focus on the left side of the pizzeria's rear wall.
4 points

Clue 104: Swing your eyes over to the right side of the rear wall to find a bright classic-Mickey star cluster.
3 points

Clue 105: Now find a three-quarter Mickey profile above the arcade games on the wall mural. (Psst! He's looking left.)
5 points

★ Wander into the **Stage 1 Company Store** and find four Hidden Mickeys.

Clue 106: Locate a classic Mickey near a bird.
2 points

Clue 107: Take a good look at the old bureau that's loaded with hats and paint cans.
3 points

Clue 108: Spot a classic Mickey on the wall.
3 points

Clue 109: Search for some famous shorts.
3 points

Clue 110: Find several Hidden Mickeys outside the store.
5 points for four or more

★ In the waiting area for **Mama Melrose's Ristorante Italiano**, search for four classic Mickeys.

Clue 111: Check out the Dalmatian.
3 points

Clue 112: Examine the plaster on the right wall.
3 points

Clue 113: Find a classic Mickey leaf near the check-in podium.
4 points

Clue 114: Now look at the plaster on the wall to the left of the check-in podium.
3 points

★ Stroll to **Radiator Springs**, where the *Cars* characters sign autographs.

Clue 115: Study Mater for a Hidden Mickey.
3 points

★ Walk down the **Streets of America**.

Clue 116: Search for a San Francisco newspaper with a Hidden Mickey.
4 points

Clue 117: Keep looking around for a reference to a Disney movie.
3 points

Clue 118: Glance at a nearby wall poster for two Hidden Mickeys.
3 points for both

Clue 119: Look for food containers along the street that form Mickey.
3 points

Clue 120: Along the street, locate a dog with a Hidden Mickey.
3 points

Clue 121: Find a Mickey Mouse watch in a window.
4 points

Clue 122: Don't miss the photo of Walt with Mickey!
4 points

Clue 123: Search for four classic characters in a window near a cruise ship.
5 points for spotting all four

Clue 124: Spot a classic Mickey in the sand in a New York window.
3 points

★ Walk past *The Great Movie Ride* to the **entrance arch to Animation Courtyard**.

Clue 125: Search the show's entrance area for Hidden Characters.
4 points for finding two characters

★ Enjoy **The Magic of Disney Animation**.

Clue 126: Look around the stage during the theater presentation for Hidden Mickeys.
5 points for two or more

Clue 127: In the theater video, watch for the cloud of smoke around Mushu the dragon.
5 points

Clue 128: Then keep watching the video for Hidden Mickeys on a mug.
4 points

Clue 129: Look around the courtyard outside the theater for Mickey.
3 points

Clue 130: Study the carpets inside as you walk toward the Character Greeting areas.
2 points

Clue 131: Search the Character Greeting areas for Hidden Mickeys and a Hidden Pluto.
5 points for Pluto and two or more Hidden Mickeys

★ Stroll **toward Hollywood Boulevard**.

Clue 132: On the way, look for Mickey in front of his Sorcerer's Hat.
3 points

Clue 133: At the intersection of Hollywood and Sunset Boulevards, discover Mickey Mouse's previous moniker. (Psst! Read the impressions in the sidewalks, near the curb.)
5 points

127

★ Look at a ***billboard above Keystone Clothiers***.

Clue 134: See any handprints in cement?
3 points

Clue 135: Walk behind Keystone Clothiers and search for a classic Mickey.
2 points

★ Study the outside display windows of ***Disney & Company***.

Clue 136: Can you spot Mickey?
2 points

★ Enter ***Mickey's of Hollywood*** to look for four Hidden Mickeys.

Clue 137: Check the posts holding up merchandise racks.
2 points

Clue 138: Now examine the racks themselves.
2 points

Clue 139: Study the cabinets in the Sorcerer section of the store. (Tip: They are near a door to the street.)
2 points

Clue 140: Next find "MICKEYS" spelled out on vertical dividers.
1 point

★ Go to the ***Cover Story store*** and take a good look at the outside.

Clue 141: See any classic Mickeys in the design?
2 points

★ Walk outside the park to the ***charter bus area***.

Clue 142: Search the cement next to a bench.
5 points

★ In the evening, stay alert during the **Fantasmic!** show for a Hidden Mickey.

Clue 143: Look for large bubbles floating up the water screen that form a classic Mickey.
5 points

Total Points for
Disney's Hollywood Studios =

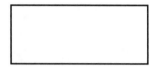

How'd you do?

Up to 205 points – Bronze
206 to 409 points – Silver
410 points and over – Gold
513 points – Perfect Score

You may have done even better if you earned bonus points in *Toy Story Midway Mania!* and/or *Star Tours*.

Notes

**Caution:
Don't peek at this
section unless you
really want help!**

- Park entrance area

Hint 1: Metal brackets at the bottoms of signs above the ticket purchase windows are shaped like classic Mickeys.

Hint 2: You'll see classic Mickeys on top of the fence at the turnstiles.

- Toy Story Midway Mania!

Hint 3: An upside-down blue paint classic Mickey is on the wall past the large map of the U.S.A. It is below a green dinosaur and an orange fish (Nemo), near the floor and behind the handrails on the left side of the queue.

Hint 4: Just as your vehicle leaves the loading area, glance back at the large "Tin Toy" book. On the back of the book, near the spine, spot full-body images of Donald Duck at the upper right corner and Mickey Mouse two figures below Donald. (Sometimes, the back of the book is positioned so that these images cannot be seen from your ride vehicle.)

Hint 5: Watch for the screen with target balloons in front of the volcano spewing lava. If you pop the middle 100-point balloon on the second tier, a light classic Mickey appears on the rear surface in the lava behind the balloons.

Hint 6: Be alert for the screen with moving white plates. At one point, a large plate aligns with smaller plates behind it to form a classic Mickey.

Hint 7: Look for the words "Circus Fun!" on the wall to your right as you rotate into position for the last screen stop. The dot below the exclamation point is a classic Mickey.

Hint 8: On the wall to the left of the ride vehicles, a classic Mickey is formed by three ovals that outline Mr. Potato Head, Slinky Dog, and Bullseye the horse. You can see this image at loading and unloading, and you can study it as you take the exit walkway.

Hint 9: On the upper spine of the large "Tin Toy" book along the exit, a tiny white classic Mickey is in a chicken's eye. It's the fourth image from the top of the spine.

Hint 10: You'll find a side-profile Mickey on a huge popcorn box that's on display across from the *Toy Story Midway Mania!* attraction. Look behind the "Hey Howdy Hey!" sign.

Hint 11: On the left lower side of a large "Prospector" plate, which stands on the left side of a shelf on the rear wall of the "Hey Howdy Hey" snack area, a horseshoe and two circles resemble a classic Mickey.

– Rock 'n' Roller Coaster Starring Aerosmith

Hint 12: Along the entrance queue, when you reach the inner room past the tile floor, distorted classic Mickeys are in the carpet.

Hint 13: On the last wall before you enter the lower level of the pre-show video room, a poster labeled "Cosmic Car Show" has a tiny classic Mickey on the bottom right under the front tire of the car. The Mickey image is at the end of the signature of "J. Mouse."

Hint 14: Cables coiled into a classic Mickey lie on the rear center of the floor in the pre-show room where Aerosmith appears.

Hint 15: You'll find three full-body Mickey Mouse stickers at the upper right and middle right side of a collage poster. The poster is on the wall to your left, at the first right turn in the inside queue near the boarding area.

Hint 16: After the right turn in the inside queue near the boarding area, about halfway to the end and above the "Compact Vehicles Only" notation on the wall, a light fixture near the ceiling sports a Mickey sticker.

Hint 17: On a wall across from the front of the loading dock area, various items are hanging from a row of hooks to the left of a wall cabinet and to the right of a garage door. One of the hanging items is a pink hat with the word "Mickey" across the front. (Note: The arrangement of these items changes from time to time.)

Hint 18: On the rear license plate of each limo ride vehicle, the year sticker at the upper right is a classic Mickey.

Hint 19: Just as people exit the ride vehicle, look for "Box #15" on the right side of the room with the guest photo screens. The "o" in "Box" is a classic Mickey.

Hint 20: In the gift shop at the exit, a female mannequin wears a black wrist bracelet that says "I love Mickey."

Hint 21: As you exit into the front courtyard, check the outside wall mural to your left for:
- a boy wearing Mickey ears.
- black classic Mickeys on a singer's light blue shirt.
- a gold "bling" Mickey on the necklace of the man in the black suit.

– The Twilight Zone Tower of Terror

Hint 22: During the pre-show film in the library, the little girl on the elevator holds a plush Mickey Mouse doll.

Hint 23: Look for sheet music on a desktop and under a trumpet to the right of the television in the left library. The words "Mickey Mouse" are part of a song title: "What! No Mickey Mouse?"

Hint 24: A black, slightly distorted classic Mickey stains the wall of the boiler room at the spot where the queue branches. He's about eight feet up from the walkway, between an "Exit" sign and a red electrical box.

Hint 25: At the first stop on the ride, a small, dark classic Mickey can be seen above the ghostly images in the lower center of the ornate design on the closest archway.

Hint 26: Also at this first stop, the little girl in the ghostly images is still holding her Mickey doll.

Hint 27: On the ride itself, you'll see a bright star field just before the doors open into the elevator shaft. Look closely as the stars you're watching converge in the middle into a small classic-Mickey shape for a split second. (Tip: You see it best from the rightmost ride vehicle.)

Hint 28: In the room below and behind the screens that show the photo ride images, look to the left to an open drawer in which gauges form a classic Mickey.

Hint 29: On the left side of the last room as you exit the ride (and before the gift shop), three distinct floor tiles form a clas-

sic Mickey. (It's not proportioned correctly but it is clearly purposeful.)

Hint 30: In the trellis-covered smoking area across from the gift shop exit, a tiny rock classic Mickey sticks out from the last arch on the left of the upper rear rock wall. It's about four feet from the end column and close to the bottom of the arch.

– Voyage of The Little Mermaid

Hint 31: Opposite the entrance doors to the inside waiting room, an ornate map of the Earth's hemispheres hangs on the left side of the wall. The brass frames encircling the hemispheres form the "head" of a sideways classic Mickey, while the decorative circular elements between them form a set of "ears." (Note: There's just one set of "ears" but two possible "heads.")

– The Great Movie Ride

Hint 32: Harry Anderson's celebrity impression is at the front left of the Chinese Theater (as you face the entrance). Look for a classic Mickey on Harry's tie.

Hint 33: Four squares to the right of Harry Anderson's impression, Carol Burnett's square has classic Mickey ears in the upper right side.

Hint 34: In the loading dock area, a shadow of Minnie Mouse's head in side profile is visible on the wall mural during loading and unloading. To find it, first spot the house in the middle of the mural. Then look above and to the right of the house to spot Minnie's shadow. She's looking to your left. Having trouble? Look at the stationary ride vehicles. The Minnie shadow is to the left of the front section of the second of the two vehicles.

Hint 35: On the right side of the loading dock mural, in the second to last house on the right, a tiny black classic Mickey peeks out of the bottom center of a top-floor window. It's on the side of the house and nearest the corner.

Hint 36: In the first part of Gangster Alley, Mickey Mouse's brown shoes and tail poke out at the lower left from under a James Cagney poster, "The Public Enemy," on the left side of the ride vehicle.

Hint 37: At the end of Gangster Alley, a silhouette of Mickey in side profile appears in the rightmost window, near the top of the "Chemical Company" building. It's to the rear left of your ride vehicle.

Hint 38: In the Western scene, look for two paper bulletins advertising "Pocahontas Remedies." One is on a wall to your right behind a barber pole. The other is to the left of your vehicle, just past John Wayne on a wood fence. (It's one of the lower bulletins on the fence and can generally be spotted toward the right of the collection of bulletins. (Note: The locations of the bulletins in this scene sometimes change.)

Hint 39: In the "Raiders of the Lost Ark" room, R2-D2 and C-3PO are together in the hieroglyphics on the left wall. Look midway between the two huge statues. The two robots are etched on the second level of panes, to the right of a kneeling figure.

Hint 40: In the "Raiders of the Lost Ark" room, a small white classic Mickey is on a broken tablet (or flat rock) that leans against the foundation that the Ark container is sitting on. Two white men are painted on the side of the container, and the tablet with the Mickey image is below and between them.

Hint 41: At the end of the "Raiders of the Lost Ark" room, Mickey and Donald can be found in the far left corner on the left wall. They're facing one another and Mickey is to the right of Donald, on the third row of panes up from the floor.

Hint 42: At the end of the right wall in the "Raiders of the Lost Ark" room, a hieroglyphic classic Mickey is at the right lower part of the first full pane above the stones on the floor. It's to the right of the lower leg of a standing figure etched in the pane.

Hint 43: In the latter part of the "Tarzan" room, a basket high in a treehouse to the

right contains three eggs that form a classic Mickey. (The eggs are all the same size, but this is a sentimental favorite Hidden Mickey among guests and Cast Members.)

Hint 44: In the "Wizard of Oz" room, several groups of flowers, among them three large blue flowers above a hut at the middle left of the room, form acceptable classic Mickeys.

Hint 45: A green classic Mickey is nestled in the top of the trees, midway along the mural above the exit from the "Wizard of Oz" room. This classic Mickey is tilted slightly to the right.

Hint 46: Near the top of the flames directly above the small gold statue that is standing over the entrance doors to the attraction, a red circle with swirls for ears resembles a classic Mickey.

– Star Tours – The Adventures Continue

Hint 47: About halfway along the outside winding queue, a white classic Mickey is high on a tree trunk, just below the walkway platform for the Ewok village above. It's on the huge central tree, directly across from the Imperial Walker.

Hint 48: Along the right side of the inside entrance queue, circles make a Mickey hat with ears on the upper part of the control panel behind C-3PO's head. It's at the lower center of the upper screen.

Hint 49: In a wall display along the entrance queue, the silhouette of R2-D2 appears several times in a continuous video loop of moving shadow figures. At one point, R2-D2 sprouts satellite ears that rotate into round "Mickey ears" for a few seconds.

Hint 50: Along the entrance queue, a robot watches a continuous scan of luggage moving along a conveyor belt. You can spot images of a plush Mickey Mouse and a plush Goofy, along with images of Buzz Lightyear, Aladdin's lamp, a Sorcerer Mickey hat, a Mr. Incredible shirt, Madame Leota's crystal ball, and some other Disney images.

Hint 51: At the end of the *Star Tours* ride, there are four classic Hidden Mickeys in the Coruscant landing sequence, which is one of three different and random end destinations for the ride. After the *Star Tours* vehicle crash lands on the platform and is lowered below into the hanger, look for four recessed panels in the top half of the back wall of the hanger. A classic Mickey is in the center of each panel. To see them, focus on the background wall instead of the droid in the foreground that's flying around with the two light batons.

Hint 52: A small classic Hidden Mickey formed of blue lights is in the gift shop at the exit of *Star Tours*. As you exit the ride, turn to face the long counter to your right. The light image is at the lower right of the counter.

Hint 53: At the "Build Your Own Lightsaber" station at the other end of the long counter in the exit gift shop, a classic Mickey is on the lower right front panel. It's formed by bullet holes with surrounding black burn marks as the "ears" and a central raised circle as the "head."

– Lights, Motors, Action! Extreme Stunt Show

Hint 54: Walk through the entrance turnstile and look through the windows of the building on your right. Classic Mickey magnets are stuck on red tool chests behind the first set of windows you encounter and behind the middle set of windows as you turn right at the first corner. These magnet Mickeys change positions on the tool chests at times.

Hint 55: In the right section of the background set, look for a window under an "Antiquities" sign and near a large "Café" sign. A full-body drawing of Mickey Mouse is near a chair in the window's lower right side.

Hint 56: A classic Mickey is behind the upper right windowpane at the rear of the set, under the sign "Motomania."

Hint 57: Near the end of the show, a fireball erupts at the front center of the stage set ("downstage center" in stage parlance). The fire forms Mickey ears for a split second.

Hint 58: As you exit, walk to the left side of the show lagoon. A dark classic Mickey formed of rocks lies in the water at the bottom.

– Disney's Hollywood Studios Guidemap

Hint 59: The face of Mickey Mouse on the upside-down park map has been distorted over time. The corners of his smile are still visible on both sides of the big Sorcerer's Hat, and his forehead "widow's peak" shows up just below where Hollywood Boulevard ends. (Look closely and you'll see that his smile and widow's peak are darker areas in the cement.) To the right, Echo Lake forms a distorted ear.

Hint 60: On the rightside-up map, a filmstrip flowerbed adorns the right side of the entrance plaza in front of the trees. A green side profile of Mickey is in the fourth square from the bottom of the filmstrip. He's looking at Minnie, who is in the third square from the bottom.

– MuppetVision 3D

Hint 61: In a fountain outside MuppetVision 3D, Gonzo is balancing on a character with bulging eyes and face who resembles Mickey.

Hint 62: On the wall near the far turn of the long outside waiting queue, you'll find a classic Mickey in the center left of a blue poster that says, "5 reasons to return . . . 3D glasses."

Hint 63: During the first part of the pre-show on the video monitors, a test pattern appears after you see the words "Video Display Test." The black lines on a white background form a classic Hidden Mickey.

Hint 64: After the cannon shoots holes in the theater and Kermit rides in on a fire truck, you can see that some of the observers outside are holding Mickey Mouse balloons.

Hint 65: An image of Cinderella Castle (a Hidden Surprise) is on a license plate at the right lower corner of the fire truck Kermit is riding.

Hint 66: Across from and outside the exit doors from the *MuppetVision 3D* theater, a poster on the right wall advertises "Rowlf." At the lower left of the poster, a classic Mickey is formed by the nose and eyes of the dog's face.

– Studio Backlot Tour

Hint 67: An advertisement with Walt Disney and Mickey Mouse is on a bulletin board behind glass, on the right side of the entrance walkway into the props area. It's in the third display board from the entrance doors. A drawing of Mickey is in the same display, to the left of the purple image of Walt and Mickey.

Hint 68: Straight ahead in the prop storage building, you'll find Mickey's gloves and then his shoes in the left display area along the first aisle.

Hint 69: On the right side of the first aisle in the movie and TV prop storage area, the front of a yellow refrigerator sports a silver classic Mickey.

Hint 70: On the left side of the second aisle of the prop storage area, a classic Hidden Mickey cactus is inside the storage bins in the first half of the aisle.

Hint 71: Also on the left side of the second aisle, a small painting of Sleeping Beauty (Princess Aurora) and Prince Philip sits in the storage bins lining the second half of the aisle.

Hint 72: Toward the end of the second aisle on the left, in the prop storage area, a framed photo of Mickey and Minnie sits inside a wire basket on top of a white bureau.

Hint 73: Inside the costuming building on the tram tour, you can spot a large Mickey clock on the far wall of the first sewing room to your left.

Hint 74: Later on the ride, you can see a small classic Mickey image inside the "D" of "Disney World" on the side of Walt Disney's airplane. (The Mickey image on the tail of the plane is decorative, not hidden.)

Hint 75: After the tram ride, look for a mural on the right wall just inside the entrance to the AFI display rooms. Just to the left of the tallest building in the mural, in the right center, is a Mickey Mouse statue on a tombstone. Atop the fourth building from the left side of the mural is Mickey's side-profile silhouette. On the right side of the fifth building from the left is a white side profile of his face.

– Studio Catering Co.

Hint 76: At the side of the restaurant, a red classic Mickey lies on a black tile under a fire alarm on the right wall of the High Octane Refreshments Bar.

– Walt Disney: One Man's Dream

Hint 77: On the left side of the display aisle (and before you are ushered into the theater), you see Walt Disney standing with a pointer in front of a wall map. On a desk to Walt's left, a coffee mug near a telephone has Donald Duck on it.

Hint 78: You can spot a green classic Mickey in the same scene. He's on the wall to the left of Walt.

– Disney Junior — Live on Stage!

Hint 79: Classic Mickeys appear at times in the lighting and stage effects as well as on various stage props during the live show.

– The Hollywood Brown Derby restaurant

Hint 80: Classic Mickeys are in the clouds on the mural on the outside wall above the restaurant. One is at the far upper right of the mural, and another is at the far mid-left of the mural, above the "Stage 5" sign.

Hint 81: On a wall to the left in the waiting area, in the second row of pictures, you'll find a caricature of Jimmy Dodd (with his Mouse ears) from the 1950s *Mickey Mouse Club* TV show.

– The American Idol Experience

Hint 82: A classic Mickey image is on the lower light brown arch in the stage backdrop, between the second and third round archway lights (counting from the lower right of the arch). Another small, faint classic Mickey image is near the top of the same arch, between the fifth and sixth round archway lights (counting from the lower left of the arch).

Hint 83: In a video toward the end of the show, female singer Jordin Sparks is wearing a necklace with classic Mickey-shaped gems.

– Sunset Boulevard

Hint 84: Midway down Sunset Boulevard toward the *Tower of Terror*, the outside scrollwork about halfway to the top of a blue building on the right side of the street has an upside-down classic Mickey in its design.

– Rosie's All-American Café

Hint 85: Mickey's smiling face is at the right lower corner of a photo collage at the left side of Rosie's leftmost food order window.

Hint 86: On the rear wall of Rosie's All-American Café, two regulators form classic Mickeys above the coffee and hot cocoa machines.

– Beauty and the Beast – Live on Stage

Hint 87: A classic Mickey is on a wind-up device on Cogsworth's back. The device has two holes for the "ears" and a larger circle for the "head." Sometimes this image is upside down.

– Hollywood & Vine restaurant

Hint 88: Outside the restaurant, a silhouette of Roger Rabbit is in a window above and to the left of the entrance.

Hint 89: On the left wall inside, the "San Fernando Valley" mural has a stick-figure Mickey on the far right, behind a pole.

Hint 90: Bushes form several classic Mickeys to the immediate left of the stick-figure Mickey and also above him.

– 50's Prime Time Café

Hint 91: In the waiting area, washers shaped like classic Mickeys secure the white tabletops.

– Mulch, Sweat & Shears

Hint 92: An orange side-profile Hidden Mickey is on the blade of a shovel that lies along the right side of the top of their vehicle.

– Backlot Express restaurant

Hint 93: Several full-body two-dimensional Mickeys are on the bulletin boards inside the Backlot Express restaurant. One bulletin board is near the exit door facing *Star Tours*. A second is close by at the side of the seating area across from the mural of the city park.

– Sci-Fi Dine-In Theater Restaurant

Hint 94: In the waiting area on the left wall (as you enter) is a poster for the movie *Attack of the 50 Ft. Woman*. A classic Mickey is behind her right knee, just off the highway.

Hint 95: Mickey Mouse in a graduation outfit is on an "Educational Reimbursement Program" notice on the lower middle of a bulletin board on a wall in the waiting area.

Hint 96: Just past the check-in counter, at the beginning of the left-side hallway, a classic Hidden Mickey is drawn on the right wall.

Hint 97: Face the kitchen, then look to the right of it at the tall fence. You'll find two Hidden Mickeys in the mural above the right side of the tall fence. Look at the treetops. A classic Mickey, tilted slightly to the right, is above the right corner of the tall fence. A second Hidden Mickey is just to the left of the first one; this one appears to be waving with his left hand.

Hint 98: In the multicolored tiles above the kitchen door entrance (on the right as you face the kitchen) is a side profile of Mickey. He is outlined in yellow tiles and appears to be looking to his left (our right). Look first for his jaw, a curving line of yellow tiles in the middle of the mosaic square.

Hint 99: Watch the movie reel for Donald Duck, Mickey Mouse, and Tinker Bell. Donald is in a cartoon segment about a secretary who is kidnapped to another planet; Donald is one of the characters who chases her. The segment follows a clip of Walt Disney. Mickey appears later in the reel, in a "News of the Future" segment; he wears a spacesuit and waves to the crowd. Tinker Bell flies around above the word "Tomorrowland."

Hint 100: Stay alert for a youngster in a spacesuit during the movie reel, when the words "Calling All Boys! All Girls!" appear on the screen. A classic Mickey formed by a circle and two knobs is on the upper chest of the spacesuit, just below the helmet.

Hint 101: Silver classic Mickeys are at the sides of the dining-car seats, on the running boards.

– The Writer's Stop

Hint 102: Some of the theater lights hanging from the ceiling sport yellow classic Mickeys.

– Pizza Planet Arcade

Hint 103: A classic Mickey is one of the constellations of stars above the counter registers. Focus on the left side of the rear wall, between Woody and the "Disney's Toy Story" sign.

Hint 104: A small, bright classic-Mickey star cluster appears above the counter registers on the right side of the rear wall. Look near the pizza-slice constellation.

Hint 105: Above the arcade games, in the moon near the top of the mural, you can spot a three-quarter Mickey profile facing left.

– Stage 1 Company Store

Hint 106: Blue birds are stuck high on side doors of one of the tall merchandise cabinets inside the store. Classic Mickeys decorate the ends of red scarves that are draped over the birds.

Hint 107: Look for an old bureau that's loaded with hats for sale and has paint cans at the very top. You'll find a green, painted classic Mickey near the center of the desktop.

Hint 108: In the middle of the store, across from the green-paint Hidden Mickey on the bureau, circles in the middle of a cloud at the upper left of a mural with a rainbow form an approximate classic Mickey.

Hint 109: Mickey Mouse's shorts (red with white buttons) are hanging on a line near one of the exit doors.

Hint 110: Walk around the outside of the Stage 1 Company Store and admire at least five Mickey images formed by yellow and purple paint that's spilled on the ground.

– Mama Melrose's Ristorante Italiano

Hint 111: Just inside the entrance, to your right, the Dalmatian has a black classic Mickey spot on its right shoulder (your left).

Hint 112: A slightly distorted classic Mickey is in the plaster of the right wall between the waiting room and the dining area. Look in the upper right corner, near the entrance door.

Hint 113: To the right of the check-in podium (as you face it), a green classic Mickey leaf is about one and a half feet above the bottom of the window, along the left edge.

Hint 114: The left wall between the waiting room and the dining area has a smaller classic Mickey plastered on the brick. You'll find it in the middle left part of the wall, just above the counter.

– Stars of Cars Greeting Area

Hint 115: The wing nut on Mater's engine air filter has Mickey ears.

– Streets of America

Hint 116: Some of the newspapers in a newsstand in the left lower area of a mural at the end of San Francisco Street feature articles about Steamboat Willie.

Hint 117: In the lower right and left sides of the same mural, some papers in a small newspaper dispenser feature articles about a Disney movie (at presstime, the movie was *Up*).

Hint 118: A poster entitled "The Osborne Family Spectacle of Dancing Lights" hangs on a wall across from the San Francisco mural. A faint image of the Earful Tower is in the lower middle of the poster, below a man wearing Mickey ears.

Hint 119: Three open silver containers form a classic Hidden Mickey in the right front display window of the China Bowl Restaurant on San Francisco Street. The image is best viewed from the right side of the window-box display.

Hint 120: Along San Francisco Street, you'll find a Dalmatian on an address plaque on the wall above a barber pole. Three black spots above its front leg form a slightly distorted classic Mickey.

Hint 121: A watch with Mickey on its face is in the window of Sal's Pawn Shop, near the passage to *Honey, I Shrunk the Kids Movie Set Adventure*.

Hint 122: On the upper left wall of the second window (on the left as you face Venture Travel Service) is a picture of Walt Disney holding a Mickey Mouse doll in his right hand.

Hint 123: The same window holds four other Hidden Characters: classic Mickey holes decorate the lower edge of a lampshade; in a photo propped on the desk below the shade, Mickey and Minnie are sitting on a bench looking out to a cruise ship at sea (we see just the backs of their heads), and small white classic Mickeys are in the corners of the window.

Hint 124: A classic Mickey sand trap is in the leftmost window as you face the New York backdrop at the end of the Streets of America.

– Animation Courtyard

Hint 125: Donald Duck and Goofy are etched on the ornamental arches that are adjacent to Animation Courtyard's main entrance arch.

– The Magic of Disney Animation

Hint 126: The stage set in front of the seating area for *The Magic of Disney Animation* theater usually includes a number of Hidden Mickeys. Check the large animator's desk for them. A coffee mug on the right side of the desk's middle shelf has a blue classic Mickey on it. The top of a pencil that's sticking out of a container on the top shelf sports a classic Mickey shape.

Hint 127: In the video shown in the theater, a classic Hidden Mickey is formed by a large cloud of smoke when Mushu the dragon is transforming into a double-headed Mushu.

Hint 128: Later in the video, a man holds a coffee mug covered with classic Mickeys.

Hint 129: Outside *The Magic of Disney Animation* theater is an interior courtyard with cement squares in the pavement that commemorate a few Disney Legends. Mickey is traced in Ward Kimball's square.

Hint 130: The circles in the carpet design near the *Animation Academy* room inside the Animation building usually include classic Mickeys.

Hint 131: In the Character Greeting areas, Mickey hats, the Earful Tower, and Pluto are in the background mural of the Sorcerer Mickey set. Pluto's outline is at the lower right of the mural.

– Toward Hollywood Boulevard

Hint 132: On the plaza, in front of Mickey's huge Sorcerer's Hat, a full-face Mickey Mouse formed by lights can often be spotted in the afternoon and evening.

– Intersection of Hollywood & Sunset Blvds.

Hint 133: On both sides of Sunset Boulevard near its intersection with Hollywood Boulevard, you'll find small impressions in the cement sidewalks, near the curb. They read, "Mortimer & Co, 1928, Contractors." 'Mortimer Mouse' was Mickey Mouse's first (and soon discarded) name; 1928 was the year he was "born." (Two more of these stamps are at the other end of Sunset Boulevard. One is near the curb just before the walkway to *Rock 'n' Roller Coaster*. The other is across the street close to the entrance walkway to the *Fantasmic!* show.)

– Keystone Clothiers

Hint 134: Outside and above the shop, a Kodak billboard shows a girl bending forward, partially covering Mickey Mouse's handprints impressed in cement.

Hint 135: At Peevy's Polar Pipeline drink service, behind Keystone Clothiers, gauges or regulators form a classic Mickey, especially when viewed from behind.

– Disney & Company

Hint 136: In an outside display window of the store, you'll find a sideways classic Mickey formed by metal circles on the side of a merchandise stand.

– Mickey's of Hollywood

Hint 137: Classic Mickey holes are drilled in some of the store's metal support poles.

Hint 138: The caps on the ends of some merchandise racks are shaped like classic Mickeys.

Hint 139: In the Sorcerer section of the store, near a door to the street, you'll find cabinets with classic Mickey shapes on them.

Hint 140: "MICKEYS" is spelled out on four vertical dividers (two on each side of the store) that separate the sections of the store.

- Cover Story

Hint 141: You'll find a design containing classic Mickeys on the outside of the store, next to The Darkroom. Look on the horizontal frieze below the second-floor windows.

- Near the charter bus area

Hint 142: Outside the park, near the charter bus area, a classic Mickey is stamped in cement. It's about nine or so benches (and three light poles) from the main entrance promenade as you head toward the walkway to the BoardWalk Resort. Look across from the "CG" marker on the cement.

- Fantasmic!

Hint 143: When animated characters float up in large bubbles on the water screen, watch for Pinocchio. His bubble forms the head of a classic Hidden Mickey. Two bubbles beside it form the ears. (Other bubbles on the screen may come together at times to form classic Mickeys.)

Disney's Animal Kingdom Scavenger Hunt

• •

★ Your first stop is **Expedition Everest** in Asia. Walk through the Oasis, turn right in Discovery Island, and follow the path to Asia. One of the queue Hidden Mickeys is only in the FASTPASS and Single Rider queues. The rest are in the regular line, which Disney calls the Standby queue because you just walk into it and stand by for the attraction. So get a FASTPASS to use later and then join the Standby queue to search for the Mickeys in Clues 1 through 12 and Clue 14. Search for Clue 13 when you come back to take the ride at your FASTPASS time.

Clue 1: In the Standby queue, search for a classic Mickey in the first sunken courtyard.
3 points

Clue 2: Locate Mickey depressions on a red wall.
4 points

Clue 3: Look around for cloud Hidden Mickeys in a mural.
4 points for spotting two

Clue 4: Keep alert for pipes on a shelf that form a classic Mickey.
3 points

Clue 5: Find small Mickey ears in this room.
4 points

Clue 6: Look for a Hidden Mickey made of light-switch devices in a display.
3 points

Clue 7: Stay alert for Mickey on a book.
4 points

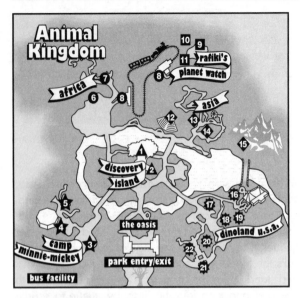

discovery island

A1 The Tree of Life
A2 It's Tough to be a Bug

camp minnie-mickey

☆ Outdoor Theater
☆4 Festival of the Lion King
☆5 Character Greeting Trails

africa

6 Kilimanjaro Safaris
7 Pangani Forest Exploration Trail
8 Wildlife Express Train

rafiki's planet watch

9 Conservation Station
10 Affection Section
11 Habitat Habit!

asia

12 Flights of Wonder
13 Maharajah Jungle Trek
14 Kali River Rapids
15 Expedition Everest

dinoland u.s.a.

16 Finding Nemo – The Musical
17 The Boneyard
18 TriceraTop Spin
19 Primeval Whirl
20 Cretaceous Trail
21 DINOSAUR
22 Dino-Sue T Rex

Clue 8: Search for Mickey on a handrail.
5 points

Clue 9: Spot a Hidden Mickey in a kettle.
4 points

Clue 10: Squint for a Hidden Mickey in an animal track.
5 points

Clue 11: Search for an animal with Mickey's ears!
3 points

Clue 12: In the last room before boarding for both the Standby and FASTPASS lines, glance around for Sorcerer Mickey near something blue.
5 points

Clue 13: In either the FASTPASS or the Single Rider queue, find a Hidden Mickey on a lantern.
4 points

Clue 14: In the loading area outside the Standby and FASTPASS lines, look for a classic Mickey.
3 points

Clue 15: After the ride starts, stay alert for a classic-Mickey melted spot in the snow.
5 points

★ After disembarking, study the photo monitors.

Clue 16: Earn bonus points if you find a Hidden Mickey in the ride photos.
4 bonus points

Clue 17: Find a small classic Mickey made of gold balls in the gift shop at the ride exit.
3 points

Clue 18: Look around the gift shop for classic Mickey circles on a brown chest.
3 points for one or more

Clue 19: Search outside, near the Serka Zong Bazaar shop, for a classic Mickey.
3 points

Clue 20: Now walk around outside the attraction to spot a classic Mickey in camp supplies near a post.
3 points

★ Stroll to Africa and enjoy **Kilimanjaro Safaris**.

Clue 21: Along the entrance queue, watch a video monitor for spots on a leopard.
5 points

Clue 22: Observe the island in the flamingo pond.
4 points

Clue 23: Near the lions, watch for Donald in the rocks.
4 points

★ Visit **DINOSAUR** next. Go back through Discovery Island and then follow the walkway into DinoLand U.S.A. Find Hidden Mickeys on paintings just inside the *DINOSAUR* building.

Clue 24: Mickey is on a tree trunk.
4 points

Clue 25: Look for Mickey ears above a dinosaur.
3 points

Clue 26: After the ride begins, be alert for a Hidden Mickey on a greaseboard. (Note: This Mickey image changes locations and even disappears at times.)
4 bonus points

Clue 27: Find a classic Mickey on the red dinosaur in the mural behind the counter in the ride's photo-purchase area.
4 points

★ Walk into the queue for **It's Tough to be a Bug!** on Discovery Island.

Clue 28: When you get inside *The Tree of Life*, look for Mickey above the handicapped entrance doors.
4 points

★ Go to **Kali River Rapids** in Asia and find a classic Mickey formed by plates on the wall of one of the rooms you pass through on your way to the ride. (You can exit when you get to the loading dock if you don't want to ride. Ask a Cast Member to point the way out.)

Clue 29: You're getting close when you see stone statues in the grass.
2 points

Clue 30: Find another Mickey nearby formed by pans.
2 points

★ Stroll over to the **Maharajah Jungle Trek**. At the tiger exhibit area, find seven classic Hidden Mickeys in the building with arches.

Clue 31: Check in the water in the painting to the right of the first arch.
2 points

Clue 32: Look for the earring Mickey on the left mural inside the first arch.
2 points

Clue 33: Find a leaf Mickey on the left mural inside the first arch.
2 points

Clue 34: Search the right mural inside the first arch for a Hidden Mickey on a man.
2 points

Clue 35: Inside the building with arches, on the right wall, check the flowers on two square panels to find classic Mickeys.
2 points for one or more

Clue 36: Look for a classic Mickey in the mountains inside the second arch.
2 points

Clue 37: Now find a classic Mickey in the cloud formation inside the same arch.
2 points

Clue 38: After you exit the temple ruins, search for two Hidden Mickeys in the leaves to your left.
8 points for spotting both

Clue 39: Scan the huge mural on the left outdoor wall at the Elds Deer Exhibit for a classic Hidden Mickey in orange flowers.
5 points

Clue 40: Further along the trail, before you get to the aviary entrance, try to spot a classic Mickey in a man's necklace in the carving on the wall.
2 points

★ Before or after an early lunch, wander over to the **Pangani Forest Exploration Trail** in Africa. Look for three Hidden Mickeys in the building with the Naked Mole Rat exhibit.

Clue 41: Find Mickey on a small box.
4 points

Clue 42: Spot a backpack with a Mickey emblem.
3 points

Clue 43: Locate Mickey on a horizontal pole.
4 points

Clue 44: Past the gorilla viewing area, search for a Hidden Jafar.
5 points

★ Eat an early lunch to avoid the crowds. The Rainforest Cafe at the park entrance is a good place to eat and has an interesting ambiance. Tusker House Restaurant in Africa serves salads and sandwiches.

★ Consult the Times Guide and pick the next convenient shows of *Finding Nemo – The Musical* and *Festival of the Lion King*.

★ See **Finding Nemo – The Musical** at Theater in the Wild in DinoLand.

Clue 45: Look around for a Hidden Mickey near the stage.
3 points

Clue 46: Find two Hidden Mickeys in the show-times signs outside.
4 points for spotting both

★ See *Festival of the Lion King* in Camp Minnie-Mickey.

Clue 47: Be alert for a classic Mickey on Timon the meerkat's float.
4 points

Clue 48: Now search for an upside-down classic Mickey on Timon's float.
4 points

Clue 49: Study the center stage for a classic Mickey.
4 points

(Tip: If Timon's float and the props are still there after the show has ended, you can look for the Hidden Mickeys in Clues 47 to 49 as you exit. If you need help, ask a Cast Member.)

★ Check other areas in *Camp Minnie-Mickey*.

Clue 50: Spot a rock classic Mickey in a wall near the *Greeting Trails*.
4 points

★ Now search the camp for a small cabin with classic Mickeys in the woodwork.

Clue 51: You'll find these Hidden Mickeys on both the front and sides of the cabin.
2 points for spotting Mickeys in both areas

Clue 52: Search the ground for a rock classic Mickey near the creek. (Psst! It's in the seating area for the food cabin that's located across from the Lion King Theater.)
4 points

Clue 53: Try to find a birdhouse with a Mickey Mouse cutout. (Note: These birdhouses are moved around to different locations in Camp Minnie-Mickey periodically.)
1 point

Clue 54: Find Mickey Mouse's head on top of a nearby flagpole.
4 points

★ Go to Africa and take the *Wildlife Express Train* to Rafiki's Planet Watch to search **Conservation Station** for a Hidden Mickey bonanza.

Clue 55: Look at the mosaic in the pavement outside the main entrance to *Conservation Station* for a tiny classic Mickey.
4 points

Clue 56: Find the Hidden Mickey profile in the changing, repeating panels inside the entrance.
4 points

Clue 57: On the wall mural just to the right, spot a Mickey Mouse profile on an opossum.
4 points

Clue 58: Look for a butterfly wearing classic Mickeys.
3 points

Clue 59: Gaze closely at a spider nearby with a classic Mickey marking.
3 points

Clue 60: Spot a classic Mickey on an ostrich.
3 points

Clue 61: Look for a classic Mickey on a green snake.
3 points

Clue 62: Search for another classic Mickey on a lizard's ear.
4 points

Clue 63: Locate a side-profile Mickey on a hippo.
4 points

Clue 64: Glance at a llama for a classic Mickey.
3 points

Clue 65: A squirrel nearby sports a classic Mickey.
3 points

Clue 66: Look for a classic Mickey on an alligator.
3 points

Clue 67: Find a frog bearing a tiny image of Mickey's face.
5 points

Clue 68: Scan a walrus for a Hidden Mickey.
4 points

Clue 69: Find the Hidden Mickey on an owl.
3 points

Clue 70: Search for the amazing Mickey image on a second butterfly!
5 points

Clue 71: Look up for a classic Mickey on a frog behind a monkey.
5 points

Clue 72: Scan the mural for a fish with a partially hidden classic Mickey.
5 points

Clue 73: Locate a butterfly with two Hidden Mickeys.
4 points for both

Clue 74: Look around carefully for a frog with a side-profile Mickey.
5 points

Clue 75: Find a yellow butterfly with a classic Mickey.
3 points

Clue 76: Look lower for a lizard with Mickey spots.
3 points

Clue 77: Scan overhead for a Mickey in tree leaves.
3 points

Clue 78: Next to the "Song of the Rainforest" area, spot a fly with a tiny classic Mickey on its back.
5 points

Clue 79: Search for a tiny flower Hidden Mickey at the first entrance to the "Song of the Rainforest" area.
4 points

Clue 80: Look for a classic Mickey indentation on a tree toward the front of the Rainforest area.
3 points

Clue 81: Don't stray far for a Mickey hole in a leaf.
4 points

Clue 82: Check the trees inside the Rainforest area for a side-profile Mickey shadow.
4 points

Clue 83: Look for the classic Mickey shadow on the ceiling near door number eight in the "Song of the Rainforest" area.
4 points

Clue 84: Now find a Hidden Mickey on a tree near door number six.
3 points

Clue 85: Search for a green moss side-profile Mickey in the Rainforest area.
4 points

Clue 86: Walk out to the front of the Rainforest area and search for a side-profile Mickey.
4 points

Clue 87: Spot a classic Mickey made of short plant stalks on the Grandmother Willow tree.
3 points

Clue 88: Also in the Rainforest area, spot a classic Mickey on a cockroach.
4 points

Clue 89: Now find a classic Mickey on a lizard on the same tree.
3 points

Clue 90: Look for a butterfly wearing a tiny Hidden Mickey on this tree.
5 points

 Clue 91: Examine the grates around the bottoms of the trees in the main lobby.
2 points

Clue 92: Locate a Hidden Mickey on a plate in a window display at the rear of the lobby.
3 points

Clue 93: Spot a reptile classic Mickey on a ledge in the rear area displays and laboratories.
3 points

★ Walk outside to **Affection Section** to spot another classic Hidden Mickey.

Clue 94: Study the animals in the petting zoo.
(Note: These Hidden Mickeys come and go.)
4 bonus points

★ Wander on over to the **Wildlife Express Train station** and look for classic Mickeys.

Clue 95: Examine the rafters inside the station.
2 points

★ Ride the train to Africa, then explore the area around **Harambe Fruit Market** to spot a large Mickey Mouse head in the cement.

Clue 96: Check the beginning of the cement and flagstone path at the side of the Fruit Market.
4 points

Clue 97: Turn left at the opposite end of the path and follow the cement walkway a few feet to find a large, faint classic Mickey in the cement.
5 points

★ Outside the **Mombasa Marketplace** store, look for a classic Mickey formed by a small utility cover and the pebbles adjacent to it.

Clue 98: It's near an entrance door to the store.
5 points

★ Stroll inside **Tusker House Restaurant**.

Clue 99: Locate a classic Mickey on an Assignment Board on a wall.
4 points

★ Go to the far side of **Tamu Tamu Refreshments**.

Clue 100: Find another classic Mickey formed by a small utility cover and adjacent pebbles.
5 points

Clue 101: Marvel at a Hidden Baloo the bear inside the small seating area behind Tamu Tamu Refreshments.
5 points

Clue 102: Search for another Hidden Character here.
4 points

★ Walk a short way down the **path to Asia**.

Clue 103: Look over to *The Tree of Life* and spot the Hidden Mickey on it. (Psst! It's near the hippo.)
4 points

★ Cross the bridge to Discovery Island and amble on into **Pizzafari restaurant** to find six Hidden Mickeys.

Clue 104: Spot Mickey in the room across from the food order counters.
3 points

Clue 105: In the first dining room to the left as you walk down the hall, search for a tiny orange classic Mickey.
5 points

Clue 106: In the Nocturnal Room (the dining room directly to the left of the food counters as you face the counters), study the firefly wings.
3 points

Clue 107: In the Nocturnal Room, look around for a classic Mickey in the trees.
4 points

Clue 108: In the large room past the Nocturnal Room, find some spots on the wall in the tree branches.
3 points

Clue 109: Study an animal near these tree branches for a classic Mickey.
2 points

★ Watch the **parade** (usually scheduled for around 4:00 p.m.).

Clue 110: Look for classic Mickey headlights and a classic Mickey antenna.
3 points for spotting both

★ Return to DinoLand U.S.A. Enter **The Boneyard** and find four classic Mickeys.

Clue 111: Look under the drinking fountains inside the entrance.
3 points

Clue 112: On the lower level, locate a classic Mickey on a fence.
4 points

Clue 113: Walk upstairs. Go to the rear and observe the small classic Mickey in an archeology display.
2 points

Clue 114: Look around the children's dig area for Hidden Mickey hard hats.
2 points

★ Walk to the **Cretaceous Trail** in the middle of DinoLand and go dino hunting.

Clue 115: Find a dark Mickey on a dinosaur's back.
3 points

★ Go to **TriceraTop Spin**.

Clue 116: Search in front of the attraction for a classic Mickey on a dinosaur with a ball.
3 points

Clue 117: Spot a classic Mickey in one of the parking spaces near the attraction.
3 points

Clue 118: Study the nearby horned dinosaur studded with gems and find a Mickey pin.
4 points

★ Check inside **Chester & Hester's Dinosaur Treasures** shop.

Clue 119: Find a marionette Mickey in the shop.
2 points

Clue 120: Study the pavement outside the store entrance that faces *Primeval Whirl* for a classic Mickey.
5 points

★ Cross back to **Primeval Whirl** and look for classic Mickeys on the outside of the attraction.

Clue 121: Check the meteors.
5 points for two or more

★ Walk along the outer walkway **behind the Fossil Fun Games area**.

Clue 122: Check out the fence signs for a classic Hidden Mickey.
3 points

★ Walk to the **Creature Comforts** shop on Discovery Island between Pizzafari restaurant and the bridge to Africa.

Clue 123: Search inside Creature Comforts for black classic Mickeys on an animal.
5 points for finding two

★ Enter the **Island Mercantile** shop.

Clue 124: Spot a classic Mickey on a wall.
5 points

★ Back outside on **Discovery Island**, find a classic Mickey made of green moss.

Clue 125: Study the front of *The Tree of Life*.
5 points

★ Stroll to the **Flame Tree Barbecue Restaurant** to find two classic Mickeys.

Clue 126: Search the ground in the food order area for a rock classic Mickey.
4 points

Clue 127: Now find a classic Mickey in the seating area outside.
2 points

★ Go to the **Rainforest Cafe entrance sign** inside the park.

Clue 128: Look for a Hidden Mickey on the sign.
3 points

★ Keep your eyes open **as you leave the park**.

Clue 129: Search the outside walls of the ticket booths for Hidden Mickeys.
4 points for two

Clue 130: Outside the entrance turnstiles, check the metal grates around some of the trees near the tram loading area.
2 points

Now turn the page and tally your score.

Total Points for
Disney's Animal Kingdom =

How'd you do?

Up to 182 points – Bronze
183 to 364 points – Silver
365 points and over – Gold
456 points – Perfect Score

You may have done even better if you earned bonus points in *Expedition Everest, DINOSAUR,* and/or *Affection Section.*

**Caution:
Don't peek at this
section unless you
really want help!**

Asia

– Expedition Everest

(Note: Hints 1 through 12 and 14 apply to Hidden Mickeys you'll find in the Standby queue. Hints 12 and 14 are for Mickeys that can be spotted in both the Standby and FASTPASS queues, while Hint 13 is a Hidden Mickey that you'll only find in the FASTPASS and Single Rider queues.)

Hint 1: A classic Mickey made of a central circle with swirls for ears hides in the base of a Yeti statue. You'll find it in a sunken outdoor courtyard past the first room (an office).

Hint 2: Just past the first room, a classic Mickey is formed by shallow depressions in the left wall of a small red building. The upright image is at the far left lower corner of the wall, below and to the left of a small curved drainpipe.

Hint 3: On the rear wall of the same red building just past the first room, classic Mickeys lie in the clouds on the left and right sides of a Yeti mural.

Hint 4: As you enter the second building (Tashi's Trek and Tongba Shop), an upside-down classic Mickey is formed by the highest pipes on the top shelf in the right corner.

Hint 5: Along the far wall of Tashi's Trek and Tongba Shop, a small white Yeti doll on the top right shelf in-side a cupboard wears black Mickey ears.

Hint 6: In Tashi's Trek and Tongba Shop, light-switch devices in a glass case on the left side of the queue form a classic Mickey.

Hint 7: Inside the Yeti Museum, on the right side of the queue after the first left turn, look for a Yeti book at the far left of the book display. A partial image of Mickey's head and ears is imprinted in the snow on the book's front cover.

Hint 8: Just past the snow Mickey of Hint 7, a classic Mickey is etched into the top of a wooden handrail.

Hint 9: Dents in a kettle in the Yeti Museum's second display form a classic Mickey.

Hint 10: Also in the museum a classic Mickey is hiding in an "animal track." It's at the lower left of a tall glass cabinet in a display labeled "Documenting Bio-Diversity." Look near the top of the third paper from the left, above the label "Small Mammal Tracks."

Hint 11: The next to last display cabinet in the museum has a photo of a bear with ears that look like Mickey's ears. The bear is on the right side of the cabinet, under the words "The Yeti, Interpreting the Findings."

Hint 12: In the last room before boarding, look for a photo of a woman in blue listening to a hand-held radio. Mickey in his Sorcerer's Hat is etched on a wall to the woman's left.

Hint 13: In the Yeti Museum as seen from both the FASTPASS and Single Rider queues, a sideways classic Mickey is formed by three dents in a lantern in the second display. (Note: You cannot spot this lantern image from the Standby line.)

Hint 14: Outside in the loading area, look for a classic Mickey in the blue scrollwork above the first window. (You can see this Hidden Mickey from both the FASTPASS and Standby queues.)

Hint 15: In the first part of the ride, as your train is climbing the mountain, a dark, melted classic Mickey-shaped spot appears in the snow to your left. The "ear" farthest away from the train is contiguous with a larger dark spot above it.

Hint 16: The ride photos from various WDW attractions often include Hidden Mickeys. Check the photos on the monitors at the unloading area. A small white classic Hidden Mickey may be present on the ground to the left of the ride vehicle.

Hint 17: Small gold balls form classic Mickeys at the bottom of both sides of a merchandise display in the middle of the gift shop at the ride exit. The display is across from the photo pickup area.

Hint 18: Brown chests sit on an upper shelf of a merchandise cabinet. The shelf faces the exit door to the left (as you exit the ride). Circles along the sides of the chests form several classic Mickeys.

Hint 19: Outside and across from the Serka Zong Bazaar shop, an upside-down classic Mickey is etched near the top of the second stone tablet from the edge closest to the shop.

Hint 20: Outside the attraction, base camp supplies hang in the Gupta's Gear area. A three-circle image hangs among these supplies, near the second post from the end nearest the restrooms.

Africa

– Kilimanjaro Safaris

Hint 21: Near the end of the entrance queue, just before you reach the final loading dock, a monitor above you shows a continuous video loop. Look for the resting orange-and-white leopard with black spots. Three spots on white fur form a classic Mickey on the left side (your right) of the leopard's neck.

Hint 22: In elephant country, and about halfway through the ride, the island in the flamingo pond is shaped like a classic Hidden Mickey. It's to the left of your ride vehicle.

Hint 23: The rocks in the lion area are arranged to resemble Donald Duck. Spot his cap first, then his face, eyes, and beak.

DinoLand U.S.A.

– DINOSAUR

Hint 24: Just inside the building entrance, on the right side of the queue, look at the tree at the far left of the painting. There is a classic Mickey on the tree trunk; it's across from a lower right branch.

Hint 25: In a painting on the wall that you face before you take the first right turn in the entrance queue, you can spot classic Mickey ears along the left side of the reddish explosion cloud above the middle dinosaur.

Hint 26: Just as the ride starts and before you travel back in time, a classic Mickey at the lower left corner of a white greaseboard appears to the left of your vehicle. (This Mickey image changes locations and even disappears at times.)

Hint 27: On the mural behind the counter in the ride's photo-purchase area, a large red dinosaur has a small classic Mickey on its lower neck.

Discovery Island

– It's Tough to be a Bug!

Hint 28: Inside *The Tree of Life*, look for the handicapped entrance doors to *It's Tough to be a Bug!* (You reach them before you get to the main entrance doors to the theater.) Look at the upper left area near the doors — and just to the right of the "Cast Members Only" door — to find a small dark classic Mickey.

Asia

– Kali River Rapids

Hint 29: Along the entrance queue, keep your eyes peeled for stone statues in the grass. As you enter the next room, look at the lower left corner of the wall. Three of the plates on the wall above the bicycle form a classic Mickey, tilted down to the right. (Note: These images change from time to time.)

Hint 30: In the right corner of the wall, above and to the right of the plates in Hint 29, three pans hanging above a chair come together to form a classic Mickey.

– Maharajah Jungle Trek

Hint 31: To the right of the first arch, swirls in the water under a tiger form a classic Mickey.

Hint 32: Inside the first arch, on the left mural, the king's gold earring forms an upside-down classic Mickey.

Hint 33: Inside the first arch, on the left mural, three leaves under the wrist of the king's extended arm form a classic Mickey.

Hint 34: Inside the first arch, on the right mural, a man is wearing an upside-down classic Mickey gold earring.

Hint 35: On the right wall inside the building with arches, two square panels are decorated with flowers. Some of the outer flowers have circles at the bases of their petals that form classic Mickeys.

Hint 36: Inside the second arch, on the left mural, there's a small classic Mickey in a brown rock formation on the left side of the mountains.

Hint 37: Inside the second arch, on the right mural, a classic Mickey appears in the upper part of the left cloud formation.

Hint 38: As you exit the temple ruins, turn to your immediate left to a large wall mural. Among the leaves is a dark green classic Mickey. It's about nine feet above the ground and one foot from the bricks at the left side of the mural. Another even darker green classic Mickey is further to the right on this mural. It's above the tiger running toward the left, and between two large, light green fan-shaped leaves.

Hint 39: In the Elds Deer Exhibit, look left to the huge outdoor mural. Mickey is hiding in the right center of the mural, below the third (from the left) of four vertical brick cracks, in some orange flowers and green leaves.

Hint 40: On a wall to the right, just before you reach the aviary entrance, you can spot an upside-down classic Mickey in the necklace of a man in the middle carving.

Africa

– Pangani Forest Exploration Trail

Hint 41: To the left of the entrance to the building with the Naked Mole Rat Exhibit, a small box of Asepso soap on a desk near a lamp has a classic Mickey as the "o" in "Asepso."

Hint 42: In the far left corner of the room with the Naked Mole Rat Exhibit, the left side of a backpack sports a small classic Mickey emblem.

172

Hint 43: In the center of the room with the Naked Mole Rat Exhibit, horizontal poles are at the side of a display cabinet. On the third pole up from the floor, a classic Mickey is traced on the end of the pole facing the exit door.

Hint 44: A three-dimensional head of Jafar is carved out of a 25- to 30-foot rock. You'll find it past the gorilla viewing area, to the right of the first section of the first suspension bridge.

DinoLand U.S.A.

– Finding Nemo–The Musical

Hint 45: Three bubbles touch to form a classic Mickey at the lower left of the stage.

Hint 46: Two sideways classic Mickeys formed by bubbles hide in each of the two outdoor signs announcing the show times for the day. One is in the bottom right corner of the signs and the other is under the 1:00 time disk. These signs are posted on both the walkway from Asia and the walkway from the rest of DinoLand U.S.A.

Camp Minnie-Mickey

– Festival of the Lion King

Hint 47: A white classic Mickey is painted on the lower middle front of Timon's (and the giraffe's) float. You can see it as the float enters the arena.

Hint 48: An upside-down white classic Mickey is on the lower right side of Timon's float, under the giraffe's front leg.

Hint 49: A classic Mickey in relief is on the lower side of the movable center stage, to the right of some steps. It is usually facing the Elephant section of the audience.

– Near the last Greeting Trail

Hint 50: A rock classic Mickey is embedded in the upper part of a short rock wall. The image is directly across from the entrance to the last *Greeting Trail*. One "ear" is light purple.

– Around the Camp grounds

Hint 51: Across from the entrance to *Festival of the Lion King*, a cabin housing an ice cream shop has classic Mickeys in the woodwork along the front and sides.

Hint 52: In the food cabin seating area, a classic Mickey made of pebbles is embedded in the ground next to the creek and close to Donald Duck. As you face the creek, look near the second fence section, in front of the third stone pillar from the left.

Hint 53: A birdhouse with a side-profile cutout of Mickey Mouse for its entrance is often hanging from the front of Chip 'n' Dale's Cookie Cabin. Similar birdhouses may be found elsewhere in Camp Minnie-Mickey.

Hint 54: A three-dimensional classic Mickey head tops the flagpole by the water well. It's opposite the entrance to the outdoor theater (and before you get to the second bridge to Camp Minnie-Mickey).

Rafiki's Planet Watch

– Conservation Station

Hint 55: A classic Mickey made of circles (two dark and one light) hides in the circular mosaic in the pavement right outside the main entrance to *Conservation Station*. Mickey is above the second "T" in "Station" and below the elephant's trunk.

Hint 56: The front wall facing you as you enter the building has a section of changing, repeating panels. A small side profile of Mickey Mouse is in the center of the orange starfish.

Hint 57: Find an opossum on the right side of the mural just inside the entrance. There is a side profile of Mickey Mouse in its eye.

Hint 58: Above the opossum, at the upper right, a butterfly has classic Mickeys on its wings.

Hint 59: About six feet up from the floor, not far from the opossum, a spider has a light pink classic Mickey marking on its thorax.

Hint 60: On the wall to the left of the restrooms, near the entrance, the pupil of an ostrich's eye is a classic Mickey.

Hint 61: Toward the middle of the mural at the front, near the entrance, a green snake sports a black classic Mickey on its upper back.

Hint 62: Near the upper right border of the changing screen, a dark classic Mickey marking is at the top of a green lizard's ear, above a deer.

Hint 63: A hippopotamus is the fifth animal from the left at the bottom of the entrance mural on the left wall. A side-profile Mickey is on its lower jaw, under the middle tooth.

Hint 64: To the immediate left of the hippopotamus, a llama sports a dark brown classic Mickey on its neck.

Hint 65: Under the hippopotamus, a squirrel's eye has a black classic Mickey pupil.

Hint 66: On the hippo's right side, an alligator has a small dark classic Mickey to the left of its green eye.

Hint 67: To the right of the alligator, Mickey Mouse's smiling face is under a frog's right eye.

Hint 68: Directly above the frog with the smiling Mickey is a walrus with a dark classic Mickey on the left side (your right) of his neck.

Hint 69: A bit farther along on this left wall mural, the pupils of an owl's eyes are classic Mickeys.

Hint 70: The entrance murals curve toward the inside of the building. On the right curving mural, look closely for the butterfly with an image of Mickey's face on its body (not on its wings!).

Hint 71: Midway along the right curving mural, high up near the ceiling, a classic Mickey-shaped marking is on the tan skin under the middle of the frog's face. The frog is behind a red-faced monkey.

Hint 72: Toward the top and near the end of the left side of the entrance mural, a dark classic Mickey, partially hidden by an octopus nearby, is on the side of a fish, to the left of the fish's fin.

Hint 73: Along the bottom of the right mural as you near Rafiki's Theater, two black classic Mickeys are near the bottom of the wings of an orange butterfly under a monkey.

Hint 74: Near the bottom of the same mural, just before the theater, a side-profile Mickey is in a silver frog's left pupil.

Hint 75: Before the first entrance to the "Song of the Rainforest" area, about halfway up the wall and above a bat, a yellow butterfly has a black classic Mickey on its left wing.

Hint 76: In the same area, a tan and green lizard has a group of spots directly behind the eye that form an upside-down classic Mickey.

Hint 77: A hole in the tree leaves overhead resembles a classic Mickey. It's directly above the first entrance.

Hint 78: The fly with a tiny classic Mickey on its back is on the left panel of the first entrance to the "Song of the Rainforest" area.

Hint 79: On the same panel, a tiny yellow-flower classic Mickey blooms on a green plant near the floor.

Hint 80: Turn to the right panel at the same entrance to the Rainforest area to see a classic Mickey indentation on a tree. It's about four feet up from the floor.

Hint 81: Look for a classic Mickey hole in a green leaf near the Mickey indentation in Hint 80.

Hint 82: Now go inside to see a side-profile Mickey shadow about seven feet up from the floor on the front of a tree inside the Rainforest area.

Hint 83: Above and in front of door number eight in the Rainforest area, you can spot a dark classic Mickey shadow on the ceiling to the right.

Hint 84: A white classic Mickey is outlined on a tree by door number six, to the left of the words "The Accidental Florist."

Hint 85: Turn around and walk out toward the lobby to look at the right side of the tree with "The Song of the Rainforest" sign (the Grandmother Willow tree). A rear horizontal panel has a green moss side-profile Mickey about six feet up from the floor.

Hint 86: A side-profile Mickey indentation appears on the same tree under the sign and to the lower right (as you face her) of Grandmother Willow's face. (Tip: You have to walk further into the lobby to spot it.)

Hint 87: Three plant stalks form a classic Mickey in the mural near the floor on the bottom left of the Grandmother Willow tree (as you face it from the lobby).

Hint 88: To the right of the Grandmother Willow tree, there is a cockroach display inside a tree in front of the "Song of the Rainforest" area. A cockroach inside and toward the back of the tree bears a dark classic Mickey on its back.

Hint 89: A lizard above the "Giant Cockroach" sign on the same tree has a classic Mickey above its front leg.

Hint 90: On the left front of the tree with the cockroach display, a light brown butterfly about six and a half feet up from the floor has a tiny black classic Mickey on its back between the wings.

Hint 91: The grates around the bottoms of the trees in the lobby have classic Mickey patterns, as do those outside by *Affection Section*.

Hint 92: A classic Mickey on a "Microtiter Plate" is usually in the first display room to the right in the rear of the lobby. Look into the second window of the "Wildlife Tracking Center." The plate changes color as you watch it!

Hint 93: A classic Mickey made of three containers with reptile skins is on a ledge in the far left window of a room with reptiles.

– Affection Section

Hint 94: One of the animals usually has a classic Mickey shaved into its coat.

– Wildlife Express Train station

Hint 95: High up in the rafters inside the train station, look for classic Mickeys where the beams intersect.

Africa

– In and around Harambe

Hint 96: At one side of the Harambe Fruit Market, a short cement and flagstone path with benches leads through some trees. A large Mickey Mouse head in the cement marks the beginning of the path. It's several feet in diameter.

Hint 97: At the opposite end of this short path, turn left onto the cement walkway and walk a few feet. Nearby you'll find a faint depression in the cement that forms a very large classic Mickey (six feet or more in diameter). This HM is best seen after a rain when the pavement is wet. It is often partially covered with parked strollers.

Hint 98: Outside, near an entrance door to the Mombasa Marketplace store, you'll find a classic Mickey formed by a small utility cover (with the letter "D" in the middle) and the pebbles adjacent to it. The cover is on the path on the side facing the Tusker House Restaurant.

Hint 99: In Tusker House Restaurant, walk to a small dining room on the left side of the hallway to the restrooms. A classic Mickey is formed by one of the magnets on an Assignment Board on a wall inside the room.

Hint 100: Near Tamu Tamu Refreshments, on the walkway that connects Africa and Asia, a small utility cover and the pebbles adjacent to it form a classic Mickey. Here, the utility cover has the letter "S" in the middle.

Hint 101: Inside the small seating area behind Tamu Tamu Refreshments, a white Hidden Baloo (the bear) is on the wall nearest the path to Asia. He's often covered by a curtain.

Hint 102: Also inside the small seating area behind Tamu Tamu Refreshments, a Hidden Scar (the lion) is on a corner wall and under vases that are in recessed openings.

Hint 103: On the back of *The Tree of Life*, and visible from the path between Africa and Asia, is an upside-down classic Mickey. Look above the eye of the hippopotamus to spot him.

Discovery Island

– Pizzafari restaurant

Hint 104: A yellow classic Mickey image is under a bat, which is on a wall in the seating area across from the food order counters. As you enter the room, turn left to face the rear wall and look for the bat on the right.

Hint 105: On the rear wall of the first dining room to the left (as you walk down the hall away from the food order area), a tiny orange classic Mickey is at the lower left of a turtle shell.

Hint 106: On the left rear wall of the Nocturnal Room (the dining room directly to the left of the food counters as you face the counters), the wings of the lower left firefly resemble Mickey Mouse ears.

Hint 107: In the same room, a classic Mickey made of tree leaves lies near a reddish raccoon. It's tilted with the "ears" to the left as you face the wall.

Hint 108: In the large room just past the Nocturnal Room, a gray spot with two white ears on the far wall forms a classic Mickey in the tree branches, to the right of the leopard.

Hint 109: On this same wall, a classic Mickey formed by black spots is directly behind the middle of the leopard's front leg.

– Parade

Hint 110: The parade (usually starting at around 4:00 p.m.) abounds in classic and décor Mickeys. The first jeep has classic Mickey headlights and the last vehicle has classic Mickey antenna dishes (forming the "ears") on the flagpole.

DinoLand U.S.A.

– The Boneyard

Hint 111: Just inside the entrance, you'll find a reddish-brown classic Mickey pattern in the flooring under the drinking fountains.

Hint 112: On the lower level, to the left of the main entrance, look for a small, fenced-in area containing archeology supplies. A white hard hat hangs on the rear fence. On the front of the hat above the letter "B," blue swirls form an upside-down classic Mickey.

Hint 113: Upstairs to the rear left, in a fenced off archeology display, three coins on a table form a classic Mickey.

Hint 114: On the right side of the children's dig area, in a small display, a fan and two hard hats form a classic Mickey.

– Cretaceous Trail

Hint 115: At one end of this short trail in the middle of Dinoland, you'll find a large dinosaur. Three dark spots on its middle back form a classic Mickey.

– TriceraTop Spin

Hint 116: In front of *TriceraTop Spin*, a green dinosaur balances a red and yellow striped ball on its horns. A classic Mickey is formed in the scales on the dino's right side, under the front horn.

Hint 117: In the parking spaces across from *TriceraTop Spin*, a classic Mickey can be found in the cement at the front of the second parking space from the horned dinosaur.

Hint 118: On the right side of the horned dinosaur (as you face it), a gold "Steamboat Willie" Cast Member pin is located on a spine on the dinosaur's upper back, near a large silver medallion.

– Chester & Hester's Dinosaur Treasures shop

Hint 119: Inside, near the middle of the shop, look up to see a Mickey Mouse marionette.

Hint 120: In front of the store, near the restrooms, a tiny orange image is embedded in the cement a few feet to the right of the leftmost post (as you face the store with your back to *Primeval Whirl*).

– Primeval Whirl

Hint 121: In the outside decorations, the sides of three meteors sport classic Mickey craters:
 - One is under "Head for the Hills."
 - Another is over the "Primeval Whirl" sign at the entrance to the attraction.

- The third *Primeval Whirl* classic Mickey crater is on the right side of the attraction near a dinosaur holding a sign.

– Behind Fossil Fun Games

Hint 122: Along the outer walkway behind the *Fossil Fun Games* area, look for a sign on the fence that says "Games of Chance." An upside-down classic Mickey made of gold spots lies on the upper left thigh of the blue dinosaur, on the right side of the sign.

Discovery Island

– Creature Comforts shop

Hint 123: Black classic Mickeys are on the backs of the large beetles that decorate some of the store's merchandise stands. One is on the mid left of a beetle under a zebra. Another beetle on the lower part of a stand (usually found at the rear of the store) has a classic Mickey on each of its wings.

– Island Mercantile shop

Hint 124: A classic Mickey made of spots is on a lower cell of an orange and blue bumblebee honeycomb on an inside post. It's on the right rear wall opposite the entrance doors closest to the walkway to the Oasis.

– The Tree of Life

Hint 125: On the front of *The Tree of Life*, facing the Oasis and about one-third the distance up the tree trunk from the bottom, is a classic Mickey made of green moss. You'll find it to the left of the buffalo.

– Flame Tree Barbecue Restaurant

Hint 126: In the food order area, rocks embedded in the ground form a classic Mickey at the front edge of the rock border and next to the second post from the right wall.

Hint 127: At the outside seating area behind the food order counters, grates on the ground near trees have classic Mickey circles. Find them near the first set of tables to the right, where there is a statue of a frog holding up a pig. These grates can also be found in other areas nearby.

Oasis

– Rainforest Cafe

Hint 128: A green lizard at the Rainforest Cafe entrance sign that is inside the park has an upside-down classic Mickey in the middle of the circles on its neck.

Outside the entrance turnstiles to the park

Hint 129: When you head out of the park, turn back as you pass the ticket booths. You'll find two rock classic Mickeys, one on the right-hand lower corner of the wall of the rightmost ticket booth and the other in the wall of the leftmost ticket booth near the ground and toward the front of the booth's left side.

Hint 130: Outside the entrance turnstiles, near the tram loading area, the metal grates at the bases of some of the trees incorporate classic Mickeys in their design.

Notes

CHAPTER 6

Resort Hotel Scavenger Hunt

Walt Disney World's resort hotels are filled with Mickeys, hidden and otherwise. The majority are what I like to call décor Hidden Mickeys, imaginative decorations that vary among the hotels and change periodically over time. Such Hidden Mickeys can be found along hotel hallways in the carpet, wallpaper, and lampshades. They appear in the guestrooms on covers for drinking glasses, bedspreads, pillows, day beds, furniture, lamps, lampshades, room curtains, shower curtains, wall pictures, wallpaper, carpets, soap, the outer wrapping of toilet paper rolls, and other items. The housekeeping staff sometimes creates Mickey images out of towels on the bed or elsewhere in your room for you to enjoy upon your return! Guest laundry rooms sometimes have Hidden Mickeys on the soap vending machines and in the bubbles on wall paintings, and resort laundry bins and carts show off classic and side-profile Mickeys.

In the restaurants, pancakes, waffles, butter pats, pasta, pizza, pepperoni on the pizza, and the arrangement of dishes and condiments, among other items, are sometimes Mickey-shaped. Sample menu displays in food order areas often have food items arranged to form classic Mickeys. Mugs, paper plates, and other items in the gift shops can sport Mickeys. Even the utilities embrace Mickey. Manhole covers and survey markers throughout Walt Disney World often have classic Mickey designs in the center.

Generally, I do not include such décor Mickeys in the scavenger hunts unless they are truly unique (as many of the carpet Mickeys are) and are easily accessible to Hidden Mickey hunters at the hotels and in other WDW areas. So don't be surprised to discover dozens of Mickeys at the hotels you visit that aren't included in this scavenger hunt. They're fun to spot but you don't get points for finding them.

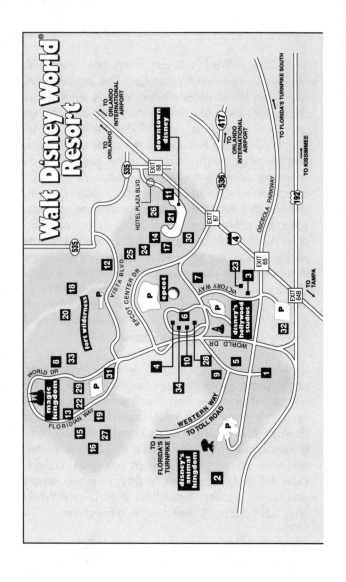

1. All-Star Resorts
2. Animal Kingdom Lodge
3. Art of Animation
4. Beach Club
5. Blizzard Beach
6. BoardWalk
7. Caribbean Beach
8. Contemporary
9. Coronado Springs
10. Dolphin
11. Downtown Disney
12. Golden Oak
13. Grand Floridian
14. Lake Buena Vista Golf Course
15. Magnolia Golf Course
16. Oak Trail Golf Course
17. Old Key West
18. Osprey Ridge Golf Course
19. Palm Golf Course
20. Pioneer Hall
21. Pleasure Island, in Downtown Disney
22. Polynesian
23. Pop Century
24. Port Orleans – French Quarter
25. Port Orleans – Riverside
26. Saratoga Springs
27. Shades of Green
28. Swan
29. Transportation and Ticket Center
30. Typhoon Lagoon
31. WDW Speedway
32. ESPN Wide World of Sports Complex
33. Wilderness Lodge
34. Yacht Club
P. Parking

The best way to hunt for Hidden Mickeys at the hotels is by car. However, buses to all the WDW hotels are available from Downtown Disney (the major bus depot is at the far end of the Marketplace). If you choose to bus around, be prepared for leisurely hunting. You won't be able to visit as many hotels in a given time frame as you would with a car.

Of course, driving means parking, and it's not always a slam-dunk. Guard gates stand watch at most WDW hotels. When you drive up, tell the guard that you're a Hidden Mickey freak and want to look for Hidden Mickeys at the hotel. You'll generally be greeted with a smile, an opened gate, and a wave — along with a "Good luck!" or "Go freak out!" to encourage you on your quest. In the event you aren't allowed to park, drive on to another hotel on the scavenger hunt and take transportation (bus, boat or monorail) to the one you want to explore. If you're really lucky, you may have a spouse, friend, or family member who is willing to drop you off and pick you up.

Again, be considerate of other guests and Cast Members. Ask permission to look around restaurants and avoid searching for Hidden Mickeys at meal times unless you are one of the diners. Even then be careful to stay out of the way — especially of waiters with full trays. Let others share in the fun by telling them what you are up to if they notice you looking around.

Two important notes:

• I've arranged this hunt in a logical, efficient progression that I imagine you could follow in a car. However, you may want to hunt just one hotel or group of sister hotels at a time. That's why I list the perfect score for each resort hotel (and hotel group) in parentheses after the hotel (or group) name in the Clues section.

• This scavenger hunt includes only those WDW resorts in which I found Hidden Mickeys. If I found no convincing (to me) Hidden Mickeys in a hotel, I didn't include it in the hunt. Keep your eyes open; you may spot one that I haven't found (yet).

★ **Bonus Points Opportunity.** During your Hidden Mickey hunt around WDW property, pay attention to the Disney buses. You may get lucky! The Disney Cruise Line bus has a Hidden Pluto on each side of the gold scrollwork on the front of the bus between the headlights. Some general Disney transport buses sometimes sport a classic Mickey on the rear of the vehicle, usually related to rear upper or lower lights. Even more subtle are faint classic Mickey images in the windows of some buses, only visible if the lighting is just right!

If you spot one or more of these images, give yourself 5 bonus points for each one.

I'll start this scavenger hunt with Animal Kingdom Lodge, but you can start (and stop) wherever you want. Have fun!

Animal Kingdom Lodge
(104 points)

Clue 1: Look up for a classic Mickey outside near the hotel's main entrance.
2 points

Clue 2: Find a classic Mickey on a mural between the outer and inner entrance doors to the main lobby.
2 points

Clue 3: Inside the main lobby, spot a classic Mickey on a chandelier.
3 points

Clue 4: Check the logs banded to wood supports around the main lobby. Find any classic Mickeys?
2 points

Clue 5: Look for a classic Mickey on the rock formation next to the short bridge on the right side of the main lobby (as you face it on entering).
4 points

Clue 6: Search the Kudu Trail at the rear of the lobby for a classic Mickey on a post.
4 points

Clue 7: Try to spot a green Hidden Mickey in side profile outside the rear doors of the main lobby. He's on the vine-covered column, on your right as you exit, and he's looking into the lobby.
5 points

Clue 8: On the trail to Arusha Rock Overlook, outside the rear exit from the main lobby, explore the decorative reliefs on the rock wall for a giraffe sporting a classic Mickey.
3 points

Clue 9: Spot another classic Mickey along the walkway in Arusha Rock Overlook.
4 points

Clue 10: Search for a classic Mickey on the rock wall as you descend the stairs from the right side of the main lobby to Boma restaurant.
4 points

Clue 11: Examine the chairs inside Boma.
2 points

Clue 12: Inside Jiko restaurant, check out the ceiling above the large oven exhausts.
2 points

Clue 13: From inside Jiko, spot a classic Mickey out the window.
5 points

Clue 14: From the path alongside the walkway to the pool's water slide, find a classic Mickey impression low on a rock.
4 points

Clue 15: Further along this walkway, around the back of the swimming pool, look for a light-colored classic Mickey cut into the rock wall.
4 points

Clue 16: From a fence at the flamingo overlook, study the rock wall for a classic Mickey.
4 points

★ Walk back to **The Mara** and then turn and walk toward the pool.

Clue 17: On your way, look down for a classic Mickey.
5 points

Clue 18: Search the wall outside in the back of The Mara eatery seating area for a classic Mickey.
4 points

★ Now find two classic Mickeys inside The Mara food area.

Clue 19: One is on the left upper wall.
3 points

Clue 20: The other is on the right upper wall.
3 points

★ *Inside the Lodge* (8 points)

Clue 21: Spot a classic Mickey in the elevator to the Fitness Center.
2 points

Clue 22: Walk around to spot some classic Mickeys in the carpet below the fifth floor as well as either on or above the fifth floor.
4 points for two or more different classic Mickeys

Clue 23: Search for Mickey near the main Zebra Trail on the third floor.
2 points

★ Walk to **Kidani Village**. (27 points)

Clue 24: Look for Mickey on a clock.
4 points

Clue 25: Search high for Mickey in the lobby.
5 points

Clue 26: Spot him as you approach Sanaa restaurant.
4 points

Clue 27: Locate Mickey on a wall inside Sanaa.
3 points

Clue 28: Study Sanaa's dining tables.
3 points

Clue 29: Now leave the restaurant and find Mickey on a rock outside.
4 points

Clue 30: Stroll the hallways for carpet Mickeys.
4 points for two or more

Disney's All-Star Resorts
(16 points)

★ *All-Star Sports Resort* (7 points)

Clue 31: Go to the main building gift shop and find classic Mickeys in the carpet.
2 points for all

Clue 32: Walk around the food court for a Hidden Mickey on the wall.
3 points

Clue 33: Find the classic Mickey in the cement outdoors behind and to the right of the registration building. (Psst! It's near the Mickey Mouse statue.)
2 points

★ *All-Star Music Resort* (5 points)

Clue 34: Examine the Jazz Inn courtyard to spot classic Mickey ears.
3 points

Clue 35: Take a look at the boots in the Country Fair area.
2 points

★ *All-Star Movies Resort* (4 points)

Clue 36: Find a classic Mickey in a display window of the gift shop.
3 points

Clue 37: Check out Andy's Room in the resort's "Toy Story" section.
1 point

Coronado Springs Resort (35 points)

Clue 38: Take a good look at the large wooden doors at the front entrance to the main lobby.
3 points

Clue 39: Search in the registration area for a spotlight Mickey.
4 bonus points

Clue 40: Now study the wooden doors at the exit labeled El Centro.
3 points

Clue 41: Admire the walls of Rix Lounge for a Mickey image.
2 points

Clue 42: Walk to the hallway outside the Veracruz Exhibit Hall in the Convention Center and look around for two classic Mickeys.
4 points for spotting both

Clue 43: Examine the cement near the Marina rental gazebo.
4 points

★ Around the **Dig Site** (19 points)

Clue 44: Spot a classic Mickey at the Dig Site swimming pool on a wall facing the lake.
3 points

Clue 45: Now find a classic Mickey on a wall facing the Dig Site pool.
3 points

Clue 46: Look for a whitish classic Mickey on a stone block on the Mayan pyramid at the Dig Site.
4 points

Clue 47: Spot Mickey near the Dig Site restrooms.
3 points

Clue 48: Locate a classic Mickey made of rocks in the sidewalk near Ranchos Building 6A.
4 points

Clue 49: Check the bus stop signs around the periphery of the resort.
2 points for one or more

Art of Animation Resort (27 points)

Clue 50: Look around just inside the entrance doors for furniture Mickeys.
3 points for all

Clue 51: In the food court seating area, study the light covers for Lightning McQueen.
4 points

Clue 52: Search for Mickey on the bottom of another light cover in the food court seating area.
5 points

Clue 53: Walk behind The Big Blue Pool and find Mickey inside the blue coral reef kids' play area.
5 points

Clue 54: Explore the Boneyard outdoors in the resort's Lion King section for a Hidden Mickey.
5 points

Clue 55: Check the hallway carpets of the various sections.
5 points for three or more

Pop Century Resort (44 points)

Clue 56: Search for a fishbowl with a Hidden Mickey near the check-in area.
4 points

Clue 57: Find Mickey behind the registration counter.
4 points

Clue 58: Look low for Hidden Mickeys at the Everything Pop Food Court.
4 points for two or more

Clue 59: Now raise your eyes up for a Mickey in the lights. (Note: It's not always there!)
5 bonus points

Clue 60: Locate Hidden Mickeys on walls in the food court.
4 points for four or more

Clue 61: In the gift shop adjoining the Everything Pop Food Court, find Hidden Mickeys on the merchandise stands.
2 points

Clue 62: Also in the gift shop, search for two classic Mickeys on the wall.
4 points for both

Clue 63: Spot a classic Mickey on a wall near the Computer Pool.
4 points

Clue 64: Now look near the Computer Pool for two Hidden Mickeys that could help you type.
2 points for both

Clue 65: Marvel at a Hidden Mickey on a wall behind Mowgli on the '60s building.
5 points

Clue 66: Find Hidden Mickeys in laundry rooms near the Hippy Dippy Pool and the Bowling Pool.
4 points for four

Clue 67: Search for Mickey's name near the Bowling Pool (and, just for fun, a reference to "Disneyland" nearby).
4 points

Clue 68: Look around for a Hidden Mickey near the bus stop out front of the Pop Century lobby.
3 points

Caribbean Beach Resort (23 points)

Clue 69: Say hello to Mickey outside the main entrance to Old Port Royale!
3 points

Clue 70: Spot a classic Mickey on the lighthouse behind Old Port Royale.
2 points

Clue 71: Search for a classic Mickey in the children's water play area near the main (Old Port Royale) pool.
4 points

Clue 72: Study the rockwork of the main pool for a classic Mickey. (Psst! Look under a cannon.)
5 points

Clue 73: Walk around just outside the main pool to marvel at this Mickey image.
5 points

Clue 74: In Shutters restaurant, find a classic Mickey in a painting.
4 points

Downtown Disney Area Resorts (103 points)

★ *Old Key West Resort* (23 points)

Clue 75: Check the fences inside Conch Flats General Store.
2 points

Clue 76: Take a close look at the fence railings in the registration area.
2 points

Clue 77: At the pool, spot a Mickey with a big mouth.
3 points

Clue 78: Find a Hidden Mickey near the steps to the water slide.
4 points

Clue 79: Notice the design of certain railings on the guest buildings outside.
2 points

★ Search for classic Mickeys formed by three shell imprints in the cement on the paths leading from parking spaces to Building 36.

Clue 80: Search the pavement on the right side of the first path for imprints.
5 points

Clue 81: On the second path, explore the corner of the sidewalk after the first right turn.
5 points

(Note: More of these amazing Mickeys may be scattered around Old Key West Resort.)

★ *Port Orleans Resort – French Quarter*
(5 points)

Clue 82: Find a classic Mickey in the registration area.
3 points

Clue 83: Look up for a classic Mickey in the food court area.
2 points

★ *Port Orleans Resort – Riverside* (11 points)

Clue 84: Look for classic Mickeys in the latticework of the registration area.
2 points

Clue 85: Also in the registration area, find more classic Mickeys near the giant fans.
2 points

Clue 86: Now spot Hidden Mickeys on the fans themselves.
3 points

★ Cross the river and visit Parterre Place.

Clue 87: Find some Mickeys outside the Parterre Place building.
4 points for all

★ *Saratoga Springs Resort & Spa* (64 points)

Clue 88: Behind The Artist's Palette shop, look around for Mickey on a door handle.
5 points

Clue 89: Notice classic Mickeys on a jacket near The Turf Club.
2 points

Clue 90: Spot Mickey on a gate.
3 points

Clue 91: Find more Mickey images inside on a wall.
2 points for one or more

Clue 92: Look around inside The Turf Club Bar and Grill for a classic Mickey on a wall.
3 points

Clue 93: Check out a statue outside the main lobby for three pairs of Hidden Mickeys. (Note: This statue also sports a décor Mickey.)
10 points for finding all six

Clue 94: Search for two Hidden Mickeys near stairs outside The Artist's Palette.
5 points for spotting both

Clue 95: Look for Hidden Mickeys on the outside wall and the downstairs entrance door of the spa.
4 points for spotting both

Clue 96: Admire the guest buildings for small Mickeys.
2 points for one or more

Clue 97: Search for a Hidden Mickey on an outdoor wall, near the check-in point.
5 points

Clue 98: Now find a similar Hidden Mickey on a wall in the Congress Park section near the Downtown Disney lagoon.
5 points

Clue 99: Check for a Hidden Mickey inside the Aquatic Play Area at The Paddock pool.
4 points

Clue 100: Look around for Hidden Mickeys on outdoor wall lights.
4 points for one or more

Clue 101: Find classic Mickeys in the Villa courtyards.
2 points for one or more

Clue 102: Locate Mickey in a gate near the Grandstand Pool.
3 points

Clue 103: Search near the Backstretch Bar for Mickey.
5 points

Epcot Resorts (124 points)

To explore the following hotels, park at one and walk around Crescent Lake to the others. Smile and tell the guards that you're searching for Hidden Mickeys.

★ *BoardWalk Resort* (37 points)

Clue 104: Spot two classic Mickeys on a horse in the main lobby.
3 points for both

Clue 105: Search for a classic Mickey on a lobby wall.
4 points

Clue 106: Find classic Mickeys on lamps in the lobby.
2 points for one or more

Clue 107: Squint to spot some classic Mickeys above an elephant.
4 points for one or more

Clue 108: Look for Mickey near the Villa elevators.
4 points for one or more

Clue 109: Check out posters inside the elevators for classic Mickeys.
3 points for two or more

Clue 110: Wander around the guestroom and elevator hallways in both the BoardWalk Inn and the Board-Walk Villas.
(Note: The images in these areas change or disappear from time to time.)
8 points for four or more different Mickey images
4 more points for a Tinker Bell!

Clue 111: Find Mickey (and his hands!) at an outside bar.
2 points

Clue 112: Check out the waiting area of Kouzzina restaurant for a classic Mickey.
3 points

★ **Beach Club Resort** (67 points)

Clue 113: Search for Mickey Mouse along the inside walkway in front of the Cape May Cafe.
3 points

Clue 114: Look around just inside the entrance to Cape May Cafe for Mickey on a plate.
4 points

Clue 115: Walk along the hallway behind Cape May Cafe and find Mickey in a painting.
4 points

Clue 116: Search for Mickey in the tile floor in the hallway to the left as you enter the main lobby. (Psst: Look near the luggage room door.)
4 points

★ Walk to the Beach Club Solarium to find more Hidden Mickeys. (Psst! Check the walls.)

Clue 117: Spot some car tires with Mickey's full face.
3 points

Clue 118: Now look for classic Mickeys in the same general area.
2 points

Clue 119: Gaze at Mickey's face in the sky.
3 points

Clue 120: Search for Mickey on the sand.
4 points

Clue 121: Now find classic Mickeys in the water.
2 points

Clue 122: Do you see other classic Mickeys floating in the air?
2 points

Clue 123: Squint for a Hidden Mickey atop a building.
5 points

Clue 124: Walk to a guestroom hallway to find classic Mickeys under your feet.
2 points for one or more

Clue 125: Now stare at the hallway walls for more.
3 points

Clue 126: Find Mickey in the Marketplace shop.
2 points

Clue 127: Look for Mickey in an elevator near the Beach Pool (aka the Quiet Pool).
3 points

Clue 128: Study the area near the entrance to the Beach Club Villas for a classic Mickey.
4 points

Clue 129: Enter The Breezeway in the Beach Club Villas and locate four Mickey images.
5 points for all four

Clue 130: Walk toward the nearby restrooms inside and find Mickey in a painting.
5 points

Clue 131: Wander into the Beaches & Cream Soda Shop to spot a tasty Hidden Mickey on the wall.
4 points

Clue 132: Now watch hamburger preparation on the Beaches & Cream grill for a classic Mickey.
3 points

★ *Yacht Club Resort* (20 points)

Clue 133: Study the globe in the main lobby.
5 points

Clue 134: Look for a cabinet in the main lobby with character names on the drawers.
4 points

Clue 135: Check out the lobby carpet.
2 points

Clue 136: Search other resort carpets for Mickeys.
4 points for two or more

Clue 137: In the Yachtsman Steakhouse, look for the photograph of (now deceased) Minnie Moo, a cow born with a black classic Mickey on her side. (You may have to ask a Cast Member where the photo is located. It's sometimes not on public display.)
5 points

WDW Dolphin Hotel (3 points)

Clue 138: Walk into the main lobby and look for classic Mickeys.
3 points

Fort Wilderness Resort (12 points)

To explore the Fort Wilderness Resort and Wilderness Lodge, take a boat from the Magic Kingdom or from the Contemporary Resort to their respective marinas, or hop on a Disney bus or into your car for transportation to their front entrances.

At Fort Wilderness, you'll need to ride an internal bus between the Hidden Mickeys at the rear near the lake (where your hunt begins) and the Hidden Mickeys near the front parking area.

Clue 139: Visit the Blacksmith (near the Horse Barn) and find a Hidden Mickey.
3 points

Clue 140: Check out Trail's End Restaurant inside for a classic Mickey.
3 points

Clue 141: Go to the Trail Ride Check-In building near the front parking area to find two Hidden Mickeys.
3 points for both

Clue 142: Stroll over to the Fort Wilderness registration building ("Reception Outpost") at the far side of the front parking area and look for Mickey.
3 points

Wilderness Lodge (127 points)

Clue 143: Check out the signs on the right side of the entrance drive.
2 points

Clue 144: Search out a classic Mickey on the guard gate kiosk.
3 points

Clue 145: Near the car unloading area, look up for a classic Mickey etched in a support pole above a black metal band.
4 points

Clue 146: Now search for a classic Mickey etched in another support pole and partially hidden under a black metal band.
4 points

Clue 147: Glance down for a tiny classic Mickey traced in the cement on a black stripe.
5 points

Clue 148: Look up again for a classic Mickey etched on a side support pole.
4 points

Clue 149: Find a classic Mickey on a large key in the registration area.
1 point

Clue 150: Look overhead for Mickey driving a bus.
2 points

Clue 151: Find a classic Mickey on the rock of the main lobby fireplace.
5 points

Clue 152: Peek at a fireplace inside the Whispering Canyon Cafe for a classic Mickey. (Ask a Cast Member to let you into the rear of the cafe.)
4 points

Clue 153: Search around the bubbling spring in the lobby for a classic Mickey.
4 points

Clue 154: Look for a classic Mickey on a wall map at the entrance stairs to the Territory Lounge.
3 points

Clue 155: Now go inside and spot a classic Mickey on a ceiling mural above the bar.
4 points

Clue 156: Inside the Artist Point restaurant, spot a classic Mickey in a large mural above the entrance to the rear left dining area.
4 points

Clue 157: Now scan another mural for a classic Mickey near the restaurant's ceiling. (Psst! Turn back toward the entrance.)
5 points

Clue 158: Next scan the walls of the restaurant for Winnie the Pooh.
3 points

Clue 159: Search inside the Roaring Fork snack bar for a Hidden Mickey in a display case.
3 points

Clue 160: Find a classic Mickey in one or more lights near the elevators close to the snack bar.
3 points

Clue 161: Glance at the hallway walls for small Hidden Mickeys.
3 points

Clue 162: Look down in the hallways for more.
2 points

Clue 163: Locate a classic Mickey near Room 6100.
3 points

Clue 164: Explore one floor down for a classic Mickey near Room 5066.
3 points

Clue 165: Find another classic near Room 4035.
3 points

Clue 166: Search for a classic Mickey in the rock outside at Fire Rock Geyser.
4 points

Clue 167: Find stairs outside an exit door from the main building (on the side toward the Boat and Bike Rental) and look up for a classic Mickey.
4 points

★ *In the Cub's Den* (8 points)

(Tip: Visit in the afternoon if possible. It's less crowded then and the Cast Members are more likely to let you in. Tell them you're searching for Hidden Mickeys.)

Clue 168: Spot a plush Mickey doll in a mural.
2 points

Clue 169: Look higher for a side-profile Mickey.
3 points

Clue 170: Find a classic Mickey in the same mural.
3 points

★ *Wilderness Lodge Villas* (34 points)

Clue 171: Search for four classic Mickeys on a wall near the Wilderness Lodge Villas lobby. (Psst! Look behind some fabric for one of the four.)
5 points for all finding all four

Clue 172: Look around the stone pillars near the Villas lobby for a classic Mickey in the rock.
5 points

Clue 173: Smile back at Mickey hiding in a hole in a beam in the lobby.
5 points

Clue 174: Locate a side profile of Mickey on a wall near the lobby.
4 points

Clue 175: Spot Mickeys around a painting in a room near the lobby.
3 points

Clue 176: Find Mickey in the rock in the Carolwood Pacific Railroad Room near the lobby.
5 points

Clue 177: Look up to spot Mickey in the hallways of the Wilderness Lodge Villas.
2 points

Clue 178: Search for Mickey on a hallway wall near Room 1507.
5 points

Magic Kingdom Monorail Resorts (150 points)

To find the Hidden Mickeys in these resorts and the nearby Wedding Pavilion, park at the Polynesian or the Grand Floridian and ride the monorail to the other two resorts and past the Wedding Pavilion. Or if you prefer, walk or drive to the Wedding Pavilion. (Note: The Polynesian has the bigger parking lot.)

★ *Polynesian Resort* (55 points)

Clue 179: On the lower level, look for a classic Mickey on the floor near the waterfall.
4 points

Clue 180: Locate four classic Mickeys in a painting at the far right behind the registration counter.
5 points for all four

Clue 181: Study the second painting from the right for Mickey ears.
5 points

Clue 182: Search the third painting from the right for two classic Mickeys.
5 points for both

Clue 183: Look for a classic Mickey in the painting at the far left.
4 points

Clue 184: Spot three Hidden Mickeys in the Tiki Boutique store.
4 points for finding all three

Clue 185: Search for another just outside the store.
3 points

Clue 186: Check two carpets near the Tiki Boutique for classic Mickeys.
5 points for five or more

Clue 187: Study the bamboo-ring wall decorations by the corner staircase.
3 points

★ Find a Hidden Mickey in Trader Jack's gift shop.

Clue 188: Look for a chair on top of a merchandise cabinet.
2 points

Clue 189: Walk by the Kona Cafe and find a classic Mickey.
2 points

Clue 190: At the Kona Island coffee bar, search for a small classic Mickey.
5 points

Clue 191: Look around inside Capt. Cook's snack bar for a Hidden Mickey that comes and goes.
5 points

Clue 192: Look down for Hidden Mickeys in hallways and elevators.
3 points for spotting them both places

★ *Wedding Pavilion* (3 points)

Clue 193: As your monorail car passes by the pavilion buildings, observe the weather vane.
3 points

(Note: A Hidden Mickey may be lurking inside, but the Wedding Pavilion isn't open to the general public.)

★ *Grand Floridian Resort & Spa* (42 points)

Clue 194: Take a good look at the weather vanes on the roofs.
3 points for one or more

Clue 195: Check the large trolley carts outside the hotel.
1 point

Clue 196: Study the lobby carpet.
2 points

Clue 197: Look at the floor tile for a classic Mickey.
2 points

Clue 198: While you're at it, check the tile for the Fab Five.
5 points for five characters

Clue 199: Look near 1900 Park Fare restaurant for a Mickey hat.
3 points

Clue 200: Also near 1900 Park Fare, find Mickey and Minnie below your feet.
2 points for both

Clue 201: Now look for other Disney movie characters, as well as Mickey and Minnie, in the floor encircling the main lobby and in front of the Grand Floridian Cafe.
5 points for five or more characters

Clue 202: Spot Mickey on the outside of the ornate lobby elevator by the stairs.
4 points

Clue 203: Look up high for Mickey on the ceiling above the main lobby.
4 points

Clue 204: Check out the classic Mickey in front of the M. Mouse Mercantile shop.
1 point

Clue 205: Find Hidden Mickeys in the hallway walls.
2 points for one or more

Clue 206: Now look down for others in the hallways.
2 points

Clue 207: Find Mickey and other characters in the lobbies of the outer buildings.
4 points for four or more

Clue 208: Walk into the Grand Floridian Convention Center's main entrance and look around for Mickey.
2 points

★ *Contemporary Resort* (50 points*)
*including Bay Lake Tower

Clue 209: From the window of the California Grill restaurant, on the top floor, spot a stretched out Mickey watchband on the ground in front of the hotel.
4 points

Clue 210: Check out the (closed) glass doors of the back room inside the California Grill restaurant. (If the doors are open, you may not see the Hidden Mickey.)
4 points

Clue 211: Go to the sixth floor and walk in the direction of the Transportation and Ticket Center to an outside balcony to spot this amazing Hidden Mickey. (Tip: This Mickey can also be seen from the resort and express monorails.)
Caution: Be sure to prop the hallway door open, as it may lock upon closing.
5 points

Clue 212: Look for Mickey's profile inside Chef Mickey's restaurant. (You'll also encounter many décor — not Hidden — Mickey images inside the restaurant.)
1 point

Clue 213: Don't miss Mickey's ears at the rear of Chef Mickey's!
3 points

Clue 214: Find Mickey on a wall near the Contempo Café.
3 points

Clue 215: Look high for a classic Mickey on an animal.
4 points

Clue 216: Search around for a stick-figure Mickey near the shops.
3 points

Clue 217: Look for classic Mickeys in The Game Station Arcade.
3 points for all

Clue 218: Ride up the monorail escalator to spot a classic Mickey on the wall. (Enjoy the five-legged goat while you're up there!)
4 points

Clue 219: Find a classic Mickey silhouette in the bricks behind the main hotel. (Psst! It's near Mickey Mouse himself.)
2 points

Clue 220: Locate a Hidden Mickey in The Sand Bar.
3 points

Clue 221: Spot Mickey in the tile at the exit from the Garden Building to the parking lot.
5 points

Clue 222: Look up for Mickey at the hotel entrance.
2 points

★ *Bay Lake Tower* (4 points)

Clue 223: Walk to Bay Lake Tower and locate Mickey from the outside. (Psst! Look high!)
4 points

Shades of Green Resort (9 points)

(Only folks with military connections are allowed into this resort.)

Clue 224: Search for four classic Mickeys in the lobby.
5 points for finding all four

Clue 225: Find a large classic Mickey outside (or on a map of the resort).
4 points

Total Points for Hotel Hunt =

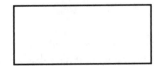

How'd you do?

A perfect score for this scavenger hunt is 777. But you may have done even better if you earned bonus points at Coronado Springs registration desk, in Pop Century's food court, and/or by spotting Hidden Characters on the WDW buses. Here is a point breakdown by resort and resort group, so that you can compare your score with the perfect score for the areas you've covered. You'll find the total points for each section in parentheses. Give yourself Gold if you scored at least 80% of the points available, Bronze if you scored at least 40%.

Animal Kingdom Lodge (104)
> Kidani Village (27)

Disney's All-Star Resorts (16)
> All-Star Sports Resort (7)
> All-Star Music Resort (5)
> All-Star Movies Resort (4)

Coronado Springs Resort (35)

Art of Animation Resort (27)

Pop Century Resort (44)

Caribbean Beach Resort (23)

Downtown Disney Area Resorts (103)
> Old Key West Resort (23)
> Port Orleans Resort – French Quarter (5)
> Port Orleans Resort – Riverside (11)
> Saratoga Springs Resort & Spa (64)

Epcot Resorts (124)
> BoardWalk Resort (37)
> Beach Club Resort (67)
> Yacht Club Resort (20)

WDW Dolphin Hotel (3)

Fort Wilderness Resort (12)

Wilderness Lodge (127)

Magic Kingdom Monorail Resorts (150)
> Polynesian Resort (55)
> Wedding Pavilion (3)
> Grand Floridian Resort & Spa (42)
> Contemporary Resort (50)

Shades of Green Resort (9)

**Caution:
Don't peek at this
section unless you
really want help!**

Animal Kingdom Lodge

Hint 1: Outside, above the lower roof, the second tall figure to the left of the car baggage drop-off area has a classic Mickey in its mouth.

Hint 2: On the right wall mural between the outer and inner entrance doors to the main lobby, an orange and brown creature sports a classic Mickey in a circle on its mid back.

Hint 3: Inside the main lobby, you can find a classic Mickey near the bottom of the second chandelier on the right (as you face in from the front entrance). The Hidden Mickey is near the bottom of one of the shields.

Hint 4: Around the main lobby, classic Mickeys are formed by logs banded to wood supports. One of the best is the second support on the right (as you enter the lobby from the front doors). It's on the second level, on the side away from the main lobby entrance.

Hint 5: On the right side of the main lobby (as you face in from the front entrance), a short bridge crosses a rockbound pool of water. A classic Mickey is visible on the rock from the side of the bridge nearest the lobby. It's toward the rear on the right side. To spot it, look for the first recess in the rock from the right edge of the pool. Mickey is at the back of this recess, above the water line.

Hint 6: Go down the staircase at the rear of the lobby. Turn left and walk down the Kudu Trail hallway. In the first small lobby, near the elevator, a classic Mickey is on the top end of a piece of wood that's roped to two giant "log" supports. Mickey is above the second rope binding, near the ceiling.

Hint 7: Outside the rear doors of the main lobby, a green Mickey in side profile hides in the decorative vines to the right as you exit. He is about two-thirds of the way up the side of the vine-covered column, above the middle horizontal brace, at the top of an open space in the vines. He's looking into the lobby.

Hint 8: Outside the rear exit from the main lobby, on the left side of the trail to Arusha Rock Overlook, check the rock wall for a decorative relief of a group of giraffes. You'll find a classic Mickey among the spots on the middle of the large giraffe in the center, above its inner front leg.

Hint 9: Along the walkway in Arusha Rock Overlook, a rock sports a classic Mickey. Look for it where the trail first turns left between rock walls. It's on the right side in the first small alcove, about six feet up from the path and under a large overhanging rock.

Hint 10: Toward the bottom of the staircase that winds from the right side of the main lobby to Boma restaurant, there's a classic Mickey on the rock wall next to a waterfall.

Hint 11: Inside Boma, you'll see classic Mickeys on some of the chairs with tall metal backs.

Hint 12: Inside Jiko restaurant, a classic Mickey is formed on the ceiling above the

two large orange oven exhausts and the white column behind them.

Hint 13: From the entrance to Jiko, walk to the third table on your left, next to the glass windows. Outside in the shallow pool area, a classic Mickey is sculpted on the first rock island from the left that has a pillar jutting out of it.

Hint 14: Outside the exit from the restaurants, a large rock on the left side of the path behind the water slide has a classic Mickey impressed on its lower half near the ground. The rock is about three-quarters of the way along the walkway to the water slide. A small light pole juts out of the top of this rock.

Hint 15: A light-colored classic Mickey is cut into a rock wall behind the swimming pool. The wall forms the back of the pool's water slide. The Mickey is several feet above the walkway, below a gazebo that marks the starting point for the water slide.

Hint 16: Walk behind the pool to the bird and fla-mingo overlook. From the rightmost "Bird Spotter Guide" on the fence along the main trail, look to your right to the opposite fence. About two-thirds of the distance along this fence from the main trail, a pinkish classic Mickey with a white right ear is about one foot down from the top of the rock.

Hint 17: A Mickey image is etched in the ce-ment outside of The Mara restaurant. Go to the walkway leading to the pool, which is directly opposite the rear exit door from the restaurant. Near the end of this short walkway, and on the left side as you stroll toward the pool, you'll find the Hidden Mickey.

Hint 18: A classic stone Mickey is on the rear of the short wall behind The Mara seating area. It's about three feet up from the ground, behind an emergency phone and a tall brown pole.

Hint 19: In the food area of The Mara, a classic Mickey is on the upper left wall in the third leaf from the left tree (in the mural of falling leaves).

Hint 20: Also in the food area, a classic Mickey hides in a leaf in the middle of the upper right mural of falling leaves.

Hint 21: As you enter the elevator to the Fitness Center, you can spot a classic Mickey on the lower left panel (as you face the rear of the elevator).

Hint 22: Many small classic Mickeys can be found in the carpet in the hallways in front of guestrooms. Classic Mickey images in the carpets below the fifth floor differ from those on and above the fifth floor.

Hint 23: On the third floor, at the end of the first short hall to the right of the main Zebra Trail hallway, an upside-down classic Mickey is formed by three plates on a wall.

– Kidani Village

Hint 24: A classic Mickey is at the 6:30 position on a large gold clock on a table just inside the entrance.

Hint 25: A white classic Mickey is on a ladybug on the middle level of the closest chandelier to the front lobby entrance.

Hint 26: At the entrance to Sanaa restaurant downstairs, a classic Mickey made of baskets is on the wall behind the check-in desk.

Hint 27: Inside Sanaa, a classic Mickey is above a booth on a white wall. It is to the left as you enter.

Hint 28: Classic Mickeys hide in the woodwork in the middle of Sanaa's dining tables.

Hint 29: Outside Sanaa, a classic Mickey is etched on the rockwork at the bottom rear of the lobby stairs.

Hint 30: A variety of small classic Mickeys can be found in the carpet in the hallways in front of guestrooms.

(Other Hidden Mickeys are in the Spa and Health Club area, but generally only Kidani Village guests are allowed to enter there.)

Disney's All-Star Resorts

– All-Star Sports Resort

Hint 31: In the main building gift shop, classic Mickeys are part of the carpet. Each is composed of a baseball with two circles for ears.

Hint 32: In the End Zone Food Court area, a black classic Mickey is on the clock on the right wall behind the clock's hands.

Hint 33: Outside, behind and to the right of the registration building, and past the buildings with surfboards, a large Mickey statue stands directly over a classic Mickey (white head and black ears) in the cement.

– All-Star Music Resort

Hint 34: In the Jazz Inn courtyard, classic Mickey ears top the cymbal stands. Each is a winged nut that holds a cymbal in place. (These nuts come and go.)

Hint 35: In the Country Fair area, you'll find classic Mickeys on the front and back of the huge boots.

– All-Star Movies Resort

Hint 36: On a mural in an outside display window in front of the gift shop next to the lobby, a small black classic Mickey hides at the lower right of the mural. It's on the front of an orange book with the title "Future Plans."

Hint 37: The large checkers in Andy's Room in the "Toy Story" section sport classic Mickeys.

Coronado Springs Resort

Hint 38: At the front entrance to the main lobby, a medallion in the upper left rectangle of the left large, open wooden door is a three-dimensional relief of Mickey's face.

Hint 39: On the far wall opposite the main entrance to the registration area, three spotlights sometimes create a classic Mickey image. The light circles change size from time to time.

Hint 40: A three-dimensional Mickey face is on the large right wooden door (as you face the doors) at the exit labeled El Centro.

Hint 41: Subtle circles form classic Mickeys in the ornate design of the outside black glass walls of Rix Lounge. They're on the walls that face the Pepper Market.

Hint 42: In the hallway outside the Veracruz Exhibit Hall in the Convention Center, a black classic Mickey pattern repeats along the sides of some of the ceiling chandeliers. Nearby, a similar Mickey pattern can be spotted on rectangular light covers that are flush with the ceiling.

Hint 43: A classic Mickey is chipped into the cement next to the lamppost nearest the Marina rental gazebo.

Hint 44: At the Dig Site swimming pool's main entrance (closest to the lake), a classic Mickey hides on a wall to your right. To spot it, check out the upper middle part of the wall facing the lake before you enter the Dig Site.

Hint 45: After you enter the Dig Site, examine the wall to your left (as you enter) that faces the pool. A classic Mickey is on the upper left side.

Hint 46: Also at the Dig Site, you'll find a

whitish, somewhat distorted classic Mickey near the very top of the Mayan pyramid, on the side facing the pool. It's on the second stone block from the left, fourth row from the top.

Hint 47: To the left of the restrooms at the Dig Site, a circular stone tablet with relief images is hanging on the wall. A somewhat distorted sideways classic Mickey hides at the lower right.

Hint 48: A section of the walkway in front of Ranchos Building 6A is made of circular flat gray rocks. Some of these rocks form classic Mickeys. You'll find one of them near the far end of the rock section. It's on the right side as you approach the Ranchos buildings.

Hint 49: Mickey Mouse (side profile) is sitting in a bus on some of the bus stop signs located around the periphery of the resort (such as at Bus Stops No. 2, No. 3, and No. 4).

Art of Animation Resort

Hint 50: In the registration lobby of Animation Hall, classic Mickeys are woven in the upholstery of benches located along the wall opposite the check-in area.

Hint 51: In the Landscape of Flavors food court seating area, an image of Lightning McQueen is in the clouds on the side of a large circular light fixture hanging from the ceiling.

Hint 52: In the same seating area, the painting on the bottom of another large circular light fixture includes a faint full-body image of Mickey Mouse. Look for Mickey near the bright light at the center of the overhead fixture. The image is in what appears to be a framed photo that is sitting on a shelf above some books.

Hint 53: Behind The Big Blue Pool is a play area for kids formed by a blue coral reef rising from the ground. Walk to the left of the slide exit and duck your head as you enter a small passageway through the coral. Halfway along the passageway, about three-quarters of the way up on the right wall, depressions in the rock form a classic Mickey.

Hint 54: Outdoors in the resort's Lion King section, there is a cave in the Boneyard play area. Walk under the elephant ribs to enter the cave on the right side and then keep your eyes peeled. About halfway through the cave, depressions in the rock form a classic Mickey on the right wall.

Hint 55: A variety of classic Mickeys hide in the hallway carpets of the resort's various sections. Each carpet design is consistent with the décor of the specific section, so these carpet Hidden Mickeys vary, too.

Pop Century Resort

Hint 56: In a small TV room near the check-in area, classic Mickey bubbles rise under a fish in a fishbowl painted on the wall.

Hint 57: In a photograph on the wall behind the middle of the long registration counter, a classic Mickey formed of moon craters is at the lower right of a television screen.

Hint 58: Several classic Mickeys are hiding on the tile floor of the food court order area. One is in the center of the order and pay area. Another is in front of the middle cash register.

Hint 59: A tiny black classic Mickey is inside one or more round lights suspended from the ceiling in the food court order area. (Note: These images change or even disappear at times.)

Hint 60: Inside the food court seating area, classic Mickeys made of circles can be found on the undulating purple, brown, blue, and green divider walls.

Hint 61: In the shop near the food court, classic Mickey holes are in the poles that hold merchandise racks.

Hint 62: Inside the gift shop, near the exit to the bus stop, check the wall behind the cash registers to spot round gift boxes that form a classic Mickey. The image appears twice in faux package-locker windows. One image is in the second window from the top of the second column of windows from the right side. The other is in the third window from the left along the top row.

Hint 63: Behind Roger Rabbit, in a mural on one of the '80s buildings near the Computer Pool, a classic Mickey is at the top of a bush beside a building. The bush's topmost leaf is just above Mickey's head and ears.

Hint 64: Two black classic Mickeys are on the keyboard of the huge computer near the Computer Pool. Both are on the lower row of keys. One is on the second key from the left and the other is on the second key from the right. (More obvious decorative classic Mickeys are in the computer monitor's screensaver.)

Hint 65: Look sharp for a faint classic Mickey in green paint on an outside wall of the '60s building, behind the Mowgli figure and just past the Hippy Dippy Pool. It's on the left side of the wall with green plants, above a vertical leaf, and almost touching the yellow beam of the walkway ceiling to your left.

Hint 66: In the guest laundry rooms near both the Hippy Dippy Pool and the Bowling Pool, bubbles form two sideways classic Mickeys. You'll find them in the same places in both laundry rooms. One is on the lower right front of the soap vending machine and the other is at the upper right.

Hint 67: "Mickey Mouse Club March" is choice "C2" on the giant jukebox near the Bowling Pool. ("I've Got a Date at Disneyland" is choice "F10.")

Hint 68: Outside the main lobby, classic Mickeys are at the ends of the guardrails near the bus stops.

Caribbean Beach Resort

Hint 69: Outside the main entrance to Old Port Royale from the parking lot, you'll find a display for Shutters restaurant on the left wall. In the lower right photo in the display, three blueberries form a classic Mickey.

Hint 70: Behind Old Port Royale, a classic Mickey appears in the "Barefoot Bay Boat Yard" sign on the side of the lighthouse near the bike racks.

Hint 71: In the child's water play area near the main pool, a classic Mickey is on the helm near the wheel of the pirate ship.

Hint 72: At the main swimming pool, a tan classic Mickey is on the rockwork of the small slide's wall. To spot it, stand at the back of the pool and look under the left cannon. Mickey is on a long rock in the second row of rocks from the bottom. This great Mickey image has almost faded away.

Hint 73: Where the sidewalk from Trinidad North meets the sidewalk outside the main (Old Port Royale) pool, they are joined by a short sidewalk that takes you to the right toward the main resort parking area. As you face the parking area from this intersection, look down at the lower right corner of the first white cement section of the short sidewalk. A small classic Mickey is etched in the pavement not far from a green lamppost.

Hint 74: In Shutters restaurant, a cloud classic Mickey hides in a painting on the left wall of the room close to the rear exit door.

Downtown Disney Area Resorts

– Old Key West Resort

Hint 75: Throughout Conch Flats General Store, the design in the fence woodwork includes classic Mickeys.

Hint 76: Classic Mickeys are worked into the design of the fence railings behind the check-in counter in the registration area.

Hint 77: At the main pool (behind the registration building), the water slide (hidden in the rock) opens into the pool through the head of a classic Mickey.

Hint 78: At the upper right of the entrance to the steps to the water slide, a classic Mickey is impressed in the white rock, above a space in the wall.

Hint 79: You'll see classic Mickeys in the outdoor railings around the guest buildings.

Hints 80 and 81: Classic Mickeys formed by three shell imprints in the cement can be found on the two paths leading from parking spaces to Building 36. On the first path, you'll find the Hidden Mickey just after the first right turn on the right side. On the second path, the three shell imprints are in the corner of the sidewalk, after the first right turn and just before the next left turn.

– Port Orleans Resort – French Quarter

Hint 82: On the third painting from the left behind the registration counter, an upside-down classic Mickey is on a man's crown.

Hint 83: Upside-down classic Mickeys made of blue and white gemstones adorn the top of a crown hanging from the ceiling on the right side of the food court seating area.

– Port Orleans Resort – Riverside

Hint 84: Above the registration area, classic Mickeys are repeated in the wooden latticework circling the central lobby.

Hint 85: In the registration area, classic Mickeys decorate the sides of the brackets that hold the giant fans hanging from the ceiling above the center of the lobby.

Hint 86: Classic Mickeys are at the base of the strapping on the big ceiling fans.

Hint 87: Small classic Mickeys are in the upper level side rails at Parterre Place.

– Saratoga Springs Resort & Spa

Hint 88: Halfway down the hallway behind The Artist's Palette shop (turn right as you enter the shop from the main lobby), a full-body impression of Mickey Mouse swinging a golf club is on a handle on the left door.

Hint 89: In the hallway leading to The Turf Club Bar and Grill, the jacket in a display on the left wall sports black classic Mickeys.

Hint 90: Just before entering the lounge area in front of The Turf Club, notice the small, ornate gate to your right, near The Turf Club menu posted on the brick wall. Examine the right half of the gate. Three small blue circles in the left middle area form a classic Mickey image tilted sideways to the left. (This image is not proportioned perfectly, but many guests and Cast Members consider it a Hidden Mickey.) Other circles on the gate also resemble classic Mickeys.

Hint 91: On a wall inside the lounge in front of The Turf Club, Mickey and other Disney characters decorate billiard balls. They are in the first display to the left as you enter from the hallway.

Hint 92: In a left wall display just inside the dining area of The Turf Club, three circles on equestrian equipment form an upside-down classic Mickey.

Hint 93: On a statue of a horse and rider outside the main lobby, the rings attaching the bridle to the reins and bit on both sides of the horse's mouth form classic Mickeys. Tiny classic Mickeys are also hidden in the roses on both sides of the horse's winner's blanket. You'll find them in the middle of the blanket in about the third or fourth row down. Finally, large blue classic Mickeys decorate the back and front of the jockey's jersey. (In addition, a blanket on the horse includes a yellow décor Mickey.)

Hint 94: As you walk away from The Artist's Palette, look for depressions in the left rock wall at the top of the stairs to the High Rock

Spring Pool. One classic Mickey is in the middle of the top horizontal rock of the wall, and a second classic Mickey is on the lower horizontal rock near the handrail post.

Hint 95: Small classic Mickeys adorn the spa signs on the wall outside and on the glass door at the downstairs spa entrance.

Hint 96: Some balcony railings on the guest buildings have classic Mickey holes.

Hint 97: In the resort's Springs section (Villas 4101 to 4436), across from the check-in parking lot, a large faint classic Mickey is on an outdoor red wall.

Hint 98: In the resort's Congress Park section (Villas 1501 to 1836), near the lagoon over which you can see Downtown Disney, another large faint classic Mickey is on an outdoor red wall. I stood near this red wall and could spot the Rainforest Cafe across the lagoon.

Hint 99: A classic Mickey is inside the Aquatic Play Area at The Paddock pool. This Hidden Mickey is formed by three stones in the middle front of a pillar that is on your right after you pass through the entrance gate.

Hint 100: Classic Mickeys can be found in the upper corners of some of the outside lights on the guest buildings, such as on the exterior of the enclosed stairways.

Hint 101: Classic Mickeys are at the bottom of obelisks in the Villa courtyards.

Hint 102: Partial classic Mickeys are in the left side of the gate to the Grandstand pool and on the back gate next to the restrooms.

Hint 103: At the Grandstand pool's Backstretch Pool Bar, a classic Mickey hides at the top of the green trees painted on the lower front wall below the bar counter.

225

Epcot Resorts

– BoardWalk Resort

Hint 104: In the main lobby, a horse on the outer ring of the small carousel has brown spots that form two classic Mickeys, one on the neck and one on the thigh.

Hint 105: In the middle painting on the wall above the middle registration counter in the main lobby, a classic Mickey is formed by the second small group of trees from the right.

Hint 106: Classic Mickeys hold the shades in place on the lamps facing the fireplace in the center of the lobby.

Hint 107: Along a side wall inside the lobby, tiny classic Mickey holes are at the very tops of the red latticework designs on all sides of the canopied seat (called a "howdah") atop the elephant.

Hint 108: On the first to the fifth floors of the Board-Walk Villas, a classic Mickey sits atop light fixtures alongside the elevators.

Hint 109: Classic Mickeys of different colors are usually hiding around the edges and in the background of some of the posters in BoardWalk Resort elevators.

Hint 110: Classic Mickeys hide in the carpet in front of some elevators and also appear in the lobby carpets and the guestroom hallway carpets in both the BoardWalk Inn and BoardWalk Villas. Also on the Inn and Villas' carpets, you'll find Tinker Bell in front of elevators.

Hint 111: Walk outside behind the BoardWalk Villas to the Leaping Horse Libations pool bar to spot a classic Mickey at the top of the wall clock behind the bar counter. Mickey's hands tell you the time.

Hint 112: As you enter the waiting room for Kouzzina restaurant, look at the right wall behind the check-in counter for a classic Mickey made of plates.

– Beach Club Resort

Hint 113: Along the inside walkway in front of the Cape May Cafe, a full length Mickey Mouse is standing in a sandcastle. It's the sculpture farthest to the left, on the wall facing the pool.

Hint 114: A classic Mickey is on a blue plate in-side Cape May Cafe. The plate is perched on a small shelf on the right wall just past the check-in podium at the restaurant's entrance. Mickey is on the inside of the plate and has a red circle for a "head" and two black circles for his "ears." The plate is evidently rotated from time to time, as this classic Mickey is sometimes upside down.

Hint 115: A gold upside-down classic Mickey hides in an old painting of Florida and its land-marks that hangs in a hallway near the back entrance to Cape May Cafe. Look to the lower left of the painting at the gazebo below the words "Cape May Point." The Hidden Mickey is above the steps to the right in the gazebo's facade.

Hint 116: In the Beach Club lobby, on the left as you walk towards the Marketplace shop, a white classic Mickey surrounded by a white circle is in-laid in a floor tile. Look for it under a light fixture and in front of the luggage room door.

Hint 117: Enter the Solarium from the Beach Club main lobby. The first painting on the wall to your left has Mickey's face on spare tires on the backs of the yellow car (left side) and the blue car (right side).

Hint 118: Classic Mickey hood ornaments adorn the blue and red cars on the right of this painting.

Hint 119: In the second painting on the left wall, you can see Mickey's face looking out at you from the clouds at the upper right.

Hint 120: In this second painting, a lady on the beach is sitting on a Mickey Mouse towel.

Hint 121: The cruise ship smokestacks in this second painting have classic Mickey decals.

Hint 122: Mickey balloons are on the right side of the third painting to your left.

Hint 123: Also on the right side of this third painting is a tiny white classic Mickey atop the front post of a small building with a brown roof.

Hint 124: The guestroom hallways have carpet segments with classic Mickeys.

Hint 125: Classic Mickeys are in the wallpaper along the guestroom hallways.

Hint 126: Sand dollars form classic Mickeys in the carpet of the Marketplace shop.

Hint 127: Check the elevator that's near both the Beach Pool (aka the Quiet Pool) and Room 1571 for an ad for the Beaches & Cream Soda Shop. Onion rings in the ad form a classic Mickey.

Hint 128: Under the Ariel statue in front of the entrance to the Beach Club Villas, seashells are embedded in the ground. One group of three shells forms a classic Mickey.

Hint 129: In The Breezeway at the Beach Club Villas, four Mickey images hide in a painting on the left wall (as you enter The Breezeway from the front doors):
- Two classic Mickeys are on a fence in the lower part of the painting.
- A full-body shadow of Mickey Mouse is in a bottom-floor hotel window in the middle of the painting.
- A subtle dark sideways classic Mickey is at the left-most water's edge facing the small red-roofed building.

Hint 130: Near the restrooms off the lobby inside the entrance doors to the Beach Club Villas, a colorful picture entitled "Cape May" is on the left wall in the short hallway to the left of the Breezeway. Look at the top border and you'll spot a train just to the left of center. A classic Mickey is formed by the coal in the car behind the engine.

Hint 131: Onion rings form a classic Mickey in one of the food images decorating the Beaches & Cream Soda Shop. The image is on the left wall as you enter, on the second panel back from the rear wall.

Hint 132: You can spot classic Mickey holes in the hamburger press used at the Beaches & Cream Soda Shop to hold the burgers on the hot griddle.

– Yacht Club Resort

Hint 133: On the globe in the main lobby, a blue classic Mickey is at the bottom right-hand corner of the sea monster, under the sea monster's head and below the island of Madagascar.

Hint 134: In a seating area in the main lobby, the names of Mickey, Minnie, Donald, Daisy, Goofy, and Huey are on small labels on the drawers of a corner cabinet. (This cabinet is moved around at times to different parts of the lobby.)

Hint 135: Near the main lobby seating area, dark classic Mickeys are in the rug.

Hint 136: Various other classic Mickey images can be found in other carpets around the resort, especially near elevators and in the guest hallways.

Hint 137: A photo of (now deceased) Minnie Moo, a cow born with a black classic Mickey on her side, often hangs in the Yachtsman Steakhouse. Examine the left wall just past the entrance podium. Minnie Moo once resided at Fort Wilderness.

WDW Dolphin Hotel

Hint 138: Walk toward the piano in the main lobby and observe the backs of the brown chairs nearby. Several classic Mickeys are formed by wooden circles on the chair backs.

Fort Wilderness Resort

Hint 139: A classic Mickey brand is on the left side of the Blacksmith sign near the Horse Barn.

Hint 140: Inside Trail's End Restaurant, a classic Mickey is formed by frying pans hanging from hooks on the wall behind the food serving station.

Hint 141: At the front parking lot, two Hidden Mickeys are on the Tri-Circle-D Ranch sign on the small Trail Ride Check-In building. They are in the middle of the scrollwork at both sides of the sign.

Hint 142: Inside the Fort Wilderness registration building ("Reception Outpost") at the far side of the main parking lot, a plush Mickey Mouse stands in a metal jug at the far left of a shelf directly over the registration counter.

Wilderness Lodge

Hint 143: On the right side of the entrance drive to the hotel, a full length Mickey Mouse is walking on top of the "Bear Crossing" sign.

Hint 144: A classic Mickey is on the slanted end of the first horizontal log beam of the guard gate kiosk as your car approaches the entrance gate.

Hint 145: As you approach the center steps from the parking lot, you'll see that the roof of the covered unloading area in front of the entrance is supported by huge wooden logs, banded together (four to a set) by black metal strips. The right rear pole of the first set to the right (as you face the entrance) has a classic Mickey etched in the wood above the upper black metal band. This Mickey faces the parking lot.

Hint 146: In the set of support poles on the left after you walk up the center steps from the parking lot, the pole in the corner closest to you and the hotel entrance has a classic Mickey etched in the wood. This Mickey is partially covered by the upper black metal band; only his head and part of his right ear are visible. This Mickey faces the steps.

Hint 147: In the cement of the car entrance drive-through, the black stripe nearest the center steps from the parking lot hides a tiny classic Mickey. From the red rectangle in the cement, follow the right (as you face the hotel entrance) diagonal crack to the black stripe. The tiny classic Mickey is traced in the cement about six inches to the right of the intersection of the crack and the stripe.

Hint 148: As you face the hotel entrance, the left rear support pole of the far left set of poles closest to the parking lot has a classic Mickey etched in the wood. It's above the lateral crossbeam on the lower part of the pole.

Hint 149: A classic Mickey hides on the left side of a large key in a wall display behind the registration counter. Look near the entrance to the Mercantile shop.

Hint 150: A sign that says "Walt Disney World Transportation" hangs from the ceiling near the Mercantile shop. Mickey (in side profile) is driving the bus at the top of the sign.

Hint 151: In the lobby, you'll find a classic Mickey on the rock in the corner to the upper right of the fireplace. Search at the level of and near the lower round wooden horizontal beam that juts toward the lobby.

Hint 152: The outer grillwork of a fireplace in the rear room of the Whispering Canyon Cafe is adorned with decorative cutouts. Bend down low and look for a classic Mickey on the bottom row. It is the third cutout from the left corner.

Hint 153: A small classic Mickey lies on the floor at the left front corner (as you face the rear of the lobby) of the rectangle of dark hardwood slats that surround the bubbling source of the water spring. The "head" is formed by a circle in the wood with small indentations in the wood for "ears."

Hint 154: At the entrance stairs to the Territory Lounge, a classic Mickey decorates a pot in the right lower section of a wall map.

Hint 155: Inside the Territory Lounge, a classic Mickey rests on the rear of a beige mule in a ceiling mural. Look above the center of the bar.

Hint 156: Inside the Artist Point restaurant, examine the large mural above the entrance to the rear left dining area. You can spot a classic Mickey in the upper part of the lowest tree on the right if you look between the third and fourth lights (counting from the left) illuminating the mural.

Hint 157: Turn left toward the Artist Point entrance and study the large mural near the ceiling and between the two front sections of the restaurant. On the clothing at the lower back of the leftmost of four horsemen is a light brown classic Mickey, tilted slightly to the right.

Hint 158: Inside the rear left dining area, the top middle part of a dark cloud in a painting on the left wall is shaped like a side profile of Winnie the Pooh. He's looking to the right.

Hint 159: A display case on an inside wall facing the entrance to the Roaring Fork snack bar contains three chestnuts arranged to form a classic Mickey.

Hint 160: You'll find classic Mickey images on a few of the wall-light covers, most often as a sideways image at the lower center of the light cover. Some of these covers are near the elevators just past Roaring Fork snack area. One or more can be found elsewhere around the hotel.

Hint 161: The wallpaper in the guest hallways on most floors (for example, near the elevators) includes classic Mickeys in the design.

Hint 162: Segments of the guest hallway carpets contain blue classic Mickeys.

232

Hint 163: A classic Mickey is etched near the bottom of a flat vertical wooden post around the corner from Room 6100 and near a green EXIT sign.

Hint 164: Near Room 5066, a classic Mickey is etched on a flat vertical wooden post about five and a half feet from the floor. It's across from an ice machine.

Hint 165: A classic Mickey is etched on a vertical wooden post about six feet up from the floor across from Room 4035.

Hint 166: Outside, from the walkway next to Fire Rock Geyser, scan the shallow stream running down from the small pool by the geyser. You'll find a slightly distorted classic Mickey with white rocks for ears in the rock of the streambed about a third of the way up to the geyser.

Hint 167: Walk toward the Boat and Bike Rental and locate stairs to an exit door in the corner of the main building. A classic Mickey is impressed in a vertical wooden beam at the left side of the exit door (as you face the door) across from the fourth-floor balcony. Mickey is on the right side of the beam, just below the log that juts out to the right.

– In the Cub's Den

Hint 168: A plush Mickey doll sits in the rightmost teepee in the mural on the right wall.

Hint 169: In this same mural, a side-profile shadow of Mickey (standing and looking right) falls on the side of a mountain to the right of the center of the mural and above the tree line.

Hint 170: On the far left of this mural, about midway up and left of the mountains, you can spot a classic Mickey.

– Wilderness Lodge Villas

Hint 171: Near the lobby elevators to the left of the entrance to the Villas, four classic Mickeys hide on the wall. One is to the right of the elevators near the lower left corner of a picture frame. Two more are part of the wall decoration between the elevators, and a fourth can be found to the left of the leftmost elevator. This last Mickey is hiding behind the red tapestry.

Hint 172: A classic Mickey made of depressions in the rock is tilted to the right on the last stone pillar to your left as you enter the Villas. You can spot this image just before you step into the lobby. It is about three feet from the floor, on the corner (facing the entrance) of the second horizontal rock from the floor.

Hint 173: Mickey Mouse is peeking out of a hole on the outer side of the first overhead beam to your right as you enter the lobby of the Wilderness Lodge Villas. The beam is jutting out into the lobby and has a rattlesnake on top.

Hint 174: A side profile of Mickey Mouse is on the upper part of a wall, between two moons, near the lobby of the Wilderness Lodge Villas (and to the right as you face the lobby).

Hint 175: Examine the art hanging in the first room to the right after you pass through the Villas' lobby entrance doors. A painting that's hanging on the room's right wall has a frame with classic Mickeys in the corners.

Hint 176: Walk to your right (as you face the Villas lobby) to the Carolwood Pacific Railroad Room. On the left side of the fireplace, a classic Mickey is embedded in the stonework at about the height of the fireplace mantel.

Hint 177: High along the hallways of the Villas, you'll find classic Mickey corner brackets.

Hint 178: To the left of the entrance doors to the Villas, in a hallway on the left past the elevators, a dark classic Mickey appears on the baseboard near the hall carpet. It's down the hallway on your right, about 8 to 10 feet before you reach Room 1507.

Magic Kingdom Monorail Resorts

– Polynesian Resort

Hint 179: On the lower level, just inside the main lobby, there's a classic Mickey design in the flag-stone tiles a few feet in front of the waterfall.

Note: Four paintings with Hidden Mickeys hang on the wall behind the registration counter. I'll start with the one at the far right (Hint 180) and end with the one at the far left (Hint 183).

Hint 180: A painting of a rocky shore with red flowers hangs at the far right. Four classic Mickeys are in the painting: one white one in the middle of the painting, another white one at the middle left, one brown one just to the left of the middle of the painting, and an upside-down brown one near the left middle.

Hint 181: In the second painting from the right, a person with Mickey ears stands at the back (aft) of the sailboat on the left.

Hint 182: In the third painting from the right, two classic Mickeys are formed in the water, one on the front of a brown rock at the left middle of the painting and another in the breaking surf in the middle of the second wave from the beach.

Hint 183: In the leftmost painting, circles in the foamy water near the shore form a classic Mickey at the lower right of the picture.

Hint 184: Inside the Tiki Boutique store on the first floor and near the various entrances, three wooden statues holding merchandise are adorned with classic Mickeys. Two of the Mickeys are blue and white while the third is red.

Hint 185: A slightly distorted green classic Mickey image is on the upper back of the Tiki statue outside Tiki Boutique. Many folks stop here for photos with the smiling Tiki guy.

Hint 186: Several different classic Mickeys hide in the carpets on the first floor. A carpet with a variety of classic Mickeys lies near the Wyland Galleries of Florida shop and to the right of the gallery entrance. Another carpet, in the kids' craft area near the front entrance, has a brown classic Mickey in the border and a blue classic Mickey on a turtle shell.

Hint 187: Along the right rear corner staircase from the lobby, bamboo wall decorations are composed of rings. Seen end on, some of the lower rings in the decoration on the right side form classic Mickeys.

Hint 188: In Trader Jack's gift shop, Mickey Mouse is sitting in a chair in front of the upper wall mural and on top of some merchandise cabinets. Classic Mickeys are on the arms of his chair.

Hint 189: The carpeting on the floor of the Kona Cafe includes many flowers. Some of the flowers contain classic Mickeys of different colors. You can see these carpet images from the railing outside the cafe.

Hint 190: At the Kona Island coffee bar, in front of the Kona Cafe, small purple tiles on top of the mosaic tile counter form a classic Mickey. You'll spot it to the left of the glass case.

Hint 191: On the "Order Here" screen at Capt. Cook's snack bar, images pan from right to left. As the image moves right, look for a palm tree with Mickey's shadow on its trunk.

Hint 192: The carpet in some of the hallways and elevators sports classic Mickeys.

– Wedding Pavilion

Hint 193: The weather vane on top of the building closest to the monorail has a full-length side profile of Mickey Mouse.

– Grand Floridian Resort & Spa

236

Hint 194: Weather vanes on various roofs at the front of the resort sport classic Mickeys.

Hint 195: The large trolley carts outside the hotel have classic Mickeys in the woodwork around the luggage storage areas at the back of the carts.

Hint 196: In the main lobby, gold classic Mickeys are in the carpet.

Hint 197: Green classic Mickeys are in the corners of the marble tile designs on the floors of the first and second levels of the main building.

Hint 198: You'll find the Fab Five Disney characters (Mickey, Minnie, Pluto, Donald, and Goofy) in the tile floor near the main lobby's front entrance — and directly above in the tile on the second floor entrance from the monorail.

Hint 199: Along the entrance hall to 1900 Park Fare restaurant, a Mickey-hat image is at the left lower corner of the left lower picture in a group of carousel pictures on the wall.

Hint 200: Minnie is here with Mickey (green full-body images) on the tile floor of the foyer in front of the dining area of the 1900 Park Fare restaurant.

Hint 201: Other Disney movie characters are in the tile floor encircling the main lobby and in front of the Grand Floridian Cafe. They include Tinker Bell, Cinderella and Prince Charming, Peter Pan and friends, Mrs. Potts and Chip, and of course Mickey and Minnie.

Hint 202: Ornate ironwork encloses the elevator out in the lobby, and the decorative sections between the floors host multiple classic Mickeys. You'll find four classic Mickeys in each ironwork panel at the intersection of the diagonal spokes and the large circle. The ears are oriented toward the center. (Tip: Stand inside the main lobby elevator for the best view of these classic Mickeys.)

Hint 203: A classic Mickey design is at the bottom of each of the four tall blue flowers in the stained-glass dome above the main lobby of the Grand Floridian.

Hint 204: On the second floor, a classic Mickey is on the top of a pole on the M. Mouse Mercantile sign in front of the shop.

Hint 205: Most guestroom hallways have classic Hidden Mickeys in the wallpaper.

Hint 206: Classic Mickeys are also in the guest hallway carpets.

Hint 207: In the lobbies of the outer guest buildings, the carpets have Hidden Mickeys as well as a Hidden Minnie Mouse, Donald Duck, Goofy, and Pluto.

Hint 208: Step into the main entrance area of the Grand Floridian Convention Center and look up for a hot air Mickey balloon painted on the ceiling.

– Contemporary Resort

Hint 209: From the window of the California Grill restaurant on the hotel's top floor, you can see a stretched out Mickey watchband on the ground in front of the building. It's among the conical-shaped trees. (You can see part of this watchband from the monorail.)

Hint 210: Inside the California Grill, the top of a classic Mickey is frosted in the design of the (closed) glass doors of the back room.

Hint 211: *(Caution: Prop the hallway door open before you step out onto the balcony to look for Mickey.)* From the sixth floor outdoor balcony closest to the front of the hotel, look left to see Mickey sitting on the edge of a roof below! This Mickey can also be spotted from either monorail just outside the hotel (the opening nearest the Transportation and Ticket Center). If you're on the resort monorail, you have to bend down to view Mickey through the lower part of the window (to the left of forward motion) and below the express monorail track next to you. On the express monorail, look to the right of forward motion.

Hint 212: Inside Chef Mickey's restaurant, a large side-profile Mickey decorates both sides of the large black, white, and red tile divider.

Hint 213: Mickey ears are atop posts at the rear of Chef Mickey's restaurant.

Hint 214: On the lower part of the wall mural facing Contempo Café, the fourth girl from the right corner of the wall has a classic Mickey on her dress.

Hint 215: High on the wall mural facing Bay Lake, a black classic Mickey is on an owl perched on a girl's head. It's on the red right wing (as you face the mural).

Hint 216: On the fourth floor, a stick-figure Mickey is in an artwork display on the side of the Bay-view Gifts store facing the monorail.

Hint 217: On the fourth floor, classic Mickeys are in the carpet inside The Game Station Arcade.

Hint 218: On the wall mural facing the monorail, an upside-down classic Mickey has a blue circle for a "head" and yellow circles for "ears." It's at the top of a tree that is positioned to the lower left of the five-legged goat.

Hint 219: Behind the main hotel, a classic Mickey silhouette can be found in the bricks under the metal Mickey Mouse sculpture. (The sculpture itself is a decorative Mickey, not a Hidden Mickey.)

Hint 220: In The Sand Bar by the pool, near the middle of the upper left wall border, one of the semaphore figures is wearing Mickey ears.

Hint 221: At the exit from the Garden Building to the parking lot (facing the monorail), a huge classic Mickey is traced in the tile under the exit canopy between the benches.

Hint 222: Large white classic Mickeys are frosted into glass partitions that support the curved roof that covers the vehicle drive-through entrance area to the hotel.

– Bay Lake Tower

Hint 223: Classic Mickeys are at the top of both elevator towers at the sides of the hotel. (Ceiling lights hang from these Mickey-shaped metal plates.) You can spot one of them from the monorail and either or both from the ground.

Shades of Green Resort

Hint 224: In the lobby, a Mickey statue stands in front of a framed picture of a blue sky with puffy clouds. Three classic Mickeys are in the clouds and another, made of fireworks, decorates the statue Mickey's right ear.

Hint 225: The Millpond pool is shaped as a classic Mickey. You can visit this pool outside or spot it on a resort map posted on hallway walls.

Hither, Thither & Yon Scavenger Hunt

A car is the most efficient method for hunting the following areas. I've planned the hunt taking time of day and location into consideration. However, some backtracking will help keep you ahead of the crowds. Don't forget to be courteous to the shoppers, diners, golfers, swimmers, other guests, and Cast Members you encounter during your hunt.

(Note: Because you may want to hunt only one area at a time, I've listed the perfect score for each area in parentheses after its name in the Clues section.)

★ **Bonus Points Opportunity.** As I advised in Chapter Six, pay attention to the Disney buses during your Hidden Mickey hunt around WDW property. You may get lucky! The Disney Cruise Line bus has a Hidden Pluto on each side of the gold scrollwork on the front of the bus between the headlights. Some general Disney transport buses sometimes sport a classic Mickey on the rear of the vehicle, usually re-lated to rear upper or lower lights. Even more subtle are the faint classic Mickey images in the windows of some buses, only visible when the lighting is just right!

If you spot one or more of these images, give yourself 5 bonus points for each one you find.

WDW Golf Courses (10 points)

If you're a golfer, look around you for the following Hidden Mickeys:

Clue 1: On the Magnolia Golf Course, find a classic Mickey sand trap.
5 points

241

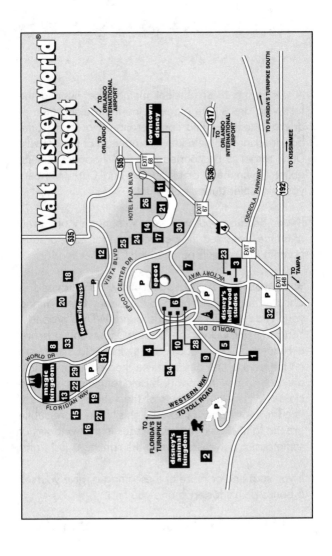

1 All-Star Resorts
2 Animal Kingdom Lodge
3 Art of Animation
4 Beach Club
5 Blizzard Beach
6 BoardWalk
7 Caribbean Beach
8 Contemporary
9 Coronado Springs
10 Dolphin
11 Downtown Disney
12 Golden Oak
13 Grand Floridian
14 Lake Buena Vista Golf Course
15 Magnolia Golf Course
16 Oak Trail Golf Course
17 Old Key West
18 Osprey Ridge Golf Course
19 Palm Golf Course
20 Pioneer Hall
21 Pleasure Island, in Downtown Disney
22 Polynesian
23 Pop Century
24 Port Orleans – French Quarter
25 Port Orleans – Riverside
26 Saratoga Springs
27 Shades of Green
28 Swan
29 Transportation and Ticket Center
30 Typhoon Lagoon
31 WDW Speedway
32 ESPN Wide World of Sports Complex
33 Wilderness Lodge
34 Yacht Club
P Parking

Clue 2: At the Osprey Ridge Golf Course look for a putting green shaped like Mickey Mouse. (Tip: You can visit this Hidden Mickey without playing golf.)
5 points

Vista Boulevard (5 points)

Clue 3: Drive east along Vista Boulevard away from Osprey Ridge Golf Course and stay alert for a classic Mickey on a sign to your left.
5 points

WDW Speedway (5 points)

Clue 4: Go to the racetrack to take a look at the lake on the infield, or more accurately, a photo of it. The lake is barely visible from the fence around the parking area for the *Richard Petty Driving Experience*. So check out a framed photo of the racetrack inside the guest sign-in building to spot this classic Mickey.
5 points

WDW Water Parks (48 points)

★ *Blizzard Beach* (15 points)

Clue 5: Take a close look at the Beach Haus store's right rear wall near the dressing rooms.
3 points

Clue 6: Inside the Beach Haus, spot Hidden Mickeys near the merchandise.
2 points

Clue 7: Hop on the *Chairlift* to spot a classic Mickey formed by three round rocks on the ground near one of the support poles for the ride. (Tip: The Singles line for the *Chairlift* is usually shorter than the Standby line.)
5 points

Clue 8: Go to the rear of the park (by tube or on foot) to find a classic Mickey with a sorcerer's hat that's formed by three stones topped by a small

triangular rock. (Psst! He's near the center of the side of a stone bridge that crosses over *Cross Country Creek*.)
5 points

★ *En Route to Typhoon Lagoon* (4 points)

Clue 9: On your way to Typhoon Lagoon from Blizzard Beach, spot Mickey on the Disney Vacation Club white tower, which will appear on your left at the intersection of Buena Vista Drive and Bonnet Creek Parkway.
4 points

★ *Typhoon Lagoon* (29 points)

Clue 10: Look around the *Crush 'n' Gusher* elevator for a Hidden Mickey.
4 points

Clue 11: Search for Mickey on a bridge over *Castaway Creek*, near *Shark Reef*.
4 points

Clue 12: Marvel at Mickey if you snorkel with the sharks in *Shark Reef*.
5 points

Clue 13: Don't pass by Mickey on the steps up to the *Storm Slides*.
4 points

Clue 14: Climb the trail up to *Humunga Kowabunga* and locate a classic Mickey along the way.
4 points

Clue 15: Spot the Main Mouse hiding under a cannon along *Castaway Creek* at the rear of the park.
4 points

Clue 16: Squint for Mickey in the wall of a cave at *Ketchakiddee Creek*.
4 points

ESPN Wide World of Sports
(15 points)

Clue 17: Search hard for a three-dimensional Mickey Mouse head near the high central ceiling of The Milk House (the Field House). He's on an upper rafter opposite the main entrance.
5 points

Clue 18: Don't miss Mickey in the outfield if you go to a game in the stadium! (Tip: You can only see this Hidden Mickey from Champion Stadium.)
5 points

Clue 19: Now head for the softball fields and check out the pitcher's mounds for possible bonus points.
5 bonus points for one or more

Clue 20: Stroll around the Sports Fields to locate a Hidden Mickey on the discus field.
5 points

Downtown Disney West Side
(72 points)

★ *Cirque du Soleil* (8 points)

Clue 21: Look down for a Hidden Mickey in the sidewalk near Parking Lot Q.
5 points

Clue 22: Head for the outside restrooms (they're under the main entrance staircase to the theater) and examine the floor in either one (men's or women's). See a small classic Mickey?
3 points for either (or both)

★ *House of Blues* (3 points)

Clue 23: Search for a classic Mickey on the ceiling.
3 points

★ *DisneyQuest* (25 points)

Clue 24: On the third floor inside, look above you in Ventureport for a Hidden Mickey.
2 points

Clue 25: Check the carpet on Ventureport's third floor.
3 points

Clue 26: Look for track lighting shaped like a classic Mickey on the second through fifth floors. (Psst! It's not on the same side on all four floors.)
5 points for spotting all four

Clue 27: Find similar lighting near *"Invasion! An Extra-TERRORestrial Alien Encounter."*
3 points

Clue 28: Spot classic Mickey markings on the back of one of the creatures you encounter during *"Aladdin's Magic Carpet Ride."* (You don't have to take the ride; you can watch the overhead video screens as others ride.)
4 points

★ Find two classic Hidden Mickeys at the *"Virtual Jungle Cruise."* (Again, you needn't take the ride; you can stand behind one of the ride pods and watch.)

Clue 29: Before the ride starts, watch the left side of the screen.
4 points

Clue 30: Keep watching the screen during the first part of the ride to see if the raft exits a glacier area. (The riders have optional routes, so they may not enter the glacier area.) If it does, watch carefully as it exits. (The ears on this Hidden Mickey aren't perfectly formed, but you'll recognize them.)
3 bonus points

Clue 31: Along the queue for *"Pirates of the Caribbean,"* examine the walls for a Hidden Mickey.
2 points

Clue 32: Check out both the trash can and the floor at the exit.
2 points for spotting Mickey on both

★ *Splitsville Luxury Lanes* (12 points)

Clue 33: Admire the mural inside on the lower level for Hidden Mickeys.
5 points for three different kinds of Mickey images

Clue 34: Find Mickey on a huge orange on the upper level.
3 points

Clue 35: Search the orange trees on the upper level.
4 points

★ *Wolfgang Puck Cafe* (5 points)

Clue 36: Study the mosaic tile pyramid behind the reception counter to find a classic Hidden Mickey.
5 points

★ *Disney's Candy Cauldron* (4 points)

Clue 37: Go inside to find a classic Mickey marking on a stone.
4 points

★ *D Street* (13 points)

Clue 38: Spot Mickey on the ceiling.
2 points

Clue 39: Search for a small classic Mickey wall impression.
3 points

Clue 40: Observe Mickey in the bricks.
2 points

Clue 41: Find a Hidden Mickey on Mickey!
3 points

248   Clue 42: Pluto is in the building!
3 points

★ *Pleasure Island Bus Stop* (2 points)

Clue 43: Look down near one of the bus stops.
2 points

Downtown Disney Marketplace
(202 points)

★ *Entrance to the Marketplace* (8 points)

Clue 44: Find Hidden Mickeys at the bus stop area
near the main entrance.
5 points for five or more

Clue 45: Check out the signs over the entrances.
1 point for one or more

Clue 46: Study the green benches for Hidden Mickeys
at the entrance and elsewhere around the Marketplace.
2 points

★ *Disney's Wonderful World
of Memories* (3 points)

Clue 47: Search for Mickey outside the store.
3 points

★ *Disney's Days of Christmas* (14 points)

Clue 48: Step inside and search for a Mickey made
of rocks.
3 points

Clue 49: Find at least one classic Mickey on each of
three large trees.
4 points total for one or more on each tree

Clue 50: Study the walls and carpet for classic Hidden
Mickeys.
3 points for two or more

Clue 51: Take a good look at the ceiling in
the rear room of the shop.
2 points

249

Clue 52: Check out the walls in the rear room.
2 points

★ *Goofy's Candy Company* (10 points)

Clue 53: Search for a Goofy shadow in the store.
4 points

Clue 54: Find Goofy and other characters on the wall.
4 points for three or more characters

Clue 55: Find Mickey in a store window.
2 points

★ *Rainforest Cafe* (3 points)

Clue 56: Look for a Hidden Mickey on the outdoor sign.
3 points

★ *Cap'n Jack's Restaurant* (3 points)

Clue 57: Step inside the restaurant entrance and spot Mickey.
3 points

★ *Sassagoula River Cruise ferry* (10 points)

Clue 58: If you have time, take the *Sassagoula River Cruise* ferryboat to Port Orleans – French Quarter, Disembark and then ride the next boat back to Downtown Disney Marketplace. During both your crossings, study the Treehouse Villas for Hidden Mickeys.
5 points for one or more

Clue 59: On the boat ride back from Port Orleans – French Quarter to Downtown Disney, don't miss Mickey on the ground under a bridge!
5 points

★ *Marketplace Carousel* (5 points)

Clue 60: Study the decorative panels on the *Carousel* for four classic Mickeys.
5 points for spotting all four

★ *Mickey's Pantry* (3 points)

Clue 61: Spot classic Mickeys on the walls.
3 points for three or more

★ *Once Upon a Toy* (38 points)

(Note: This store sports numerous Mickeys and other Disney characters in the décor in addition to the Hidden Mickeys below.)

Clue 62: Examine the interactive fountain near the store. (Note: Two Hidden Mickeys are there all the time, a third appears only when the water is on.)
4 points for two
5 points for spotting all three

Clue 63: Find a classic Mickey in the cement outside.
5 points

Clue 64: Outside the main entrance, look for classic Mickeys with tires for ears.
2 points for one or more

★ Now enter the store and keep your eyes open.

Clue 65: Gaze up for classic Mickeys.
2 points for one or more

Clue 66: Check out the tops of merchandise stands. (Only some sport Hidden Mickeys.)
1 point for one or more

Clue 67: Now examine the bottoms of these stands.
1 point for one or more

Clue 68: Search for a classic Mickey on a sandal in the middle of the first room.
3 points

Clue 69: In the first room, find a tiny Mickey near Mrs. Potato Head.
4 points

Clue 70: Examine the mural behind the service desk in the same room.
2 points for two or more images

251

Clue 71: Look at the upper beams of the wooden merchandise displays.
1 point for one or more

Clue 72: Now observe the bolts on those displays.
1 point for one or more

Clue 73: Study the floor for a Mickey.
3 points

Clue 74: Find a classic Hidden Mickey cloud in a central room.
3 points

Clue 75: Look for a Mickey shadow in a central room.
3 points

Clue 76: Look for Hidden Mickey lollipops.
2 points for one or more

★ *Disney's Pin Traders* (5 points)

Clue 77: Spot a Hidden Mickey on a Mickey statue inside the store.
3 points

Clue 78: Find another Mickey on the Donald statue.
2 points

★ *Tren-D* (22 points)

Clue 79: Look around for white classic Mickeys on the side and legs of a merchandise table.
3 points for both

Clue 80: Check out Mickey in wallpaper.
2 points

Clue 81: Find Mickey on a mannequin.
4 points

Clue 82: Look for a Mickey ring on Minnie Mouse, a Mickey watch on another Minnie, and a gold Hidden Mickey on a third Minnie.
5 points for all three

Clue 83: Spot a blue Hidden Mickey on the wall inside the store.
5 points

Clue 84: Locate Mickey on a countertop.
3 points

★ *Team Mickey Athletic Club* (6 points)

Clue 85: Find a classic Mickey in the Disney Vacation Club (DVC) display near Team Mickey.
2 points

Clue 86: Observe the pillars outside.
1 point

Clue 87: Find classic Mickeys in the Caricature Booth nearby.
3 points for one or more

★ *Ghirardelli Ice Cream & Chocolate Shop* (4 points)

Clue 88: Locate Mickey on a wall inside.
4 points

★ *Near the lake* (3 points)

Clue 89: Do you see any chairs with Hidden Mickeys outside the Ghirardelli Shop?
2 points

Clue 90: Spot Mickeys in the fence around the lake.
1 point

★ *World of Disney* (55 points)

Clue 91: Look up for Mickeys on the store sign.
1 point

Clue 92: Find light brown Mickeys outside the store.
2 points

Clue 93: Inside one of the store entrances, study the wall near the jail cells for a classic Mickey.
4 points

Clue 94: Look for classic Mickeys in some of the clothing racks.
2 points

Clue 95: Examine some of the indoor signs for an image of Mickey.
2 points

Clue 96: Find a classic Mickey emblem on the Chinese Theater in a mural in the high-ceilinged central room.
4 points

Clue 97: In the same room, find an upside-down classic Mickey on the Pocahontas airship.
4 points

★ Now find two classic Mickeys on the Tweedle Dee and Tweedle Dum mural in the same room.

Clue 98: Look for a flag.
2 points

Clue 99: Check out an apron.
2 points

Clue 100: Study the mannequins in this room.
4 points

Clue 101: Find Mickey near Cinderella Castle.
4 points

Clue 102: Search for two different classic Mickeys inside shadowboxes on the wall.
3 points for both

Clue 103: Look for Hidden Mickeys on a curtain.
2 points

Clue 104: Spot classic Mickeys on paintings in the central Genie Room.
2 points

Clue 105: In the same room, observe the "antique" maps decorating the walls. (Psst! Think character profiles.)
5 points for three or more

Clue 106: Next door in the Villain Room, spot Cruella DeVille's Hidden Mickey.
3 points

Clue 107: Look down for Mickey under merchandise.
3 points

Clue 108: Now find Mickey on a wall near the restrooms.
3 points

Clue 109: Outside the store, in an entrance area to the Marketplace, look around for a classic Mickey.
3 points

★ **T-REX** (10 points)

Clue 110: Admire a classic Mickey near the bar area.
5 points

Clue 111: Find a Hidden Mickey just outside the main entrance.
5 points

WDW Casting Center (3 points)

Clue 112: Drive to the Casting building, across the road from the rightmost Downtown Disney Marketplace entrance, to locate more classic Mickeys. (These Hidden Mickeys can also be spotted from Interstate 4.)
3 points

Miniature Golf Courses (22 points)

You can find these Hidden Mickeys while you play the courses. Or you may be able to walk the courses without playing if it's not crowded, due to rain or luck. (Tell the attendants that you're hunting Hidden Mickeys and ask if you can take a look around.)

★ *Fantasia Gardens* (4 points)

Clue 113: Check the tee-off areas.
1 point

Clue 114: Take a good look at the 12th hole on the Gardens Course.
3 points

★ *Winter Summerland* (18 points)

Clue 115: Find Mickey on the third hole.
3 points

★ Now head straight for the 16th holes.

Clue 116: Spot Goofy on the 16th hole of the Winter Course.
3 points

Clue 117: Now check around the same hole for a Mickey Mouse gingerbread cookie.
2 points

Clue 118: Find Mickey and Minnie on the 16th hole of the Summer Course. (Psst! This Hidden Mickey is also visible from the 16th and 17th holes of the Winter Course.)
3 points

Clue 119: Wait for Mickey on the 17th hole of the Winter Course.
1 point

Clue 120: Study the Christmas tree on the 17th hole of the Summer Course for Hidden Mickeys.
3 points for three Hidden Mickeys

Clue 121: Look around for Mickey near the 18th tee for the Summer Course.
3 points

Near Celebration, Florida (4 points)

Okay, I admit it; this Mickey isn't hidden. Just the op-posite, in fact. But it is unique. So I decided to include it anyway. You'll find a huge classic Mickey near Celebration, Florida, on the west side of Interstate 4.

Clue 122: Look for it as you get close to Exit 62.
4 points

Near the Magic Kingdom (5 points)

Clue 123: You can only see this classic Mickey made of tree groves from the air or on an image from a Google search. It's a few miles northwest of the Magic Kingdom. Good luck!
5 points

Total Points for Hither, Thither & Yon =

How'd you do?

A perfect score for this hunt is 391. You may have done even better if you earned bonus points in ESPN Wide World of Sports, DisneyQuest, and/or by spot-ting Hidden Characters on the Disney buses.

You'll find a breakdown by area below, so that you can tally your score for only those places you've cov-ered. Give yourself Gold if you scored at least 80% of available points, Bronze if you scored at least 40%.

The Golf Courses (10)
  Magnolia Golf Course (5)
  Osprey Ridge Golf Course (5)

Vista Boulevard (5)

WDW Speedway (5)

WDW Water Parks (48)
Blizzard Beach (15)
En route to Typhoon Lagoon (4)
Typhoon Lagoon (29)

ESPN Wide World of Sports (15)

Downtown Disney West Side (72)
Cirque du Soleil (8)
House of Blues (3)
DisneyQuest (25)
Splitsville Luxury Lanes (12)
Wolfgang Puck Cafe (5)
Disney's Candy Cauldron (4)
D Street (13)
Pleasure Island Bus Stop (2)

Downtown Disney Marketplace (202)
Entrance to the Marketplace (8)
Disney's Wonderful World of Memories (3)
Disney's Days of Christmas (14)
Goofy's Candy Co. (10)
Rainforest Cafe (3)
Cap'n Jack's Restaurant (3)
Sassagoula River Cruise ferry (10)
Marketplace Carousel (5)
Mickey's Pantry (3)
Once Upon a Toy (38)
Disney's Pin Traders (5)
Tren-D (22)
Team Mickey Athletic Club (6)
Ghirardelli Ice Cream & Chocolate Shop (4)
Near the Lake (3)
World of Disney (55)
T-REX (10)

WDW Casting Center (3)

Miniature Golf Courses (22)
Fantasia Gardens (4)
Winter Summerland (18)

Near Celebration, Florida (4)

Near Magic Kingdom (5)

**Caution:
Don't peek at this
section unless you
really want help!**

The Golf Courses

– Magnolia Golf Course

Hint 1: A sand trap at the sixth green is shaped like a classic Mickey.

– Osprey Ridge Golf Course

Hint 2: The practice putting green is shaped like a side profile of Mickey Mouse.

Vista Boulevard

Hint 3: If you drive east from Osprey Ridge Golf Course along Vista Boulevard, you can spot a sign for the Golden Oak Resort on your left. A classic Mickey is hidden in the tree of Golden Oak's logo.

WDW Speedway

Hint 4: A lake on the infield is shaped like a classic Mickey. You'll barely see the lake, let alone the Hidden Mickey, from ground level. To marvel at its full effect without paying admission, walk inside the guest sign-in building and look at the framed photo on the wall.

WDW Water Parks

– Blizzard Beach

Hint 5: Find a lighting fixture on the wall at the right rear of the Beach Haus store near the dressing rooms. There's a painting on the cover in which a small classic Mickey is formed by rocks at the lower center of an outdoor mountain scene.

Hint 6: As in many WDW shops, one or more of the merchandise stands has classic Mickey-shaped holes on its center pole.

Hint 7: From the *Chairlift* ride that takes you to the water slides, look to the ground on the second level of the mountain just past support pole #4 (counting from the beginning of the lift) and below the right side of your chairlift to spot a classic Mickey made of three round rocks.

Hint 8: At the rear of the park, a classic Mickey is formed by three stones jutting out from near the top edge of a stone bridge crossing *Cross Country Creek*. It is on the side of the bridge, near the center. A small triangular rock over this Hidden Mickey gives it the appearance of wearing a sorcerer's hat.

Tip: You can see this Mickey from the water or dry land. It is visible from the floating tubes as you approach the bridge by water. On land, you can see it through the trees (past the "Runoff Rapids Tube Pickup" area) either from just past the *Runoff Rapids* "Red Slope" entrance sign or from several points on the walkway on the other side of the bridge.

– En Route to Typhoon Lagoon

Hint 9: Classic Mickey holes are in the railing around the Disney Vacation Club (DVC) white tower that stands to the left of Buena Vista Drive at its intersection with Bonnet Creek Parkway.

– Typhoon Lagoon

Hint 10: At *Crush 'n' Gusher*, on the upper floor near the elevator, paint circles on the cement form a classic Mickey.

Hint 11: Mickey ears are at the bottom of a vertical strut in the railing of a bridge. You can see the ears if you enter *Castaway Creek* at Shark Landing (near *Shark Reef*) and look behind you as you float under the first bridge. The ears are toward the right side of the bridge. You can also usually see the ears if you walk downstream on either side of the creek and look back at the bridge.

Hint 12: As you snorkel along in *Shark Reef*, you can often see a classic Mickey resting on the bottom of the swim route. Recently, the Mickey was located on the right side, about halfway along the route after the island.

Hint 13: About halfway up the wooden steps to the *Storm Slides*, Mickey ears are on the left side of a walkway slat, just before the anchor on the right side of the path.

Hint 14: Near the end of the long trail up to *Humunga Kowabunga*, three of the last short logs in the ground under the rope fence to the left of the walkway form an upside-down classic Mickey when viewed from above. (Note: You may spot other groups of short logs in the ground along walkways that resemble classic Mickeys.)

Hint 15: You'll find a classic Mickey formed by cannonballs along *Castaway Creek*. He's on your left by the second cannon past the waterfall if you're drifting in the creek. If you're walking on the nearby trail, you'll see him just past *Forgotten Grotto* in the rear of the park as you walk alongside the drifters.

Hint 16: In the walk-through cave at the rear of *Ketchakiddee Creek*, there is a classic Mickey impression in the rock. It's on the back wall of the cave, about one and a half feet up from the ground, and near the drain at the right side of the cave as you enter the cave from the water.

ESPN Wide World of Sports

Hint 17: A three-dimensional Mickey Mouse looks out over the court from near the high central ceiling in The Milk House (the Field House). He's on an upper rafter above the sign, "The Milk House," in front of a yellow triangular wall partition that is opposite the main entrance. I spotted him to the upper left of the lower seats of section 104.

Hint 18: A large, pale green classic Mickey image lies in the outfield grass in the Wide World of Sports Champion Baseball Stadium.

Hint 19: On some days, you may spot classic Mickey circles around the pitcher's mounds on the nearby softball fields.

Hint 20: Walk past Champion Baseball Stadium, the Field House, and several multipurpose Sports Fields to the Track and Field Complex way in the back. A clever classic Mickey forms the base of the discus-throwing launch pad. (Tip: You can get a better vantage point for viewing this Mickey image by climbing up into the nearby bleachers.)

Downtown Disney West Side

– *Cirque du Soleil*

Hint 21: A classic Mickey is etched in the sidewalk near *Cirque du Soleil*, on the second slab back from Parking Lot Q, just past a manhole cover and near the grass.

Hint 22: Under the main entrance staircase to the show are restrooms for men and women. You will find tiles laid to approximate a small classic Mickey on the floor of each restroom, in a corner just inside the entrance doors. These circles don't touch, but the design is convincing to my eyes.

– House of Blues

Hint 23: Walk through the front door and down the right side aisle. A classic Mickey is on the ceiling past the first server's station.

– DisneyQuest

Hint 24: At the bottom of the large three-dimensional ray gun poised over the lobby of Ventureport, three spheres form a classic Mickey from certain perspectives.

Hint 25: Symbols and figures that include classic Mickey designs are woven into the carpet on the third floor in Ventureport. (You can also spot these images on the fifth floor in the FoodQuest seating area.)

Hint 26: Track lighting shaped like a classic Mickey hangs above the elevator doors on floors two, three, four, and five. You'll find it near the *"Mighty Ducks Pinball Slam"* (on the third floor) and near *"Ride the Comix"* (on the fourth and fifth floors). On the second floor, near *"CyberSpace Mountain,"* the lighting is above an elevator door on the opposite side of the elevator bank.

Hint 27: Similar track lighting can be found in front of pod 4 of *"Invasion! An ExtraTERRORestrial Alien Encounter."*

Hint 28: During *"Aladdin's Magic Carpet Ride,"* the golden beetle you encounter bears classic Mickey markings on its back.

Hint 29: At the *"Virtual Jungle Cruise,"* classic Mickey-shaped balloons periodically float up from the left side of the screen, in front of the castle, before the ride starts.

263

Hint 30: On the screen in the first part of the *"Virtual Jungle Cruise"* ride, the raft may exit a glacier area under a distorted classic Mickey-shaped ice bridge over the river.

Hint 31: In the wall murals along the queue for *"Pirates of the Caribbean,"* the rightmost bunch of palm tree coconuts near the stairs is shaped like a classic Mickey.

Hint 32: You can spot the DisneyQuest classic Mickey logo on trash cans (like the one near the exit). It is also illuminated on the floor of the exit walkway and, at times, on the walkways outside DisneyQuest.

– Splitsville Luxury Lanes

Hint 33: In the right wall mural inside the main entrance on the lower level, you can see the Mickey Earful Tower, balloons with Mickey ears, and classic Mickey holes in a red bowling ball.

Hint 34: On the upper level near the escalator, holes form a classic Mickey in a huge "orange" in the left wall mural.

Hint 35: A few classic Mickeys are formed by groups of oranges in the trees in the upper level left mural.

– Wolfgang Puck Cafe

Hint 36: Behind the reception counter, about two thirds of the way up the mosaic pyramid, a white tile and two smaller black tiles form a classic Mickey.

– Disney's Candy Cauldron

Hint 37: Inside the store, on the upper wall above the candy display, a dark marking on a stone near the ceiling forms a classic Hidden Mickey.

– D Street

Hint 38: Above you, various Mickey images float as clouds on the ceiling just inside the store entrance.

Hint 39: A somewhat distorted image on the wall to your immediate left as you enter the store resembles a classic Mickey.

Hint 40: A large classic Mickey image is formed by exposed bricks on the wall behind the main counter and across from the store entrance.

Hint 41: On the wall to the right of the exposed-brick classic Mickey, a full-body menacing Mickey has a black classic Mickey on his belt buckle.

Hint 42: A Hidden Pluto made of exposed bricks is on the right front wall of the store.

– Pleasure Island Bus Stop

Hint 43: A large classic Mickey hides in the cement between Bus Stops 5 and 6, across from Planet Hollywood restaurant.

Downtown Disney Marketplace

– Entrance to the Marketplace

Hint 44: Coca-Cola vending machines stand near Bus Stops 2, 3, and 4 in the Downtown Disney Marketplace Bus Stop area. In colorful paintings on these machines, one full-body Mickey is pouring water and several classic Mickeys can be found on signs, a tower, and an awning.

Hint 45: Signs over the entrances to the Marketplace sport classic Mickeys at their sides.

Hint 46: Green benches with classic Mickey emblems on the top and sides are scattered around the Marketplace and the interactive fountain.

– Disney's Wonderful World of Memories

Hint 47: The sign on the store contains a full-figure Hidden Mickey on the page of a book.

– Disney's Days of Christmas

Hint 48: A large dark brown circular rock and two smaller rocks for "ears" form a classic Mickey on the middle side of the "chimney" inside the store. You'll see Dalmatians on the mantelpiece around this chimney.

Hint 49: Inside the shop, three large trees surrounded by merchandise have classic Mickeys carved in their bark near the tops of their trunks. The trees are not Christmas trees, and each of the three has one or two Mickey carvings.

Hint 50: Various sections of wallpaper and carpet often hide classic Mickeys.

Hint 51: In the rear room of the shop, classic Mickeys hide in the scrollwork on the ceiling.

Hint 52: Also in the rear room, you'll find small white classic Mickeys in the wallpaper near the ceiling.

– Goofy's Candy Co.

Hint 53: A shadow of Goofy is on the upper back wall of the store, behind the large Krispy Treat display.

Hint 54: Goofy, Mickey Mouse, Pluto, and other characters hide in the light brown mural on the upper wall around the store.

Hint 55: Classic Mickey circles are part of the design in the middle of the side window that faces the lagoon.

– Rainforest Cafe

Hint 56: A green lizard on the outside sign for Rainforest Cafe has an upside-down classic Mickey in the middle of the circles on its neck.

– Cap'n Jack's Restaurant

Hint 57: Three glass or plastic balls in a net form a classic Mickey behind the check-in counter that's just inside the restaurant.

– Sassagoula River Cruise ferry

Hint 58: From the boat dock to the right of Cap'n Jack's Restaurant, take the ferryboat to Port Orleans – French Quarter and then back to Downtown Disney Marketplace. Both ways, spot small white classic Mickeys in some of the Treehouse Villas' windows.

Hint 59: On the ferryboat ride back from Port Orleans – French Quarter to Downtown Disney Marketplace, look to your right as you pass under the first bridge to spot a classic Mickey made of coiled rope lying on the ground.

– Marketplace Carousel

Hint 60: At least four classic Mickeys are hiding on the inner and outer decorative panels on the Carousel near Disney's Days of Christmas store.
- A blue classic Mickey is on the sign under Minnie Mouse.
- Two light green classic Mickeys are on the dragon's nose.
- Two tiny classic Mickeys are on the pink window awnings on the right side of the panel that shows part of the store from a distance.
- Pink classic Mickeys formed of roses hide in the upper part of the panels in the center of the Carousel.

– Mickey's Pantry

Hint 61: You'll find classic Mickeys of different sizes and colors in the wall decorations around the store.

– Once Upon a Toy

Hint 62: In the interactive flat fountain near the Once Upon a Toy store, water-tube heads are shaped like classic Mickeys, recessed lights in the cement are arranged in a classic Mickey shape, and the fountain water collects into a huge classic Mickey on the cement!

Hint 63: Outside the store, you'll find several faint classic Mickeys in the cement near the side entrance.

Hint 64: Outside the store's main entrance, classic Mickeys are formed by truck tires (the "ears") atop Lincoln Logs.

Hint 65: Classic Mickey pincers or clamps (holding toys) circulate on a track that hangs from the ceiling in the room with Mr. Potato Head.

Hint 66: Tinker Toys on top of merchandise stands around the store form classic Mickeys.

Hint 67: At the bottom of these merchandise stands, you'll find classic Mickey supports.

Hint 68: Two black classic Mickeys are on blue sandals on one of the Mr. Potato Heads in the first room just inside the store's main entrance.

Hint 69: In the center of this Mr. Potato Head display in the first room, a tiny white classic Mickey adorns the clasp of Mrs. Potato Head's handbag. Note: She's holding decorative Mickey balloons.

Hint 70: In this same room, the mural behind a service desk includes a classic Mickey balloon, several pairs of Mickey ears, and a Mickey ice cream bar.

Hint 71: The centers of the upper beams on wooden merchandise displays sport classic Mickey shapes.

Hint 72: On the same merchandise displays, large wing nuts on some of the bolts form Mickey ears.

Hint 73: Across the first and second rooms (as you enter from the front main entrance), large letters in Scrabble tiles on the floor spell "MICKEY."

Hint 74: In a central room of the store, a classic Mickey cloud appears in a window in a mural behind the service desk.

Hint 75: In the same room, a partial classic Mickey shadow is at the top of a wall mu-

ral. It's to the left of the classic Mickey cloud and above a checkout counter.

Hint 76: In the rear room, lollipops are arranged to form classic Mickeys on the outside of merchandise stands.

– Disney's Pin Traders

Hint 77: On the large statue of Mickey and Minnie, Mickey wears a classic Mickey pin on his tie.

Hint 78: On Donald's statue, a red, white, and blue classic Mickey pin is on the upper right side of Donald's duffel bag.

– Tren-D

Hint 79: Several small white classic Mickeys hide in the white dots along the side of a red merchandise tabletop and on the table's legs. (Other merchandise tables display decorative Mickey images.)

Hint 80: Classic Mickeys are repeated in sections of framed wallpaper artwork inside the store.

Hint 81: A tiny black classic Mickey is on a female mannequin's cheek, under the left eye.

Hint 82: Minnie Mouse is painted on several columns inside the store in a variety of costumes and poses. In three of these paintings, she sports accessories adorned with Hidden Mickeys. In one, she wears an upside-down classic (Hidden) Mickey ring and clothing with purple decorative classic Mickeys. In another, she wears a Mickey watch and enjoys a decorative Mickey lollipop. In a third painting, Minnie's necklace has a small, gold classic Mickey pendant that stands out against her green outfit.

Hint 83: A blue paint-splash classic Mickey is high on the wall inside the store near the entrance from Team Mickey Athletic Club. If you enter the store from the main promenade, the image is on the upper wall to the right.

269

Hint 84: On the check-out countertop to the right as you enter from the promenade, circle impressions form a classic Mickey. (The circles are all the same size, but this image is accepted by guests and Cast Members as a Hidden Mickey.)

– Team Mickey Athletic Club

Hint 85: Outside the entrance to Team Mickey, you'll find a classic Mickey repeated in the white picket fence bordering the Disney Vacation Club display.

Hint 86: Classic Mickeys are on the bases and tops of the shop's outside pillars.

Hint 87: Classic Mickeys hide in the clouds in the background of several paintings on the rear wall of the Caricature Booth near Guest Relations.

– Ghirardelli Ice Cream & Chocolate Shop

Hint 88: A dark side-profile image of Mickey looking to the left appears as a shadow in a painting on a rear wall of the shop (to the left as you enter). Look for a streetcar in the painting. The shadow is in the streetcar's second window from the left.

– Near the lake

Hint 89: Green chairs with classic Mickeys on top are scattered around outside in the Marketplace and near the Ghirardelli shop.

Hint 90: Several sections of the green fence around the lake have repeating classic Mickeys near the top of the railing.

– World of Disney

Hint 91: Blue classic Mickeys are on the far sides of the World of Disney entrance signs.

Hint 92: Light brown classic Mickeys can be found near the tops of the columns outside the store.

Hint 93: Inside the store entrance with the pirate figures behind prison bars, some of the circular impressions in the stone walls outside the prison cells form classic Mickeys. Look along the stone wall on the far right (as you enter) to find a sideways classic Mickey slightly below eye level.

Hint 94: Classic Mickey holes are drilled in some of the metal posts that support the clothing racks.

Hint 95: Some of the indoor signs for the various store sections include Mickey and other Hidden character images.

Hint 96: In the high-ceilinged central room, behind the three little pigs floating overhead, a wall mural has a classic Mickey emblem above the doors of the Chinese Theater.

Hint 97: In the same room, the Pocahontas airship has an upside-down classic Mickey at the very bottom of the rear vertical tail fin, near where the tail fin connects to the body of the airship.

Hint 98: In the same room, you'll find a classic Mickey on a flag in the background of the Tweedle Dee and Tweedle Dum wall mural.

Hint 99: That mural also includes a classic Mickey on Tweedle Dee's apron.

Hint 100: In the same room of the store, some of the female mannequins have classic Mickey freckles under their eyes.

Hint 101: In the large central room, the clouds that encircle the model of Cinderella Castle hide a small classic Mickey.

Hint 102: In the large central room, you'll find several wood-framed shadowboxes decorating the walls. Each one contains a framed full-body white silhouette of Mickey Mouse (a décor Mickey) positioned against a red background in a fancy black diamond-shaped frame.

A small red classic Mickey hides in the black frame's bottom tip. In the background, white classic Mickeys form the centers of black stylized flowers in the black and white paper that lines the shadowbox and forms the background for the black frame and its contents.

Hint 103: Look for one or more white curtains with black designs hanging along the sides of the central room. White classic Mickeys lie in the middle of black flowers.

Hint 104: On the walls in the central Genie Room, blue classic Mickeys can be spotted in the compass paintings.

Hint 105: Also on the Genie Room walls, antique-looking maps on wood panels painted to look like tapestries have land masses that resemble the side profiles of Mickey Mouse, Winnie the Pooh, Goofy, and possibly Donald Duck. (Donald is a bit of a stretch.)

Hint 106: On the wall in the Villain Room, next door to the Genie Room, Cruella DeVille's left wrist is wrapped with fur that has a classic Mickey dark spot on the side.

Hint 107: Classic Mickey "feet" are at the bottom of display tubs that hold merchandise in some of the rooms (and decorative classic Mickeys may surround the top edges of these tubs).

Hint 108: Near the restrooms at the far end of the store, a picture frame on the wall is lined with small classic Mickeys.

Hint 109: Near the World of Disney store, in an entrance to Downtown Disney from the parking lot, there is a fountain surrounded by colorful flowers in clay pots. The fountain is composed of pots and bowls of varying sizes and shapes arranged so that water flows from one to another. A decorative topiary Mickey pours water into the topmost pot. Lower down, three clay pots form a classic Mickey when viewed from above.

– T-REX

Hint 110: Just inside the entrance and over the bar, a pink classic Mickey hides on the body of an octopus across from a green praying mantis.

Hint 111: A classic Mickey is formed by a clearing in the dirt (or sawdust) in the covered truck bed at the rear of the truck parked outside and to the right of the restaurant entrance.

WDW Casting Center

Hint 112: Classic Mickey holes can be seen in the upper outside walls of the Casting building. (These Hidden Mickeys can also be spotted from Interstate 4.)

WDW Miniature Golf Courses

– Fantasia Gardens

Hint 113: The tee-off areas on both courses are marked with classic Mickeys.

Hint 114: On the Gardens Course, the green at the 12th hole is shaped like a classic Mickey.

– Winter Summerland

Hint 115: On the third hole of the Winter Course, candy canes, milk, and gingerbread men pop out of "Defrosty" (the cooler). One is a gingerbread cookie featuring Mickey ears.

Hint 116: On the 16th hole of the Winter Course, you'll find a Goofy nutcracker on the left side of the mantelpiece.

Hint 117: A Mickey Mouse gingerbread cookie pokes out from a stocking hanging on the right side of the same mantelpiece.

Hint 118: On the left side of the 16th hole of the Summer Course, Mickey and Minnie are sitting in a sleigh on the mantelpiece, along with Pluto. Since the 16th holes of both courses are close together, this mantelpiece is also visible from the 16th and 17th holes of the Winter Course.

Hint 119: Mickey pops out of the present on the 17th hole of the Winter Course when you putt the ball under the gift box. This Mickey is big, but he is hiding most of the time!

Hint 120: At least three classic Mickey ornaments hang on the Christmas tree at the 17th hole of the Summer Course.

Hint 121: A red classic-Mickey Christmas ornament hangs from a rafter above your right shoulder as you face the 18th tee of the Summer Course.

Near Celebration, Florida

Hint 122: On the west side of Interstate 4, south of exit 62 near Celebration, you'll find a huge classic Mickey atop an electrical transmission line pole.

Near the Magic Kingdom

Hint 123: A few miles northwest of the Magic Kingdom, a huge green classic Mickey made of groves of trees can only be seen from the air (or on a Google image). The Hidden Mickey is in a field just off Highway 27 and near the 192 merge.

CHAPTER 8

Other Mickey Appearances

••••••••••••••••••••••••••••••

These Hidden Mickeys won't earn you any points, but you're bound to enjoy them if you're in the right place at the right time to see them.

★ Look for holiday Hidden Mickeys if you're at WDW during the Christmas season or any major holiday. For example, the "Osborne Family Spectacle of Dancing Lights" along the Streets of America in Disney's Hollywood Studios includes many hiding Mickeys.

★ Other "Hidden" Mickeys — décor and deliberate — appear with some regularity throughout WDW. Notice the Mickster on popcorn buckets, WDW brochures, maps and flags, Cast Member name tags, guestroom keys, pay telephones and phone books, and restaurant and store receipts. The restaurants sometimes offer classic Mickey butter and margarine pats, pancakes and waffles, pizzas and pasta, as well as Mickeys on napkins and food trays. They also arrange dishes and condiments to form classic Mickeys, and some condiment containers are shaped like Mickey.

The Mickey hat and ears on top of the "Earful Tower" are obvious to every visitor in the vicinity of Disney's Hollywood Studios. Many road signs on WDW Resort property sport Mickey ears and classic Mickey images, and WDW vehicles and monorails have Mickey Mouse images and insignia.

Cleaning personnel will often spray the ground, windows, furniture, and other items with three circles of cleaning solution (a classic Mickey) before the final cleansing. Or they may leave three wet Mickey Mouse circles or other Disney character images on the pavement after mopping! Mickey even decorates manhole covers, survey markers, and utility covers in the ground, as you've had a chance to find out for yourself on some of the scavenger hunts.

Enjoy all these Mickeys as you explore WDW. And if you want to take some home with you, rest assured that you can always find "Hidden" Mickeys on souvenir mugs, merchandise bags and boxes, T-shirts, and Christmas tree ornaments sold in the Disney World shops. So even when you're far away from WDW, you can continue to enjoy Hidden Mickeys.

CHAPTER 9

My Favorite Hidden Mickeys

In this book, I've described over 1,200 Hidden Mickeys at Walt Disney World. I enjoy every one of them, but the following are extra special to me. They're special because of their uniqueness, their deep camouflage (which makes them especially hard to find), or the "Eureka!" response they elicit when I spot them — or any combination of the above. Here then are my Top Ten Hidden Mickeys and, not far behind, Ten Honorable Mentions. I apologize to you if your favorite Hidden Mickey is not (yet) on the lists below.

My Top Ten

1. Once-a-Year Mickey. *Under the Sea ~ Journey of The Little Mermaid*, Fantasyland, Magic Kingdom. Each year around noon on Mickey Mouse's birthday (November 18), sunlight shines through holes in the rock to form a classic Mickey on the wall of the inside entrance queue. Stay alert because Mickey might show up here at other times of the year! (Chap. 2, Clue 19).

2. Fern Mickey. Garden Grill restaurant, The Land, Epcot. This Mickey hides behind a fern in the big mural inside the restaurant. When I outline this Mickey (a Cast Member often helps me by handing me a broom to reach it and highlighting it with a flashlight), I have witnessed folks in the restaurant smile and shout, "I see him; look, there's Mickey!" (Chap. 3, Clue 103)

3. Minnie Mouse's Shadow. *The Great Movie Ride*, Disney's Hollywood Studios. This shadow on the mural by the loading dock is hard to spot, but once you see Minnie, you'll never forget her. (Chap. 4, Clue 34)

4. Golf Ball Mickey. *Soarin'*, The Land, Epcot. Your first reaction is to duck down to avoid the ball that's flying right at you. But

277

stay still and don't blink, or you'll miss this great Hidden Mickey! (Chap. 3, Clue 12)

5. Jafar Rock. *Pangani Forest Exploration Trail*, Africa, Disney's Animal Kingdom. This three-dimensional head of Jafar is one of the most remarkable sculpted characters you'll see anywhere on Disney property. (Chap. 5, Clue 44)

6. Bush Rock Mickey. Japan, World Showcase, Epcot. This is one amazingly well concealed rock Mickey! (Chap. 3, Clue 65)

7. Steamboat Willie Mickey. *Under the Sea ~ Journey of The Little Mermaid*, Fantasyland, Magic Kingdom. The Imagineers sculpted Mickey in his Steamboat Willie persona on a series of large rocks at the exit of the attraction. A tour de force in the world of Hidden Mickeys! (Chap. 2, Clue 24)

8. Light Cover Mickey. Art of Animation Resort. In the food court seating area, don't miss this faint image of Mickey Mouse smiling down on you. (Chap. 6, Clue 52)

9. Beam Mickey. Wilderness Lodge Villas. This Hidden Mickey peeks out of a hole in an overhead beam in the Villas lobby. Outstanding effect! Most folks don't even know he's up there, hiding! (Chap. 6, Clue 173)

10. Roof Mickey. Near the Contemporary Resort. Sitting on the edge of the roof of a backstage building next to the Contemporary Resort, this playful Mickey welcomes you to the Magic Kingdom. When you're on the monorail, show this Mickey to fellow travelers so they can join in the fun! (Chap. 6, Clue 211)

Ten Honorable Mentions

1. Grim Reaper Mickey. *Haunted Mansion*, Liberty Square, Magic Kingdom. A classic, this wonderful Mickey image has survived refurbishments and seems even better and spookier than ever! (Chap. 2, Clue 43)

2. 3-D Volcano Mickey. *Toy Story Midway Mania!*, Pixar Place, Disney's Hollywood Studios. While you're racking up points in the game, stay alert for this Hidden Mickey behind the target balloons. A convincing 3-D effect! (Chap. 4, Clue 5)

3. Sorcerer Mickey. At the rear of Blizzard Beach, Sorcerer Mickey is formed by stones jutting out from a bridge over *Cross Country Creek*. Very clever! (Chap. 7, Clue 8)

4. Purple Tile Mickey. A classic Mickey in tile is on the counter of the Kona Island coffee bar, Polynesian Resort. This one's a real winner, especially when you point it out to folks who've never seen it. It's hiding in plain sight! (Chap. 6, Clue 190)

5. Tattered Fabric Mickey. Be Our Guest Restaurant, Fantasyland, Magic Kingdom. While you're marveling at the décor inside this restaurant, make a point of strolling through the West Wing room to enjoy this subtle classic Mickey hiding high above you. (Chap. 2, Clue 117)

6. Tiny Fly Mickey. "Song of the Rainforest" area, *Conservation Station*, Rafiki's Planet Watch, Disney's Animal Kingdom. Journey to spot one of the smallest classic Mickeys ever created. (Chap. 5, Clue 78)

7. Aquarium Rock Mickey. *The Seas with Nemo & Friends*, Future World, Epcot. At the bottom of the aquarium lies one or more classic Mickeys formed of rocks. Cast Members (and guest divers) do a great job of maintaining these images. (Chap. 3, Clue 87)

8. Vine Mickey. Animal Kingdom Lodge. This green classic Mickey hides on the vine-covered column outside the rear lobby doors. Well-camouflaged and hard to find, but fun to spot. (Chap. 6, Clue 7)

9. Octopus Mickey. T-REX restaurant, Downtown Disney Marketplace. The octopus over the bar has many colorful spots, including one cool Hidden Mickey. (Chap. 7, Clue 110)

10. Star-Field Mickey, *Buzz Lightyear's Space Ranger Spin*, Tomorrowland, Magic Kingdom. Ride the attraction several times if you need to; this tiny Hidden Mickey is worth discovering! (Chap. 2, Clue 78)

CHAPTER 10

Don't Stop Now!

Hidden Mickey mania is contagious. The benign pastime of searching out Hidden Mickeys has escalated into a bona fide vacation mission for many Walt Disney World fans. I'm proud to include myself among them. Searching for images of the Main Mouse can enhance a solo trip to the parks or a vacation for the entire family. Little ones delight in spotting and greeting Mickey Mouse characters in the parks and restaurants. As children grow, the Hidden Mickey game is a natural evolution of their fondness for the Mouse.

Join the search! With alert eyes and mind, you can spot Hidden Mickey classics and new Hidden Mickeys just waiting to be found. Even beginners have happened upon a new, unreported Hidden Mickey or two. As new attractions open and older ones get refurbished, new Hidden Mickeys await discovery.

It may be just my imagination but I swear that every time I visit Walt Disney World, I spot a Hidden Mickey up in the clouds, watching over his domain! Do you think the Imagineers might actually have some influence on the atmosphere over Walt Disney World?

The Disney entertainment phenomenon is unique in many ways, and Hidden Mickey mania is one manifestation of Disney's universal appeal. Join in the fun! Maybe I'll see you at Walt Disney World, marveling (like me) at these Hidden Gems. They're waiting patiently for you to discover them.

Acknowledgements • • • • • • • • • •

No Hidden Mickey hunter works alone. While I've discovered many of the Hidden Mickeys in this book on my own — and personally verified every single one of them — finding Hidden Mickeys is an ongoing group effort. I am indebted to the following dedicated Hidden Mickey lovers for alerting me to a number of Hidden Mickeys I might otherwise have missed. Thanks to each and every one of you for putting me on the track of one or more of these WDW treasures and, in some cases, also helping me verify them. Extra special thanks to Sharon Dale for spotting over 225 Hidden Mickeys and to Jesse Kline for finding over 100 of these elusive gems!

Names in bold have spotted 10 or more. You can find each person's contribution(s) by visiting my website, HiddenMickeyGuy.com.

Candi A., Maxine A., Nancy A., Frank Abbamonte, Scott Abney, Alex Abrahamzon, Debbie Acres, Jonah Adams, Kaitlyn Rae Adams, Ron Adams, Sarah Adams, Nancy Ahlsen, Michael Akers, Lindsey Albrecht, James Algatt, Matt Allgaier, Anthony Almeyda, Jordan Altug, Eric and Danielle Ambielli, Cathy Ames, John Ames, Amy Amyot, Alex Anderson, Chelsea Anderson, Michelle Anderson, Robert Anderson, Sarah Anzjon, Kristin Archibald, Elena Argaluza, Jennifer Ashley, Mark and Dean Ashwaite, Michelle Astuti, Tacey Atkinson, Chloe Augustine, Barb B., Dan B., Devon B., Jason B., Jessica B., Andrew Babb, Priscilla Baer, Sarah Bagwell, Tony and Matthew and Caroline and Stephanie Banzer, Salina Barbosa, Angie Barclay and kids, Daniel Barrach, Steven Madison Barrett, Vickie Barrett, Chris Barry, Diana Barry, Diane Barry, Samantha Barry, Nicholas Bartoli, Johnny Bartolomeo, Fred Bastien, **James Baublitz**, Sarah Baywell, Penny and Jeff Beam, Mike Beckerman, Brittany and Craig Bedelyon, Jonathan Beer, Leila Beikmohamadi, **Annmarie and David and Josh and Rick Benavidez**, Rich Benneau, Steve - Colleen - Michaela and Amanda Benson, Richard Bent, Clark Benton, Jeffrey Berg, Patti Berg, Bryan and Stacy and Jenna Berger, Terry Berringer, David Berry, **David and Celia Berset**, Jenny Bess, Tom Binder, Andy Birkett, Murray

281

Bishop, Roberta Blackburn, Mark Blackie, **Erin Blackwell**, Trevor Blair, Louis Blanco, **Nancy Blevins**, Laurie and Rebecca Bloodworth, The Bodmann Family, Jennifer Bogdan, Tyler Bolton, Rich Bonneau, Michael Bonnett, Jr., Kevin Booton, Storie Borgman, Katie Borland, Craig Boudreaux, Alicia Bourne, Wendy Bowen, The Bowles Family, Holly Bowling, Elizabeth Bowman, Nicole Bowman, Donna Brackin, Alan Brainard, Brent Brandon, Tina Brannen, Todd Breakey, Matthew Brennan, J. Bridge, Christine Bristow, Patrick Broaddus, Colin Brooks, Larry E. Brooks, Stuart Brooks, Daniel Brookwell, Stephen Brookwell, Chrissy Brown, Jaye Brown, Jeff Brown, Karen Brown and daughter, Peter Brown, Roberta Brown, The Brown Family, Emily Brubaker, John and Susan P. Bruederle, Paul Brune and family, Erica Bryant, The Buaas Family, Cheryl Buchanan, Matt Buchanan and son, Earl Burbridge, Nancy Burke, Lisa Burleson, Todd Busby, Jon Bushee, Brett Butcher, Ruth Butler and daughter, Giovanni C., Villa Cadlle, Bret Caldwell, **Peter Caldwell**, Kerri Callahan, Sarah Callanan, Anne Campbell, Lisa Campbell, Rob and Annabel Campbell, Michael-Lindsay-Alex and Hailey Campe, Craig Canady, Jason Cannons, Todd Carballo, Stan Carder, Chris Carlson, Deborah Carpenter, Gary Carr, Kacey Cassette, Robbie Castro, Jade and Dominic Cavalco, Alexis Cavileer, Mary Anne Ceci, Christina Cella, Kelly Challand, Austin Chanu, J. Chappa, Julie Chappa, Chloe Charette, Catherine Chiarello, Dana Christos, Alyssa Ciaccio, Vito Ciaccio, Michael Ciampi, Anne-Marie L. Clanton and family, Matt Clarke, Matthew Clemons, Malcolm Cleveland, John Clover, Alexa Cohen, Serena Anne Cohen, Rob Coile and daughter, Elizabeth Coler, John Coliton, Kent Collins, Mary Jo Collins, Michael Collins, Jason Colpitts, Eleanor Coltman, Greg Conlin, Joey Connors, Jeffrey Contompasis, Lindsay Contreras, Timmy Coogan, Ian Cordle, Colleen Costello, Calvin Cotanche, Bill Cote, Angela Coutavas, Sara Cox, Karen Crabtree, David Craig, George Crippen, Rob Croskery, Lydia and Michael Cross, Catherine Crouch, Kasie Culp, Erica Culver, Nancy Curl, Brian Currier, Traci Curth, Curtis D., Katie D., Nick D., Marie and Bruce Daigneault, **Sharon and Chloe Dale**, Christina Darce and brother, Jim Darling, Christopher Dash, Shannon DeAraujo, Anthony Dearman, Bob Decker, Keenan DeFrisco,

Amy Degenstein, Dwayne Degler, Michele DeGrace, Bethany and Christine DeLaurentis, Robert Delgado, Sarah Del Grande, Dottie Del Signore, Mike Demopoulos, Michael DeRose, Stephen DeSanto, Rich DeTeresa, Wanda Deveau, **Tim Devine**, Dania Dewese, Sondra Dewey, James Dezern, The DiBenedetto Family, Cara Di Cicco, Maryt DiEuliis, The Digon Family, Doug Dillard, James and Jennifer DiMaggio, Suzannah DiMarzio, Max Dinan, Sam Dinan, Mark Dingman, Mario DiPlacido, Alexander Disney, Calvin Dolsay, Gina Dorkins, Jim Doyle, Sarah Dozert, Kelsey Draves, Laura Dubberly, Angelica Dufer, James Duggan, Joey Duggan, Tom Durr, Abby Dwyer, Alex Dwyer, Ian Dwyer, Robert E., John Early, Jason Ebels, Linda Eckwerth, Susan Edgington, Erik Edstrom, Seth Edward, Nicholas Elardo, M. Eldred, Amber Ellis, Eric England, Lillie England, Ben English, David and Elizabeth Epley, Kelly and Kimberly Erickson, Michael Ethridge, Nick Exley, Eric Fabian, Nick Falco, Adam Fanjoy, Ken Fanti, Ronald and Gianna Fazio, Joshua and Krystina Fears, Alan and Craig Fergus, Ronald Ferraco, Kathy Fetters, Dom Fiandra, Kenney Fichter, Jim Finley, John Finley, Elaine Finnigan, Ashley Rae Fischer, Dennis Flath, Sharon Flood, Jessica Flowers, Dave Flynn, Stephanie Foley, Carlos Font, Melissa and Jacob Forbes, Chet Ford, Joseph Fortenbaugh, Joe Franceschino, Sr. and Joe Franceschino, Jessica and Brent Fraser, Debbie Frazier, Eden Frazier, Matt Freeman, Connie Freese, T.J. Frey, Devon Friedman, Rachel Friedman, Ryan and Fairen Frisinger, Jake Fruci, Diane Furtado, Eric Gagnon, Michelle Gala, **Jason Gall**, Jack Gallaher, Dave Gallant, Chrystine Gallegos, Justine Gamale, Traci Garber, Brad Garfinkel, Marilyn Garfinkel, Scott Garland, Gunnar Garner, Tony Garon, Melissa Garrigus, Kristen Gartrell, Terry and Julia Garvey, Christy Gattis, Anthony Gentile, Pauline Gibson, Kaela and Ryan and Jake Gilbert, Owen Gilley, Tyler Glynn, Chase Goeser, Mark Goldhaber, Nathan Goley, Jeremiah Good, Ty Goode, Andrew Goodwill, Jack Goodwill, June Goodwill, William Goodwill, Vanessa Gordon, Trevor Goren, James and Edward Goring, Ryan Goukler, Josh Graham, Jeff and Joyce Grant, Tim Grassey, Dani Gray, Jim Greenhouse, Mark Greenwald, Rick Gregg, Adam Gregorich, Bill Griffin, Robert Grohman,

Werner Grundlingh, Louis Guidry, Lorri Gumanow, Amanda Gunn, Elizabeth Gutman, Ryan Gutzat, Chris and Cindy H., Christine H., Cindy H., Rick Haas, Daniel Hadden, Brandi Hall, Byron Hall, Melanie Hall, Mike Hamilton, Shannon Hamilton, Theresa Hamway, Jake Hardin, Donna Hardter, Ray Harkness, Ed Harriger, Stephen Harris, Brian Harshberger, Grant Hart and brother, David Hartzell, Bernice Hasher, Laura and Ross Haston, Bryan Hauser, Abbi Hawthorne, Debbie Hayden, Colin Healy, Sean Heard, Ryan Hecht, Mary Heidenberg, Kurt Heinecke, Haley Heintz, Claudia and Ralph Hemsley, Brian Henry, Liz Hernandez, Otto Hernandez, Louise Herrick, Ricky Hett, Beth Higginbotham, Aaron Hill, Jamie Lee Hindes, Jim Hines, Joan Hinkle, Mark Hitt, Jay Hobson, Matt Hochberg, Rick Hoefinghoff, Ed Hoffman, Paul Hoffman, sdmt Hogan, Chip Holland, Vivian Holland, Matt Holley, Michael Hollingsworth, Joyce Holroyd, Jamie Holz, Craig Hood, Evelyn Horton, Kim Howe, Erik Hubbard, Josh Hudson, Tony Hudson, Emily and Lynette Huey, Elton Hughes, Brennan Huizinga, William Huntley, Kaitlyn Husak, Cameron Hutt, The Huwar and Fabanich Family, **Bill and Donna Iadonisi**, Dawn and Megan Ilsley, The Ilsley Family, Alex Inman, Andy Inserra, Mike Ireland, Sarah Ireland, James Ivers, Ashley Izzo, Andy Jackson, Mark Jackson, Scott Jackson and niece, Andy Jasinski, Mark Jeffries, Troy Jewell, Chris Johnson, Jessica Johnson, KJ Johnson, Trisha Johnson, Samantha and John and Brian Jonckheere, Laura Jones, The Jones Family, Tim Jones, Michelle June, Michael Kania, Gary Kaplow, Debbie Karnes, Ray Kastner, Constance Katsafanas, Kathy Katsafanas, Brent William Kee, Aaron and Evan Keller, Gayle Keller, Jennifer Keller, Robert Keller, Declan Kelly, Jim Kelly, Melanie Kemper, The Kemper Family, Deb Kendall, Jasmine Kennedy, John Kessel, Brian Keys, Sam Kimport, Bonnie King, James King, Chris Kirchein, Rachel Kirk, Maggie Kirkwood, Rochelle Klay, Aaron Klein, Cheryl Klein, Hilary Klein, Patty Klein, Patty and Patrick and Adam and Megan Klein, Paul and Michelle Klein, Mitchell Michini Klepac, **Jesse and Jordan Kline**, Jordan Kline, Sarah Kline, Steve Knapp, John Koerber, Deb Koma, Gloria Konsler, Rich Kordalski, Shirley Kordalski, Jack Koss, Jack and John and Christine Koss, Wendy Kraemer, Amy Krauss, Monte Kremin, Tim Kress, Chris Kretzman, Austin

Kruckmeyer, Mikey Laing, Paul Lalli, Kim Lamb, Anne Langlotz, Brian Lanier, Meris Larkins, **Bev and Scott and Dick Larson**, Tim Larson, Richard Lathrop, Allison Laudage, Rebecca Lawler, Daniel Lawson, Lea Ann Lavy, Dr. E. Kye Layton, Melanie LeBlanc, Russell LeBlanc, Will LeBlanc, Joshua Lehrer, Becca Leipzig, Justin Lemonds, Lisa Leonard, Jennifer Leone, Linda Lesar, Angie Leslie, Jessica Levenson, Justin Lewicki, Billy Lewis, Bradley Lewis, Luke Licygiewicz, Taricia Lightfoot, Kyle Lighting, Beth Lindemann, Chuck Lionberger, Jeffrey Lipack Sara Lodgen, C. Loesch, Bryan Long, Christie Long, Kristen Long, **Marc and Josiah Lorenzo**, Jeff Love, Stephen Lovelette, John Lovett, Kent and Pam Low, Ashley Lowe, Nick Lowman, The Luckner Family, Ash Lux, Jennifer Lynch, Jim Lyon, Will Lyon, Linda Mac, Alexander Mack, Chris Macri, Michelle MacVane, Keri Madeira, Cholle Madere, Dusty Madere, Hope Madere, Karen Madere, Mason Madere, Shane Madere, Beci Mahnken, John Majcherek, Austin Malone, Katherine Manetta, Sharla Manglass, Brent Manley, Adam Manno, Kristy Mantarro, Frank Marando, Vanessa Marquez, John and Stephanie Marshall, Drake Martin, Jeffrey Martin, Breanne Martine, Brian Martsolf, Jake Massoni, James Massoni, Brooke Matinides, Pam May, Allison and Andy Mayo, Greg Mazzella, Kelly McAdams, Isaiah McAllister, Aurora McBride, The McCully Family, Mark McCurry, Chris McDaniel, Fawn and Holden McDonald, Mark McDonald, Chris McDonnell, Jessica McGilvary, Sarah McGovern, Saffron McGregor, Billy and Zoe McInerney, Andrea McKenna, Carrie McLaren, Ryan - Rachel - Samantha and Robert McMillan, **Donna McMurrey**, Allissa McNair, Michala McNair, JerriAnne and Susan McPherson, Jill Meadows, Mark Medley, Joseph Mehr, Matt Mellarkey, Amy Mentz, Brian Mentz, Tammy Metz, Sharon Meyer, Kim Michaux, H. Mildonian, Bill Miles, William Miles, Geoff Miller, Herb Miller, Krista and Maeve Miller, Rich Miller, Todd and Jennifer and Sean Miller, Stephen and Brianna Millevoi, Patti Minden, Sandy Modesitt, Aruna Mohan, Perry Molinoff, Kelly Monaghan, Claire Monahan, Lou Mongello, Michele Moody, Jennifer Moon, David Moore, Sharon Moore, Ron Moorhouse, Denise Morelli, Mickey Morgan, The Moriarty Family, Rick Morin, Patti Lel Morris, Joseph Moschinger, Phil Motto, Scott Mueller, The Muklewicz Family,

Ed Muller, Brodie Mumphrey, Baseer Muqri, Lori Murch, Christine Murphy, Marty Murray and son, Brenda N., L. Naizer, Lindsey Naizer, Kurt Nank, Michael Nemeroff, Brayson Nesbitt, Mandy Newby, Jeff Newcomb, Mary Newell, Victoria Newhuis, Benjamin and Aden Newman, Devon Newport, Debbie Newton, Darrin Nilsson, Joe Nixon, Ashley Nolf, Dennis Nordling, Annette Nuenke, Cheryl Nutter, Andrew and Matthew Nypower, Denise O., Erin O'Brien, George O'Brien, Scott O'Donnell, Eileen Knight Ogle, Steve Okeefe, Jeff Oldham, David Oliver, Mitch Oliver, Giovanni Oliveras, Beth Olliges, Kim Olsen, Bob Ondercik, Bobby Ondercik, Rita Ondercik, Sheri Ondercik, Susie Ondercik, A. O'Neill, Jim Opaleski, Lisa O'Reilly, Justin Orilio, *Orlando Attractions* Magazine, Katie Ortynsky, Greg Ostravich, The Outra Family, Denise Owen, Annette Owens, Charles Owens, Jake Owens, Curtis P., Dom P., Kristin P., Melissa P., Glenn and Vickie Pacheco, Bill Padonisi, Doreen Pakidis, Brad and Brittany Paliswat, Jessica Paneral, Benoit Paquin, Nancy Paris, Caleb Parry, Calley Pate, Bob and Maryellen Paton, Chad and Megan Paton Evans, Sam and Lucy and Kimberly Paton Vegter, Alex Patrick, Brian Patterson, Drew Patterson, Kyla and Jen Patton, Lori Payne, Denise Peczinka, Jonathan Peczinka, Tawny L. Peedin, Glenn Peeters, Natalie Pence, **Maya Perez, Octavio Perez, Suzanne Perez**, Todd Perlmutter, Caleb Perry, Jenny Perry, John Perry III, John Perry IV, Mark Petar, Sheila Peter, Kristina Peterson, Lucy Peterson, Tony and Kara Peterson, Steve Petty, Patrick Phelan, Martin Pierce, Victoria Pike, Ray Pilgrim, Brooke Pimental, Linda Pinto, Sara Pirraglia, Tony Pirrelli, Susan Pitts, Linda Pizzuro, Amanda Plante, Cynthia Platt and family, Krista Porter, Roberta Powers, Al Prete, Karen and Grace Price, Katherine Price, Kirby Price, Nathan Price, Walt Prindle, Hayden Pronto-Hussey, Caleb Pryor, Matt Pucci, Wendy Pugh-Hummel, Todd Pushman, Erica R., Tessa R., Tim Rachuba, Richard Rando, Nicholas Ranger, Carol Ray, Sharon Reedy, Stacy Reedy, Derrick Rees, Lynne Reilly, Johnny and Jyle Reis, Michael Remy, Kathy Riccardi, Chris Ricci, Nik Ricci, Mikey Ricco, Richie Rich, Bob Richmond, D. Richmond, Richard Rick, Chuck and Sharon Ridgely, Brian Rigsby, Ron Riley, Antonio Riquelme, Jose Riquelme, Rob and Kathy Risavy,

Bryan Rivera, Joy E. Robertson-Finley, Andy and Jay and Angel Robey, Joseph Robinson, Lauren Robinson, Lawrence Robinson, Lawrence Robson, S. Rodriguez, Lauren Roeser-Nordling, Geoff Rogos, Terry Rohrer, Robyn Romine, Clara Rosadas, Emily Rose, Matt Roseboom, Nancy Rosenberg, Trent Routien, Teresa Rovery, Timothy Rowe, Mitch Rozetar, Chris Rudolph, James Rudolph, Jim Rudolph, Annmarie Rumford, Shauna Rupert-Sessions, Ed Russell, Christine Russo, Steve Russo, Heather S., Ken S., Steve S., Tom S. and Terri, Robin Sackevich, I and Y Sakurada, Andy Salerno, Anthony Salzano, Sheila Sanders, Tami Sanker, Christina Santoro, Hannah Savage, Rachel Savage, Andrew Savers, Dee Dee Scarborough, Jackie Scheibis, The Scheuher Family, John Schiaparelli, Josh Schickler, Matt Schimkus, Ashlea Schneider, Julie Schneider, Sherrie Schoening, Ashley Schultz, Hank Schultz, Steve Schultz, Spencer Schweinfurth, Bethany and Michael Scibetta, Carol Scopa, Mike Scopa, Jeri Scott, Keira Scott, Liam and Michelle Scribner-MacLean, Todd Seales, Jack Seidenberg, Steve Seifert, David and Aubree Serkoch, Debbi Sessa, Trent Sexton, Khrys Sganga, Chris Shank, Leslie Sharkey, John Sheehan, Randy Shelton, Yinan Shentu, Susan Shirey, Bob Shoemaker, Bret Shortall, Andy Shull, Bill and Kim Shultz, Stephanie Shultz, Scott Siblovin, Josh Siegel, Scott Sigouin, Deb Silhan, Tyler Silhan, Stephen Simmons, Steve Simmons, James Simon, **Jimmy Sisson**, Alexander Sjursaether, Bridget Skallet, The Skazick Family from the UK, Mike Sluss, Michael Smart, Byon Smiddy, Laurie Smiley and grandsons, Bonnie Smith, Elaine Smith, Neil Smith, John Snider, Michele Snoddy, Jack Sorensen, Benjamin Soto, Roy Souders, Zach Souders, Douglas Southworth, Kitty Spangler, Megan Spellman, Ryan Spellman, Erica Spencer, Steve Spevak, Michele Sponagle, Kailah Spratt, Megan Stallings, Todd Standley, Rich - Diane - Andrew and James Stangle, Michael and Emily Steele, Kevin Stein, Joshua Steiner, Sharon Stevenson, Lori Stewart, Mark Sties, Skip and Susan and Jack Stinson, Heather Stone, **Jay Stonefield**, Ben Stowell, Branson Strawderman, Allen Stroud, The Suarez Family, Jill Sullivan, Chris and Cathy Sutherland, David Sutton, Dan Swain, Jeff Swearingen, Jordan and Kenya Swiss, Joey Sylvester, Kathy Szczerba, Brittani T., Jen T., Jenni Tackett, Alex Taday, Sharon Tamplain,

287

Joe Tanzillo, Jordan Taylor, Karen Taylor, Leanne Taylor, Len Testa, Samantha and Mikayla Tewksbury, Alayna Theunissen, Brian Thomas, Kimmie Thomas, Roni Thomas-Patterson, Patsy Thomasson and family, Brian Thompson, Jake Thompson, Laura Thompson, Thomas M. Thompson, Emily and Kate Thorington, Albert Thweatt, Erin Tickno, Paige Tiffany, Martha Tischler, Kristy and Scott and Jim and Kim Todd, Debra Tolsma and Alex, Holly Tomashek, Frank Tonra, Frank Tonra Jr., Frank Tonra III, Kevin Toomey, Whitney Townsend, Lauren and Steven Tracy, Kendra Trahan, Scott Trask, Nathan Trent, Jessica Trentacosta, Marcel Troost, Beverley Tuck, Brandon Tucker, Ashley Kennedy Turner, Glenn Turner, Terry Ulrich, Melissa Uzzilia, Nicole V, Stephen Valente, Sandra Valgardson, Shivani Varma, Max-Emanuel Vingerhoets, Aninka van Staden, Frank van Wijk, Chris Vaughn, **Wayne and Angie Vaughn**, Tairyn Velie, Tracy Vesel, Jim Vignola, The Vitrano Family, Jared Voegele, Fred Vosecky, Christpher and Alisha Vozella, Deven Wagenhoffer, Maureen Wahtera, Harry Walker, Jeanne Walker, Amanda Wallace, The Walsh Family, Grace Walter, Christine Wang, Matthew Wang, Jonathan Ward, Rachel Ward, Sharon Ward, Kathy Warner, Matthew Watson, Mary Weaver, Dena Weber, Rebecca Webster, Scott Weideman, Fred Weiner, Joshua Weiss, Cheri Weitkamp, Max Weitkamp, The Welch Family, Carrie Welf, Matt Wells, Robert Wescovich, Michelle Wesolowski, John Weyrich, Craig Wheeler, John Wheeler, Shona Whiddon, Jennah and Noah Whitcomb, Jared White, Jeff Whitlock, Katarina Whitmarsh, Sharon Whitney, Patricia Whitson, Jack Widman, Andrew Wierzbicki and sister, Victoria A. Wieting, Becky Williams, Carla Williams, Chris Williams, Jason Williams, Kevin Williams, Scott Williams, Susan Williams, Ida Williamson, Garrett Willis, Deb Wills, Amory Wilson, Debbie Wilson, Jeannette Winner, Darren Wittko, Chrissy Wooding, Barb Wooldridge, Harry Wootan, Marli Worden, Elizabeth Worth, Kassidy and Cody Wright, Jeanine Yamanaka, Lynn Yaw, Trevor Yeatts, Callum Young, Heather Young, Jonathon Young, Robert and Mary Jo Young, Alexandra Z., Adam Zaner, Meghann Zanotta, Eric Zech, Christianna Ziccardi, Lea Zich, Kristine Zolciak, Catherine Zori, and

Aaron, Aimee, AJ, Al, Alan, Alanna, Alex, Alexis, Alison, Allie, Allison, Alpha, Alyssa, Amelia, Amy, Andy, AnimeHockeygrrl, Ann, Anonymous, Anubis316, Ariel, Austin, Barbara, Benjamin, Beth, Bill, Blair, Brad, Brad & Courtney, Brandon, Brandy, Brian, Brianne, Brooke, Bryan, Bryan@allaboutthemouse.com, Caitlin, Caitlyn, Captain Mike, Carlos, Caroline, Casey, Catherine, Cathreine, Caylie, Charlene, Charles, Charlie, Charlotte, Cheryl, Chloe, Christopher, Christy, Cindy, Claire, Claudia, Cole, Colin, Colin - Kevin - Connor - Jodi - Nana and Pops, Colleen, Corey and mother-in-law, Courtney, Crispynoodle, C.T., Darren, Dave, David, Debbie, Denise, Devon, Donna, Ear to There Tours, Eloy, Emily, Emma, Eric, Erik, Evan, Fernando, Foxx, Gage, Gen, Gilbert, Giorgio, Giovanni, glaslady, Gracie, Graffix, Grant, Greg, Hanah, Hannah, Hidden Kid, Hidden Mickster, Hoffman, Imercado, Jackie, Jake, Jake of Lake Mary, Jamie, Janelle, Jared, Jason (TrendyMagic), JB, Jeanette, JE.D, Jennah, Jennifer, Jeremy, Jessica, Jim, Jodi and Nana and Pops, Joe, Jonathan, Joseph, Josh, JP and son, Julie, Justin, Jyl, Kaela, Katie, Kelly, Kelma, Ken, Kent, Keri, Kerri, Kimberly, Kimmie, Kira, Kitzzy, Kristin, Kristy, Kyle, Laura, Laura and Joe, Lauren, Laurie, Lea, Lea Ann, Lisa, Luis, Luke, Lyinel, Lynn, Makenzie, Marc, Maria, Marissa, Mary Ann and daughter, Mason, Matt, Matthew, Maureen, Max, Megan, Melissa, Memoree, Michael, Michelle, Mike, MOEMOE55, Natalie, Nick, Nickole, Nicole, Noah, Patti, Peter, Quinten, Rich, Rick, Rikki, rjf1423, Roman, Ronald, Rumbanana, Sam, Samantha, Sarah, Sean, Shannon, Sharon, Sharon from Auburn, She-Knows-CA, Sheri, Skiyalater, Snickers, Someone, Sonali, Stacey, Stacy, Stephanie, Taricia, Taylor, Thomas, Tim, Tony, Toontownkid4, Trevor, Tricia, Trina, Tyler, Vicki, Vickie, Victoria, Wendy, Wendy and her Stepmom, Zach, and Zachary.

Index to Mickey's Hiding Places

Note: This Index includes only those rides, restaurants, hotels, and other places and attractions that harbor confirmed Hidden Mickeys. So if the attraction you're looking for isn't included, Mickey isn't hiding there. Or if he is, I haven't yet spotted him. — *Steve Barrett*

The following abbreviations appear in this Index:

AK - Disney's Animal Kingdom
DD - Downtown Disney
E - Epcot
HS - Disney's Hollywood Studios
MK - Magic Kingdom
WP - Water Park

A

Adventureland (MK) 26–27, 36–38
 bridge to the "hub" 38
 Jungle Cruise 37
 near The Magic Carpets of Aladdin 36
 Pirates of the Caribbean 26–27
 Swiss Family Treehouse 37
 Tortuga Tavern 36
 Walt Disney's Enchanted Tiki Room 36
Affection Section (AK) 161
Africa (AK) 153–154, 156, 161–162
 Harambe Fruit Market 161
 Kilimanjaro Safaris 153–154
 Mombasa Marketplace store 161
 Pangani Forest Exploration Trail 156
 path to Asia 162
 Tamu Tamu Refreshments 162
 Tusker House Restaurant 161
All-Star Resorts. See Disney's All-Star Resorts
American Adventure, The (E). See The American Adventure (E)
American Idol Experience, The (HS) 122
Animal Kingdom Lodge 189–192

Animal Kingdom Lodge, cont'd.
    Arusha Rock Overlook area 190
    Boma 190
    Jiko 190
    Kidani Village 191–192
        Sanaa 191–192
Animation Courtyard (HS) 127
Ariel's Grotto (MK) 24
Art of Animation Resort 194
Asia (AK) 151–153, 154–156
    Expedition Everest 151–153
    Kali River Rapids 154–155
    Maharajah Jungle Trek 155–156
Astro Orbiter (MK) 30

B

Backlot Express (HS) 123
Backlot Tour, Studio (HS) 120
Barnstormer, The (MK) 33
Beach Club Resort 200–202
    Beach Club Solarium 200–201
    Beach Club Villas 201–202
    Beaches & Cream Soda Shop 202
    Cape May Café 200
Beauty and the Beast — Live on Stage (HS) 123
Be Our Guest Restaurant (MK) 34
Big Thunder Mountain Railroad (MK) 24
Blizzard Beach (WP) 244–245
BoardWalk Resort 199–200
    Kouzzina restaurant 200
Boneyard, The (AK) 163
Bonjour Village Gifts (MK) 34
Buzz Lightyear's Space Ranger Spin (MK) 29–30
    FASTPASS machine for 28

C

Caffe Italiano cart (MK) 40
Camp Minnie-Mickey (AK) 157
    Festival of the Lion King 157
    near the Greeting Trails 157
Canada (E) 79–80
    Le Cellier Steakhouse 80
Cap'n Jack's Restaurant (DD) 250

Captain EO (E) 74
Caribbean Beach Resort 196
  Shutters restaurant 196
Carousel of Progress, Walt Disney's (MK) 28–29
Casey Jr. Splash 'N' Soak Station (MK) 33
Castle Couture shop (MK) 32
Celebration, Florida: near to 257
Charter bus area outside the Studios (HS) 128
Chester & Hester's Dinosaur Treasures (AK) 164
China (E) 76
Cirque du Soleil (DD) 246
Club Cool (E) 85
Columbia Harbour House (MK) 26
Conservation Station (AK) 158–161
Contemporary Resort 210–211
  Bay Lake Tower 211
  California Grill 210
Coronado Springs Resort 193–194
Cover Story store (HS) 128
Creature Comforts shop (AK) 164
Cretaceous Trail (AK) 163
Crystal Arts store, outside of (MK) 39
Crystal Palace, The (MK) 39

D

DinoLand U.S.A. (AK) 154, 156, 163–164
  Chester & Hester's Dinosaur Treasures 164
  Cretaceous Trail 163
  DINOSAUR 154
  Finding Nemo–The Musical 156
  Fossil Fun Games area, behind 164
  Primeval Whirl 164
  The Boneyard 163
  TriceraTop Spin 163–164
Discovery Island (AK) 154, 162–163, 164–165
  Creature Comforts shop 164
  Flame Tree Barbecue Restaurant 165
  Island Mercantile shop 164
  It's Tough to be a Bug! 154
  Pizzafari restaurant 162–163
  The Tree of Life 164
Disney & Company (HS) 128
Disney Junior — Live on Stage! (HS) 122

Disney Traders store (E) 80
DisneyQuest (DD) 247–248
Disney's All-Star Resorts 192–193
    Movies 192–193
    Music 192
    Sports 192
Disney's Candy Cauldron (DD) 248
Disney's Days of Christmas (DD) 249–250
Disney's Pin Traders (DD) 252
Disney's Wonderful World of Memories (DD) 249
Downtown Disney Area Resorts 196–199
    Old Key West 196–197
    Port Orleans Resort – French Quarter 197
    Port Orleans – Riverside 197–198
    Saratoga Springs 198–199
Downtown Disney Marketplace 249–255
    Cap'n Jack's Restaurant 250
    Disney's Days of Christmas 249–250
    Disney's Pin Traders 252
    Disney's Wonderful World of Memories 249
    entrance to 249
    Ghirardelli Ice Cream & Chocolate Shop 253
    Goofy's Candy Company 250
    Marketplace Carousel 250
    Mickey's Pantry 251
    near the lake 253
    Once Upon a Toy 251–252
    Rainforest Cafe 250
    Sassagoula River Cruise ferry 250
    Team Mickey Athletic Club 253
    Tren-D 252–253
    T-REX 255
    World of Disney 253–255
Downtown Disney West Side 246–249
    Cirque du Soleil 246
    D Street 248
    DisneyQuest 247–248
    Disney's Candy Cauldron 248
    House of Blues 246
    Pleasure Island bus stop 249
    Splitsville Luxury Lanes 248
    Wolfgang Puck Café 248
D Street (DD) 248
Dumbo the Flying Elephant (MK)
    FASTPASS area for 33
    near 33

E

Electric Umbrella (E) 85
Emporium store (MK) 39
Enchanted Tales with Belle (MK) 19
Entrance/exit areas
    Disney's Hollywood Studios 111
    Disney's Animal Kingdom 165
    Downtown Disney Marketplace 249
    Magic Kingdom 19, 41
Epcot Character Spot (E) 87
Epcot Guidemap 87
Epcot Resorts 199–202
    Beach Club 200–202
    BoardWalk 199–200
    Yacht Club 202
ESPN Wide World of Sports 246
Expedition Everest (AK) 151–153

F

Fairytale Garden (MK) 32
Fantasia Gardens 256
Fantasmic! (HS) 129
Fantasyland (MK) 19, 22–24, 31–34
    Ariel's Grotto 24
    Be Our Guest Restaurant 34
    Bonjour Village Gifts 34
    Casey Jr. Splash 'N' Soak Station 33
    Castle Couture shop 32
    Dumbo/Barnstormer FASTPASS area 33
    Enchanted Tales with Belle 19
    Fairytale Garden 32
    Fantasyland Train Station exit area 33
    Gaston's Statue 34
    "it's a small world" 32
    Mickey's PhilharMagic 31
    near Dumbo the Flying Elephant 33
    near Peter Pan's Flight 32
    Peter Pan's Flight 19, 22
    Pete's Silly Sideshow 33
    Pinocchio Village Haus restaurant 31–32
    Sir Mickey's Store 32
    Storybook Circus area 33
    The Barnstormer 33

Fantasyland (MK), cont'd.
  The Many Adventures of Winnie the Pooh 22
  Under the Sea ~ Journey of The Little Mermaid 23–24
Ferryboats
  from MK to Transportation and Ticket Center 41
  Sassagoula River Cruise (DD, R) 250
50's Prime Time Café (HS) 123
Finding Nemo–The Musical (AK) 156
Flame Tree Barbecue Restaurant (AK) 165
Fort Wilderness Resort 203
Fossil Fun Games area, behind (AK) 164
France (E) 79
  Impressions de France 79
Frontierland (MK) 24–25, 27, 36
  Big Thunder Mountain Railroad 24
  Frontierland Shootin' Arcade 27
  Frontier Trading Post 36
  Pecos Bill Tall Tale Inn and Cafe 36
  Splash Mountain 24–25
  Tom Sawyer Island 31
Frontierland Shootin' Arcade (MK) 27
Frontier Trading Post (MK) 36
Future World East (E)
  Mission: SPACE 72–74
  Spaceship Earth 84
  Test Track 69
  Universe of Energy 84–85
Future World West (E)
  Epcot Character Spot 87
  Imagination! 74, 83–84
  The Land 69, 72, 81–83
  The Seas with Nemo & Friends 74, 80–81

G

Gaston's Statue (MK) 34
Germany (E) 76
Ghirardelli Ice Cream & Chocolate Shop (DD) 253
Golf courses 241, 244
  Magnolia 241
  miniature. See Miniature golf courses
  Osprey Ridge 244
Goofy's Candy Company (DD) 250
Grand Floridian Resort & Spa 208–210
  Convention Center entrance 210
  Grand Floridian Café 209
  1900 Park Fare restaurant 209

Gran Fiesta Tour Starring the Three Caballeros (E) 75–76
Great Movie Ride, The (HS) 116–118

H

Hall of Presidents, The (MK) 30
Harambe Fruit Market (AK) 161
Haunted Mansion (MK) 25–26
Hollywood Brown Derby, The (HS) 122
Hollywood & Vine restaurant (HS) 123
House of Blues (DD) 246

I

ImageWorks (E) 84
Imagination! (E) 74, 83–84
    Captain EO 74
    ImageWorks 84
    Journey Into Imagination with Figment 83
Impressions de France (E) 79
Innoventions East (E)
    Electric Umbrella 85
Innoventions West (E)
    near to (Club Cool) 85
    "The Great Piggy Bank Adventure" 85
    "Where's the Fire?" 85
Island Mercantile shop (AK) 164
Italy (E) 77
    Tutto Italia Ristorante 77
"it's a small world" (MK) 32
It's Tough to be a Bug! (AK) 154

J

Japan (E) 78
    Mitsukoshi store 78
Journey Into Imagination with Figment (E) 83
Journey of The Little Mermaid, Under the Sea (MK) 23–24
Jungle Cruise (MK) 37

K

Kali River Rapids (AK) 154–155
Kilimanjaro Safaris (AK) 153–154

L

Land pavilion (E). See The Land (E)

Le Cellier Steakhouse (E) 80
Liberty Square (MK) 25–26, 27, 30, 35
    Columbia Harbour House 26
    Haunted Mansion 25–26
    Liberty Square Riverboat 27, 30
    Liberty Tree Tavern 35
    The Hall of Presidents 30
    The Yankee Trader shop 35
    Ye Olde Christmas Shoppe 35
Liberty Square Riverboat (MK) 30
    entrance 27
Liberty Tree Tavern (MK) 35
Lights, Motors, Action! Extreme Stunt Show (HS) 119

M

Maelstrom (E) 74–75
Magic Carpets of Aladdin, near The (MK) 36
Magic Kingdom Monorail Resorts 207–211
    Contemporary 210–211
    Grand Floridian 208–210
    Polynesian 207–208
Magic Kingdom Monorail Resorts area
    Wedding Pavilion 208
Magic of Disney Animation, The (HS) 127
Magnolia Golf Course 241
Maharajah Jungle Trek (AK) 155–156
Main Street Bakery (MK) 39
Main Street Confectionery (MK) 39
Main Street Electrical Parade (MK) 41
Main Street Train Station (MK) 19, 40
Main Street, U.S.A. (MK) 34–35, 39–40
    Caffe Italiano cart 40
    Crystal Arts store, near 39
    Emporium store 39–40
    horse-drawn trolley 40
    Main Street Bakery 39
    Main Street Confectionery 39
    Main Street Train Station 40
    Mickey's Meet 'N' Greet 34–35
    The Crystal Palace 39
    Tony's Town Square Restaurant 40
    Town Square plaza 40
    Town Square Theater 34–35
Mama Melrose's Ristorante Italiano (HS) 125
Many Adventures of Winnie the Pooh, The (MK)
    22

Marketplace Carousel (DD) 250
Merchant of Venus shop (MK) 38
Mexico (E) 75–76
    Gran Fiesta Tour Starring the Three Caballeros 75
    San Angel Inn 75–76
Mickey's Meet 'N' Greet (MK) 34–35
Mickey's of Hollywood (HS) 128
Mickey's Pantry (DD) 251
Mickey's PhilharMagic (MK) 31
Mickey's Star Traders shop (MK) 38–39
Miniature golf courses 255–256
    Fantasia Gardens 256
    Winter Summerland 256
Mission: SPACE (E) 72–74
Mombasa Marketplace store (AK) 161
Monsters, Inc. Laugh Floor (MK) 28
Morocco (E) 78
MouseGear shop (E) 86
Mulch, Sweat & Shears (HS) 123
MuppetVision 3D (HS) 120

N

Norway (E)
    Maelstrom 74–75

O

Odyssey Center building (E) 74
Old Key West Resort 196–197
Once Upon a Toy (DD) 251–252
Osprey Ridge Golf Course 244
Outpost between China & Germany (E) 76

P

Pangani Forest Exploration Trail (AK) 156
Parades
    Disney's Animal Kingdom 163
    Magic Kingdom: evening 41
Pecos Bill Tall Tale Inn and Cafe (MK) 36
Peter Pan's Flight (MK) 19, 22
    near to 32
Pete's Silly Sideshow (MK) 33
Pinocchio Village Haus restaurant (MK) 31–32
Pirates of the Caribbean (MK) 26–27

Pizzafari restaurant (AK) 162–163
Pizza Planet Arcade (HS) 124–125
Pleasure Island bus stop (DD) 249
Polynesian Resort 207–208
    Kona Island coffee bar 208
Pop Century Resort 194–195
Port Orleans Resort – French Quarter 197
Port Orleans Resort – Riverside 197–198
Primeval Whirl (AK) 164

R

Radiator Springs (HS) 126
Rafiki's Planet Watch (AK) 158–161
    Affection Section 161
    Conservation Station 158–161
    Wildlife Express Train station 161
Rainforest Cafe (DD) 250
Rainforest Cafe entrance sign inside park (AK) 165
Rock 'n' Roller Coaster Starring Aerosmith (HS) 114–115
Rosie's All-American Café (HS) 122–123

S

Saratoga Springs Resort & Spa 198–199
    The Turf Club Bar and Grill 198
Sassagoula River Cruise ferry (DD, R) 250
Sci-Fi Dine-In Theater Restaurant (HS) 124
Seas with Nemo & Friends (E). See The Seas with Nemo &
    Friends (E)
Shades of Green Resort 211
Sir Mickey's Store (MK) 32
Soarin' (E) 69, 72
Sorcerer's Hat, plaza in front of (HS) 127
Spaceship Earth (E) 84
Splash Mountain (MK) 24–25
Splitsville Luxury Lanes (DD) 248
Stage 1 Company Store (HS) 125
Star Tours — The Adventures Continue (HS) 118–119
Streets of America (HS) 126
Studio Backlot Tour (HS) 120–121
Studio Catering Co. (HS) 121
Studios Guidemap (HS) 119–120
Sunset Boulevard (HS) 122
    intersection of Hollywood & Sunset Blvds. 127
Swiss Family Treehouse (MK) 37

T

Tamu Tamu Refreshments (AK) 162
Team Mickey Athletic Club (DD) 253
Test Track (E) 69
The American Adventure (E) 77–78
    Fife and Drum Corps 78
The American Idol Experience (HS) 122
The Barnstormer (MK) 33
    FASTPASS area for 33
The Boneyard (AK) 163
The Crystal Palace (MK) 39
The Garden Grill (E) 82
The Great Movie Ride (HS) 116–118
"The Great Piggy Bank Adventure" (E) 85
The Hall of Presidents (MK) 30
The Hollywood Brown Derby (HS) 122
The Land (E) 81–83
    "Behind the Seeds" tour 83
    entrance doors 82
    interior railing 82
    Living with the Land 81–82
    outdoor sign 82–83
    Soarin' 69, 72
    The Garden Grill 82
The Magic Carpets of Aladdin, near (MK) 36
The Magic of Disney Animation (HS) 127
The Many Adventures of Winnie the Pooh (MK) 22
The Seas with Nemo & Friends (E) 80–81
    Turtle Talk With Crush 74, 81
The Tree of Life (AK) 164
The Twilight Zone Tower of Terror (HS) 115–116
The Writer's Stop (HS) 124
The Yankee Trader shop (MK) 35
Tomorrowland (MK) 27–30, 38–39
    Astro Orbiter 30
    Buzz Lightyear FASTPASS machine 28
    Buzz Lightyear's Space Ranger Spin 29–30
    Merchant of Venus shop 38
    Mickey's Star Traders shop 38–39
    Monsters, Inc. Laugh Floor 28
    Tomorrowland Speedway 27
    Tomorrowland Transit Authority PeopleMover 38
    Walt Disney's Carousel of Progress 28–29

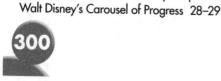

Tomorrowland Speedway (MK) 27
Tomorrowland Transit Authority PeopleMover (MK) 38
Tom Sawyer Island (MK) 31
Tony's Town Square Restaurant (MK) 40
Tortuga Tavern (MK) 36
Tower of Terror, The Twilight Zone (HS) 115–116
Town Square plaza (MK) 40
Town Square Theater (MK) 34–35
Toy Story Midway Mania! (HS) 111, 114
Transportation and Ticket Center 41
Tren-D (DD) 252–253
T-REX (DD) 255
TriceraTop Spin (AK) 163–164
TTC. See Transportation and Ticket Center
Turtle Talk With Crush (E)
    show 74
    waiting area 81
Tusker House Restaurant (AK) 161
Typhoon Lagoon (WP) 245

U

Under the Sea ~ Journey of The Little Mermaid (MK) 23–24
United Kingdom (E) 79
Universe of Energy (E) 84–85

V

Vista Boulevard 244
Voyage of The Little Mermaid (HS) 116

W

Walkway to World Showcase (E) 86
Walt Disney: One Man's Dream (HS) 121–122
Walt Disney's Carousel of Progress (MK) 28–29
Walt Disney's Enchanted Tiki Room (MK) 36
Water parks, WDW 244–245
    Blizzard Beach 244–245
    Typhoon Lagoon 245
WDW Casting Center 255
WDW Dolphin Hotel 202
WDW Railroad (MK) 40
WDW Speedway 244
Wedding Pavilion 208
"Where's the Fire?" (E) 85

Wilderness Lodge 203–207
   Artist Point restaurant 204–205
   Cub's Den, in 206
   Fire Rock Geyser 205
   Roaring Fork snack bar 205
   Whispering Canyon Café 204
   Wilderness Lodge Villas 206–207
      Carolwood Pacific Railroad Room 206
Wildlife Express Train station (AK) 161
Winter Summerland 256
Wishes fireworks show (MK) 41
Wolfgang Puck Cafe (DD) 248
World of Disney (DD) 253–255
World Showcase (E) 74–80
   Canada 79–80
   China 76
   France 79
   Germany 76
   Italy 77
   Japan 78
   Mexico 75–76
   Morocco 78
   Norway 74–75
   Outpost between China & Germany 76
   Showcase Plaza: Disney Traders store 80
   The American Adventure 77–78
   United Kingdom 79
Writer's Stop, The (HS) 124

Y

Yacht Club Resort 202
   Yachtsman Steakhouse 202
Yankee Trader, The (MK) 35
Ye Olde Christmas Shoppe (MK) 35